MUTATIONS

MUTATIONS

THE MANY STRANGE FACES OF HARDCORE PUNK

SAM MCPHEETERS

RARE BIRD BOOKS
LOS ANGELES, CALIF.

Publisher's Cataloging-in-Publication Data
Names: McPheeters, Sam, 1969–, author. | Vail, Tobi, foreword author.
Title: Mutations: The Many Strange Faces of Hardcore Punk / Sam McPheeters;
Foreword by Tobi Vail.
Description: First Trade Paperback Original Edition | A Genuine Rare Bird
Book | New York, NY; Los Angeles, CA: Rare Bird Books, 2020.
Identifiers: ISBN 9781947856981
Subjects: LCSH Punk rock music—History and criticism. | Punk rock
musicians. | Punk culture. | BISAC MUSIC / Genres & Styles / Punk
Classification: LCC ML3534.3 .M46 2020 | DDC 781.66—dc23

For Tolga and Orkun
Thanks again

You can't stop people who are never embarrassed by themselves.

—Norman Mailer

CONTENTS

PROBLEMS

FOREWORD

by Tobi Vail

MUTATIONS IS AN ANTI-MEMOIR by an unsentimental participant of hardcore punk, written during an era when nostalgia for the late twentieth century sells out music venues and festivals on a daily basis and auto-fiction is trending in the publishing industry. Instead of writing a glorified heroic narrative of his own life story told in the predictable chronological order through a narcissistic psychological lens, Sam McPheeters has chosen to reflect on his memories and experiences in their specific cultural context in ways that not only illuminate our understanding of the past but also encourage us to reflect on how history shapes our own lives and has created the current political moment. This is refreshing and also in character, as Sam is an outsider who is definitely not capable of being trendy, is a staunch contrarian, and has never been one to approach a creative work with a market-driven motive such as selling books, as a look at his total body of work quickly shows: he's not in it for the money.

Which brings us to the first question you may be asking yourself as you browse the new bookshelf at your local independent bookseller, or perhaps unearth a dusty copy of this relic in a public library years from now:

Who is Sam McPheeters?

IF YOU KNOW, YOU know and you can skip this part, but if you don't know (or even if you do), you are in luck, as this book will answer that question in depth. But first, allow me to introduce you to the guy, as he is an old pen pal of mine from the 1990s, when we were both active in what he insists on calling hardcore punk and I, like our mutual friend Aaron Cometbus, prefer to call underground music. We met when Sam was singing for one of the only good political hardcore bands that I knew about at the time, Born Against, and I was playing drums for Bikini Kill, a feminist punk group that was actively trying to reinvent both feminism and punk to be more inclusive of young women. Sam mentions our memorable first encounter when both bands briefly toured together in his essay on The Casual Dots so I will skip that here and he is emblematically self-deprecating about how we eventually became friends despite an initial fissure between our scenes, which intersected and clashed but really it makes sense. We are ultimately both self-reflexive fanzine nerds who take things way too seriously, tend to get stressed out and obsessive about music and its surrounding culture to the point of neuroses, and found a way to escape the existential horror of the world using bands and fanzines as cultural tools to overcome the mundane limitations of everyday life under capitalism. Our friendship was documented and preserved in the letters we wrote each other back then, which I still have, and they are funny little time capsules now.

For example, on November 23, 1993, Sam wrote: "It was very good and surprising to get a letter from you—I had actually assumed that everyone in Bikini Kill hated us on account of some fanzine weirdness two years ago. I guess not." Born Against had just moved to Richmond, Virginia, from New York City, finding themselves in a geographically isolated, insular punk scene, similar to the one I had recently returned to in Olympia after Bikini Kill had been living in Washington, DC for a year and a half. At that moment we both felt like exiles from scenes we had helped create and were trying to start over. I had written to Sam's label Vermiform asking if they wanted to advertise in my fanzine, *Jigsaw*. Sam declined, claiming that funds were low, but this was the beginning of a lengthy correspondence that lasted for several years and by early '94, after becoming trusted confidantes, he did submit an ad to *Jigsaw*. I don't remember exactly what the beef was between our two groups, but we wrote it off as a "non-controversy" at the time of our reconnection. I valued Sam's support of Bikini Kill from that moment on, as he perceptively assured me that Born Against had gone through "a micro-version of what Bikini Kill went through, namely people adopting rigid interpretations of what they thought the band's approach or attitude or whatever was supposed to be and often making wrong, mean spirited assumptions about us as a kind of punk caricature."

At the time, most guys I knew in bands were definitely not actively going out of their way to support feminist punk, and what has become known as Riot Grrrl, was widely hated, actively demonized, and generally misunderstood as man-hating or separatist, neither of which was actually 100 percent true or false. Obviously, it was more nuanced, specific, and varied than that, but most people didn't get that far because they had ideological blinders on that amounted to fingers in their ears. They couldn't hear us, we couldn't reach them, yet we wouldn't go away. Despite incessant, nonconsensual mainstream media coverage, we were basically invisible and yet punished for simply existing, refusing to conform to society's bullshit rules about what young women could and couldn't do with their bodies in public space. This is what it's like to be a woman trying to have a voice under patriarchy, and punk was no exception. Sam will be the first to admit that he didn't necessarily get any of that right away, but eventually he opened his ears and tried to hear to us, and I was grateful for his support. That is the kind of person he is. A tolerant, critical thinker who listens and tries to figure out what things mean beyond appearances and pushes past the status quo to gain a counter-hegemonic understanding of culture and politics.

Bringing us to the next question you might have, as you start to turn the pages:

Why read this book?

WE ARE CURRENTLY LIVING in a different time period than the one discussed in this book, as Sam's focus is mostly on the years of his involvement in hardcore punk, which took place from 1984–2004. Since that time, we have entered a period of what he aptly calls taste fragmentation. Punk has not ceased to exist, and, in fact, it could be argued that hardcore is more popular than ever before and no less viable as a cultural tool that empowers young people to have a voice and connect with each other outside of the music industry. In the past ten years, women, queers, people of color, and trans kids have moved from the margins to the center of hardcore. There are hardcore punk festivals all over the world that new and old bands play, and as an evolving form, the scene is arguably more all ages than ever before as the kids in eighties bands grew up they weirdly didn't quit playing in bands and you can still see bands like Negative Approach on tour, yet there are also new groups everywhere. I don't pretend to understand any of the nuances of egg and chain, as an "old punk," but Sam didn't even know about "meme-punk" until a few months ago when I asked him about it. His response was classic Sam: "Any explanation would ruin this," so I didn't bother to try to decode it for him. So what do us old guys have to say that could be of interest or use to the next generation? I really don't know, but this book is hilarious, amazingly well-written, and asks deep, probing questions about the nature of consciousness (is it a solitary experience?), whether or not music is actually communal, and what it all means. If you need specifics, this book contains the most extensively well-researched piece on Doc Dart from The Crucifucks that I have ever read, amazing insights on Die Kreuzen and Discharge, and celebrates one of the greatest bands in modern memory, The Casual Dots. If that sounds intriguing, you are in for a wonderful treat.

Since dropping out of the scene in 2004, Sam has focused on writing fiction, and this book demonstrates a very skilled command of language. His sentences are beautifully constructed. I laughed out loud several times reading this book to the point of tears. I argued with his conclusions and bizarre opinions (in no way is the *Age of Quarrel* LP better than the demo, sorry) but I was deeply entertained and engaged with every single sentence of this book. It is a good one. I hope you enjoy it as much as I do. But the first thing that you should do is skip the entire book and turn to page 160 where the Endnotes begin. Just read it from beginning to end, or at least until you get to the endnote about Void, which contains the best writing on hardcore punk that I have ever read.

PREFACE

FOR TWENTY YEARS, I immersed myself in aggressive underground music. I never considered myself a punk rocker, or even a "punk," although this was obviously the turf on which I operated. Even now, I'm still trying to make sense of the nuances and mutations of this subculture. It hasn't gotten simpler with hindsight. "Punk" isn't a porous subject; it's completely fluid. Writing about it in any meaningful way is like trying to document one particular part of a lake.

For example, the word itself has no set definition. Depending on who and where you are, "punk" can be a lifestyle; cosplay; design element; powerful ideal; lazy cliché; magical realism; badge of authenticity; pantomime social movement; withering mockery; ironclad conviction; lucrative career; vow of slovenly poverty; incubator of brilliance and/or mediocrity; rite of passage; riot of violence; ferocious hokeyness; suicide hotline; sales category; community glue; license to wallow; mass catharsis; a refuge for smart people and/or playground for dumb people; boisterous escapism; marketable nostalgia[1]; belligerent incompetence; self-satire (intentional or otherwise); assault on falseness; or adult-sized, psychic diapers that can be worn until death. And if someone has a strong belief about what it is, odds are they have an even stronger opinion about what it is not. How can so many people pledge allegiance to something with no fixed meaning?[2]

And yet pledge they do, generation after generation identifying with a musical subgenre so powerful *that it has the ability to change listeners' identities.*

•••

I INTERSECTED THIS WORLD through hardcore (the "hardcore" version of punk rock[3]). Starting with the Dead Kennedys tape I bought in 1984 and ending with the last show I played live in 2004, I tried to sample every possible expressive outlet within this subculture. I fronted three bands, one (Born Against) that got a lot of attention within its circuit, and two more (Men's Recovery Project, Wrangler Brutes) that did not. Between one bungled night as a college radio DJ and fifteen years of touring, I also made fanzines, booked shows, ran a record label, co-owned a record store, and designed my fair share of merchandise and ephemera.

For years, hardcore punk was the best game in town, despite the consensus that its golden age lasted from 1980 to 1986. So I never outran the feeling that the scene's finest days had ended just as I'd gotten in.[4] Entering this subculture in the wrong year, however, gave me an odd bird's-eye view of its central players. Many of them had moved on by the time I'd signed up, but they were never that far away. I had access to most of the people who'd immediately preceded me, a bit of fortunate timing for which I will always be grateful.

I've now spent as much time outside this world as I did as a touring band member. Many of punk's battles—against white supremacy, or the eternal churn of leftist infighting—have migrated to the national stage. A much larger, less defined battle against the forces of mass insanity also looks increasingly familiar. The more time passes, the less the whole thing feels like nostalgia than it does a prelude. But to what, exactly?

Sam McPheeters
October 2019

QUESTIONS

NETWORKING UNDER
THE ESP STATION

What do People Even Write?

In 1978, the state of New York completed the Empire State Plaza (ESP), a hundred-acre government complex dominating the skyline of the capital city, Albany. The Plaza's forty-four-story Tower Building—seemingly named in the grand, bland tradition of Soviet architecture—loomed over the nearby Mansion Hill like a conquering spaceship. When I moved to the neighborhood that same year, it was still an enclave of old Italian families, remnants of the Little Italy obliterated to make room for the gleaming new behemoth. Klieg lights kept the Tower Building luminous after dark. When it snowed, the night sky glowed with power.

The Plaza's multilevel concourse served as a vast playground for my kid self, a Hundred Acre Woods of concrete, marble, and glass I was allowed to roam alone. With its colossal corridors and brutalist architecture, the Plaza looked like the kind of place one would go to receive further instructions. Which is what it became; opening a mailbox in its tiny post office, the ESP Station, was one of my first grown-up acts.

After getting dumped in eleventh grade, I washed dishes seven days a week and somehow saved enough to buy a pea green 1974 Chevy Impala with vinyl bench seats the size of church pews. My high school was off the highway and the highway cut through the ESP parking levels. After school, I would park underground, grab my mail upstairs, then read letters and listen to tapes in the Empire State Plaza's upper parking level.

It was here, in the diving bell privacy of the Impala, using my massive car dashboard as a desktop, that I first reached out into the wider world. I had nothing to sell, no persona to advance, no grudges to stoke. I just liked getting mail. I perused pamphlets from the Karen Carpenter fan club, and Wiccans, and Church of the Subgenius, and Satanists. For a while, I fielded replies from a bunch of teen girls who'd written to *Archie* comics as kids in 1975 and were thus roughly my age. My best friend Jason and I had written each one that we were doing some sort of "ten-year follow-up study" (to meet girls?), although I have no idea how we got their home addresses.

The *Archie* girls were, surprise, totally boring lamers who did not like my favorite band, the Cro-Mags. But I did snag a pen pal who liked the Cro-Mags, a college girl from Sarah Lawrence I met in the personal ads of *Flipside* fanzine. I wrote a lot of people from fanzines. I didn't know it at the time, but I was entering something new and breathtakingly potent: the network of hardcore punk.[5]

Those two words weren't synonymous, but became entwined in ways that flattened them to outsiders.[6] Punk tried to crack the code of the music industry; hardcore never had that option. It would have been absurd for any major label to sign—or any radio station to play—loud, violent bands made up of loud, mentally ill people who gleefully "sang" about every possible taboo.

The extremism of hardcore forced its fans to do everything themselves. The opportunity of hardcore was the same opportunity once offered by running off to join the circus: horizontal ambition, not vertical. This was the chance to bypass the music industry altogether, to tour, release records, and network—to make music for its own sake, to have adventures for their own sake.

The self-reliance of hardcore had American fingerprints all over it. The earliest versions of these networks, painstakingly built by just a handful of bands, channeled the energy of past spurts of American ingenuity, both cultural (Chautauqua, the Chitlin Circuit, 1960s underground media) and industrial (the sheer endurance required to clear and pave wilderness). The global success of hardcore punk has masked its identity as an American art form, one as homegrown as vaudeville, jazz, or rap.[7]

Oddly, the people who still pay reverence to this art form do so, I think, for largely personal reasons. Many people who submerge themselves in this subgenre describe it as the most positive experience of their lives. Not many people recognize the rarity of a self-generated, self-reliant network, which is probably a tribute to the power of the art form and its sprawling network of music and literature and ideas, rapidly spreading to every corner of western civilization.

•••

I CAN PINPOINT THE moment I entered this network as a participant. For a homework assignment, I'd copied a chapter from *The Federalist Papers* in my school library. I included the cover because I liked the art: cartoony figures of three founding fathers, loitering on the street like people outside a show.[8] Its awkwardness, its *offness*, resembled the Raymond Pettibon drawings I had only recently learned to appreciate. All it needed was a creepy caption.

I folded the pages and smiled in realization. I was holding what looked like a small photocopied magazine. What if I made my own small photocopied magazine? I'd done lots of little projects and cartoons and calendars as a child, including several copied comic books I forced on my relatives. I had no idea yet that fanzines were already an existing thing (in issue one, I used the word as a joke, although I didn't quite get its meaning). Thus, Jason and I launched *Wretched* fanzine.

Wretched bypassed the burden of content by being mostly graphics. Jason drew comics, I made collages. Although the first issues were 80 percent him (he was a far better artist and writer[9]), each slender fanzine provides a tiny ice core sample of our shared tastes: Bible tracts and Book of Revelations quotes, drawings of skeletons and skateboarders,[10] *Archie* comics,[11] absurdist newspaper clippings, jokes about the Contras and the Challenger explosion, and CPR line art of boys performing mouth-to-mouth on each other with little cartoon hearts drawn around them, which, for the anti-gay 1980s, seems oddly ballsy.

My mom bought a Canon PC-14 to use for her own art. One of the first personal copiers (eight pages a minute!), it was too small and fragile for print runs, but perfect for making layouts and degrading the quality of graphics. By issue four, I was seventeen and driving, the PO box was open for business, and we were ready to start writing about things like a real fanzine.[12]

This point was a micro-crisis, as I had no idea what people wrote in real fanzines. The twin mediums of hardcore journalism—review and interview—seemed completely beyond me. I didn't know how to review records, and the idea of interviewing people from actual bands seemed as realistic as interviewing astronauts. I remember asking Jason the question aloud: "What do people even write?"[13]

I'd penned a few other bits for *Wretched*, but it didn't feel like these bits conformed to real zine standards. And as I got deeper into the scene, I wanted to make something more accessible to that scene. Issue four finally featured my first record review:

<u>CRO-MAGS "Age of Quarrel" LP</u>

"Blazing" NYHC sound, combined with the best apocalyptic lyrics ever thought of, make this the greatest record <u>ever</u> recorded. In fact, you WILL buy it. I'm not offering you a choice...[14]

I vaguely recall not being thrilled with this review, or any other piece of writing I did for a long time after.[15] It took even longer to grasp that I was going to be doing a lot of bad writing, and that most of this writing would be done in public formats (it took a quarter century for me to realize I could just write things and not show them to anyone). This wasn't what we now think of as a readership, the infinity of online eyeballs that sees everything, but only stripped of context. This was an actual audience, tiny but engaged, and one that could be coaxed to grow through nothing more than persistence. As I slowly learned how to write, I did so in a self-consciously public manner.

Wretched begat *Plain Truth*, a real fanzine that interviewed real bands. *Plain Truth* begat *Dear Jesus*, the fanzine where I started to push a persona, that of an obnoxious, mentally ill hardcore band guy.[16] After a bandmate expressed frustration with inaccuracies in a tour diary, I moved toward conspicuously falsified personal histories; impossible shows, fake backstories, dialogue with real-world celebrities I clearly did not know.

In hindsight, these experiments were my first fumbling toward writing fiction, the same general path I'm on today.

•••

BACK TO THE EMPIRE State Plaza. One detail from those days glints with significance. Most correspondents would leave off the "ESP Station" part of my new address. It took me a while to understand that many of the people I communicated with thought I was being needlessly weird. This became a theme of my adult life.

The acute constraints of hardcore punk, in all its formats—zines, bands, records, record labels—always struck me as challenges. The price of experimentation is failure, so I frequently missed the mark in my output and developed a reputation as someone being needlessly weird.

This isn't a complaint, just an observation. There are worse reputations to get. The intensity of wrestling with ideas in public can often look ridiculous to those outside the process. At a certain point, I realized I was getting my mail anyway, so I simply ceased caring.

FROZEN PITS

Why be in a Band?

NOT LONG AFTER I'D called it quits as a performer, I drove into LA to catch a band I liked. My former band had played the same venue a few months earlier, spurring an onstage panic attack. I'd managed to bluff my way through the set, but my confidence had taken a hit. Returning to this room felt like trying to resume a relationship after the kind of screaming blowout no relationship ever really recovers from.

The headlining band played loud, aggressive music. At some point during their set, I shifted my gaze from stage to crowd. No one moved. No one did anything. I found myself surrounded by blank faces. Now it was the audience who were bluffing, and bluffing badly. I found myself wondering if music fans had always been so disengaged, if my own emotional investment in bands had blinded me to this mass disinterest. It was spooky.

A week later, flipping through TV channels, I paused on a Foo Fighters concert. I'd arrived mid-song to find frontman Dave Grohl rocking out, one foot up on a monitor, wild mane of hair swooshing as he soloed with virile abandon. The entire spectacle was self-evidently absurd. Why wasn't he laughed off stage? The thought became a loose thread that, when tugged, led to an unraveling. Had I ever looked this piously pompous when performing?

And if I could no longer summon faith in my own live music, how could I muster interest in anyone else's live music? I'd already known that I wouldn't be in any more bands. Now I realized I wouldn't even be able to watch other bands. This change was so bizarre, so abrupt, it felt like a brain injury. Something that had overwhelmed my life for twenty years no longer made sense. I can remember those earlier emotions, the way live music was like fresh-squeezed juice to the canned concentrate of a recording. But I can no longer feel them.[17]

•••

THERE WAS A TIME when music made me submerge myself in mobs. Bands and songs were the drivers, but photography was the lure. Audiences were (and are) part of punk's sales pitch. The big visuals from this era are of stagedivers. Photographer Ed Colver set the template with one infamous photo taken at a LA show in the early eighties. In Colver's picture, a stagediver in Vans and a sleeveless tee hovers four or five feet over the crowd, curled upside down like a human pill bug. Although the landing is clearly going to hurt (at least for the people below), the instant captured is strangely serene. A man floats, bystanders watch. Even today, the best stagediving photography follows Colver's template—people leaping from dangerous heights, visually isolated from the waiting throng.

In *Loud 3D*, stagedivers plunge *into* crowds. As the title suggests, this slender, long out-of-print book of photography (self-published by Mike Arredondo, Rob Kulakofsky, and Gary Robert in 1984) comes with a pair of cheap cardboard glasses that convert each red and blue photo into a mesmerizing little still life.[18] Every picture showcases that peculiar contradiction of pre-digital black-

and-white 3-D, pairing the distance of sepia with the immediacy of depth. A small glossary of visual info lost in traditional photography—texture, sweat, hollows of shadow—lends the photos a fascinating density.[19]

This collection of photos chronicles hardcore punk concerts ("hardcore rock'n'roll," according to the book's cover) in San Francisco between 1982–1984. Meaning, the book covers the very best years of hardcore punk in a national hub for local and touring groups. Blue chip bands (Black Flag, Minor Threat, Dead Kennedys) share space with forgotten acts (Sado-Nation, Black Athletes, Stranglehold). Few books of music photography can match its urgency.[20] Singers shriek and launch themselves at audiences, creating bizarre dioramas of feigned violence. In one picture, a stream of beer hangs in mid-air, connecting the hand of Fuck-Ups singer Bob Noxious to the gaping mouth of a fan. In another photo, Dead Kennedys' frontman Jello Biafra bestows water on outstretched arms, the droplets neatly suspended in zero gravity. Viewed without glasses, the guitarist of NYC's Cause For Alarm is apparently getting punched in the face. In 3-D, the fist is shown jovially punching the air in front of him as he body slams his own instrument.

Audience shots take up more than a third of the book. Slam dancers pose, halted in time, the billows of their plaid shirts suspended like puffs of smoke in an old stereoscope. One man seems to register shock that he has just been leapt upon. Another man puffs his cheeks out, as if a trap door had dumped him into a pit of writhing bodies. These hurtling, plunging, stampeding masses say more about the era than even the band shots. There is none of the indifference of modern concert-goers. These people seem involved in an epic struggle with an eternally off-screen antagonist, their efforts closer to news footage than concert photography.[21]

On one page, the singer of Deadly Reign has been shot mid-mosh, high stepping, arms swinging, his *Rollerball* T-shirt ripped on both sides to expose strong, bare shoulders. The pose resembles Eugène Delacroix's "Liberty Leading The People." It is martial yet joyous, and oddly sensual. It looks like sexy propaganda. This book is full of good-looking young men striking poses for each other's enjoyment. Although bare male torsos were staples of early eighties hardcore photography, a certain amount of sexual energy evaporates in the physics of two dimensions. In the depths of these photos, men strut and flex and glisten in physical space. It's a sales pitch for a lifestyle brand.

On the opposite page, we see Keith Brammer, bassist of Die Kreuzen, frozen in the throes of performance. This is early in the band's career; he must be playing very fast. Viewed flat, he is clearly a handsome young man. Seen in 3-D, the viewer can discern the jut of his chin, the fullness of his lips, the distinct knob of his Adam's apple. He peers upward, over the photographer, through a mane of slick wet hair. The look on his face could easily be mistaken for private adult sexy times.

It's a theme. Sothira Pheng from Crucifix, lithe and feline, arches backward in his black tank top. Henry Rollins—half naked, but not yet in his short shorts phase—bends toward the viewer like a randy Stanley Kowalski.[22] Fear's Lee Ving mugs for the camera, looking like a bare-chested wrestler. The camera even catches Jello Biafra shirtless and horizontal, exposing an upside-down cross shaved into the fur of a surprisingly taut stomach (the clear indentations of a six-pack are visible with the glasses).[23]

Where do the ladies stand with all this sexy stuff? There are so few it's hard to know. Women are vastly outnumbered in the world chronicled by *Loud 3D*.[24] Halfway through the book, there is one nicely worded block of text from Mordam Records' Ruth Schwartz, who defends the scene from accusations of chauvinism with a level of maturity that is slightly jarring in its context. "The generation of women in punk (13–30, mostly) are the hardest working, most ardent feminists/humanists I've ever met," writes Schwartz. "Most women I know are not just dealing with their oppression as females, but also as people. This is a step beyond the liberation and feminism our mothers (bless them) fought for."

Perhaps to punctuate this quote, Lewd bassist Olga deVolga appears on the opposite page decked out in a bondage harness and wrist spikes.[25] Her costume muddies the book's chronology. These aren't the freewheeling days of late seventies American punk, when audiences dressed up like Rocky Horror enthusiasts.[26] It's the eighties. There are dress codes. Crowds wear flannel shirts or leather jackets. The only facial hair belongs to two of the Dead Kennedys (who all sported silly mustaches and goatees for their second tour, a rebuke of the rigid new styles).[27] Toward the middle of the book, writer Jennifer Blowdryer nicely sums the slippery conformity of nonconformity: "Those gorgeous young creatures are not wearing casually slapped together outfits. Fashion exists even—especially—for the roughest, toughest skinhead."[28]

Fashions date this book, but so do the faces. This was an age when band members recognized their role as visual performers. Singers work their mics with the facial expressiveness of silent movie stars,[29] and the full-body physicality of Japanese actor Toshiro Mifune, leaping and yelling like samurais, like people engaged in combat.[30] In 1952, French photographer Henri Cartier-Bresson coined the concept of "the decisive moment," a combination of timing, intuition, skill, and patience. But for Arredondo, Kulakofsky, and Robert (and Joe Rees, of Target video, who makes a cameo filming the Circle Jerks), decisive moments were there for the taking, song after song. These pictures were my propellant, an ideal of performance that I referred back to for years.

•••

IN THE DECADES SINCE *Loud 3D* came and went, fans of hardcore punk found other motives. The tangible lures of eighties hardcore (photography, fashions) gave way to fuzzier bait, things like "community" and "communication" and "release," all concepts peripheral to the theatrical art at the heart of the music.

Once, in one of those immense airport corridors, I saw a group of young men walking toward me from a great distance away. As they approached, I could make out their shirts and patches, and hear them exuberantly discussing bands I knew. I watched them pass, a stationary tracking shot where only the camera swivels. They were a group—a band—high on camaraderie and headed for adventure. No amount of money would have made me switch places, but I envied their drive.

Sometimes motives aren't so clear. There was the night, years ago, on a long solo drive down the coast, when I stopped for gas on a lonely highway in Oregon. I started the pump, then saw a young guy fueling up a Ford Econoline van at the pump opposite. Through the van's back window, I could just make out a sleeping body slumped up against the glass. I'd intersected someone else's tour.

I remembered this part of touring. This was the moment when I would stand with a gas pump at three in the morning, staring off into the cold darkness of an unknown state, mentally curating the sense-memory into a much larger narrative about something important I was doing with my life. For the briefest of moments, I had the sensation of being a time traveler, of viewing my younger self, of seeing those gorgeous blue and red *Loud 3D* photos in the cartoon thought balloon floating over my younger self's head.

The pump clicked. I got back in my car and drove off.

THE HEIST

Why Rob a Record Store?

2013

HOW DO YOU EXPLAIN to people that you once robbed a record store? I've been thinking about this a lot after the store, New York's Bleecker Bob's, closed last year. My hope is that my one small contribution to "shrinkage"—as theft is dutifully acknowledged on the balance sheets—did not ultimately contribute, decades later, to the store's downfall. But I'm not an economist. I don't know how the butterfly effect works.

In the twenty-teens, record stores are fragile businesses. Robbing one now would be morally equivalent to replacing all the candy bars in a Red Cross packet with animal droppings. I try to convey my sincerity when retelling the story. Yes, Bleecker Bob's was a good store, with knowledgeable staff and a great selection. Yes, I genuinely regret my actions. Sometimes my own deep shame forces a defensiveness. "Look, it was the eighties," I explain. "Everyone was doing it."

Some context: by 1989, it had been two decades since a sanitation strike ushered in an era of Big Apple apathy, crime, fear, and filth. New York had long since become known as a place where normal rules of conduct had been suspended. Films of the seventies and eighties documented the defensive measure required to live in this city, all those comical locks and deadbolts and roll gates covered in misspelled graffiti. But there's far less documentation of all the offensive measures taken by New Yorkers. It seemed like everyone carried some sort of weapon. There was the classmate with a hammer in his backpack, and the bike messengers who brandished locks and chains like gangs in a sci-fi apocalypse. There was the time my taxi driver produced a crowbar to fight a rival cabbie, as if he'd taken a wrong turn and ended up in *Grand Theft Auto*. Everyone was angry.

Even though I was in college and lived in a luxury apartment, I too felt I had the right to be angry. For one thing, the luxury apartment was a scam. In order to afford the $1,300 rent on the two-room unit, my two roommates and I took on two extra roommates. I'm sure the five of us thought we were scamming the landlord, but one could also argue that we'd perpetrated a much larger scam on ourselves by converting a classy condo into a *Gangs of New York*-era tenement.[31]

Certainly our neighbors felt scammed. They were the ones paying exorbitant rents to share a building with a frat house/flophouse. Visitors to our fraphouse would write their names in the elevator with markers. Strange men who lived in abandoned buildings would pop by late at night to avail themselves of our shower, or the building's communal laundry room. We recorded several demos for fake punk bands in the apartment, each involving real guitar amps. At some point, fellow tenants piled up bags of trash in front of our door as a sort of micro-sanitation strike.

The main culprits here were my two original roommates. Bill—not his real name—and Neil—very much his real name— were the guys who would bust in breathless, demanding that

I immediately come to the roof to "see what we did" as police sirens grew louder in the distance.[32] Some of their shenanigans bordered on the irresponsible. Together, they would light discarded Christmas trees on fire, or hurl objects off the roof, or roll barrels down subway steps.

To their credit, neither Bill nor Neil were the worst behaved gentlemen in our larger social circle, let alone the city itself. In this same way, their hijinks provided a valuable service within the tiny ecosystem of the apartment. For all my own bad behavior, I still wasn't as bad as them.

Although I had my moments. For example, I accidentally smashed out Bill's front teeth with a frying pan. I don't mean "accidentally" in that sarcastic, sinister, organized crime way. It was a genuine accident. We were playing the Let's Throw Progressively Larger Objects At Each Other game, and, you know: oops.[33] It could easily have been me who'd inexplicably failed to catch that cast iron skillet. Afterward, while all of us were trying to figure out how Bill was going to make it through a three-day weekend with a mouthful of exposed nerve endings, I offered him any one rare record, from my own collection, that might take away a bit of the pain.

I mention this detail to underscore the importance of vinyl (both albums and seven-inch EPs) to all of us. I was building what turned into a formidable record collection, one that was "sourced ethically," meaning original price, trade, or—in early 1989— liberated from any store I deemed evil. Ten years later, when anti-Napster record executives would invoke visions of reckless music thieves, they would more or less be talking about me and my pals. We believed we had the right to illegally download physical records from the stores that supplied them. I didn't partake in any of the outright robberies, but there were several incidents of employee-assisted 98 percent-discounts that I can't say I'm proud of. Could our illicit shopping sprees have contributed to the death of Tower Records seventeen years later? Again: not an economist. I hope not.

Our beef against record stores felt ideological.[34] We believed that many of these records had been overpriced. Our confiscation of such incorrectly priced consumer goods had the delusional feel of a civic duty, not unlike the time, years later, when Neil would destroy an uncooperative payphone with a claw hammer. So when Bleecker Bob's eventually drifted onto our radar, at no point did anyone discuss stealing money. That would have been gauche. Our target was the store's collection of rare hardcore punk seven-inches. These were split alphabetically. The box we wanted was labeled A-M.

We knew this box was the juiciest catch because we'd done reconnaissance. And we'd put in the reconnaissance time because it was my plan. I brought a measure of cautious prudence to the group. For example, before we'd embarked on the prank call marathons that came to replace television as a communal roommate activity, I was the one who insisted we first check with the operator to see if a crank call could be traced. "But my life was threatened!" I pleaded. "Are you really telling me there's NO way you can find out who did this?"

So I planned the robbery with the care of a professional jewel heist. Our raid would take place during the Super Bowl, when the fewest people would be out. Neil would go to the counter, ask for the A-M box, and casually flip through the records. We practiced his casual flipping. At a prearranged time—I had us synchronize watches—I would call the store from a payphone, distracting the clerk. Neil would grab the box and sprint. Bill would be standing by the bulletin board near the front door. His role was the clueless bumbler, a random stranger who would "accidentally" get in the clerk's way as he attempted to give chase. This time I did mean the word with underworld sarcasm.

On Sunday night, the streets were indeed empty. I walked to my predetermined pay phone in a funk. TV screens illuminated the windows of apartments, and it occurred to me that Super Bowl XXIII was an odd parallel to what we were doing. I'd diagrammed our moves like a coach. It was as if the three of us were one team and society was the other team, and society, being composed of everyone, had an insurmountable advantage. I'd picked the safest role in the caper, but could I be sure they couldn't trace pay phones? Could they lift fingerprints from the receiver? What was I doing?

I placed my call, and walked a long route home. I tried to picture Neil running victorious through the streets, his box of A-M records tucked under one arm, unconsciously imitating 49ers running back Roger Craig as he led his team to victory in Miami. But the image seemed bogus. I'd done something irreparably wrong. The moment was creepy.

Back at the apartment, Bill and I waited. And waited. I did my job on the phone, he'd done his job with the bumbling. Had Neil been caught? If caught, would he name names? If the cops came, would I be able to keep my cool and work the plausible deniability angle? *No, officer, I don't know either of these men, despite the fact that they live here. A lot of people live in this apartment, and I can't be expected to keep track of each and every one.*

Neil did finally arrive, sweaty and shaken. At the last moment he'd gotten spooked, grabbed as many records as he could stuff down his pants, and dashed out the door. In his panic, he'd forgotten the route I'd so carefully mapped out, bolting in blind criminal terror through the deserted streets of the East Village. Two cops stopped him. When asked where he was going in such a rush, he said "home," and when asked where that was, he found he could no longer remember. Unwilling to search his pants, they instead took down his ID information, promising a visit if anyone reported anything suspicious.

We inspected the haul in demoralized silence. He'd grabbed five records, all from the D section. Four were garbage. It's remarkable how many truly terrible punk bands start with the letter D. But the fifth record, Discharge's *Never Again*, was a decent catch. I went to cheer the group up by playing this record, only then noticing that it had gotten gouged on Neil's belt buckle. We'd destroyed something beautiful and finite. My only hope was when the cops came, I could use this sorrow to leverage some sort of plea deal. And although the Internet informs me that the statute of limitations has long since run out on this particular crime, I've gone straight ever since.

A CONVERSATION WITH
AARON COMETBUS

What is all This Stuff?

MY EARLIEST MEMORY OF Aaron Cometbus is of arriving home
in Richmond, VA, to find a body lying face down on my living
room floor. I remember understanding that this was a corpse and
thinking, *okay, this is it, it's finally happened*. But the body was Aaron,
and Aaron was alive. He'd arrived exhausted from somewhere else,
and needed a floor to crash on.

How long did Aaron stay at that house? How long did he live in
Richmond? My life as a Virginian had a strange purgatory vibe—I'd
freed myself from the expense and stress of New York, but at the
cost of a chronic aimlessness that stretched the lazy days into years.
My memories from that time are jumbled. Surely I must've met
him years earlier, on one of my many visits to the Bay Area, either
at the Gilman Street club, or in one of the apartments or houses
or lofts I tromped through, hunting for similar corners of similar
living rooms in which to fling my own sleeping bag.

Although only a year older than me, Aaron made a name for
himself at a much younger age and in a much larger scene than
I, and he appears to have never slowed. He's published *Cometbus*

(with a few name changes) for over thirty-five years, performed with Crimpshrine and Pinhead Gunpowder, toured with Green Day, and labored on Gilman Street. One of his countless printed projects includes a 608-page collection of fanzine highlights. In our many conversations and occasional collaborations, it's never been entirely possible for me to separate Aaron the charming person from Aaron the dauntingly prolific institution. And yet Aaron has always treated me as a peer, not a poseur. I have no intention of ever correcting his mistake.

•••

Sam: Every year or so, you and I meet up and have long, weirdly complex conversations about all this stuff. But I can't quite figure out what *all this stuff* actually is. You seem comfortable with the word "underground," which for me has always had the ring of a placeholder. In the era of omnipresent social media, can anything actually *be* underground anymore? I've been using "hardcore punk," which is equally constricting, but in the opposite way: it's far too small a term. It's like we're a couple of mob goombahs, talking in hushed tones about *our thing*. So, I'm curious, how would you define all this stuff? Where are the fence posts?

Aaron: Underground has always been an exciting word for me, just like "downtown." It gives a sense of secrecy, but also the feeling of exploring subterranean worlds. It never meant that something was inaccessible, just that it wasn't shoved down your throat. But I'm surprised to hear you talking about hardcore. It seemed like you fled from that scene decades ago. Why return to the subject now?

S: I only fled New York City, not hardcore. When we met—in '93?— I'd recently moved to the South after having been kicked out of the NYC scene. It was a painful time in my life, and I probably gave you the impression that I was starting over. But I still had another decade of label work, touring, and zines ahead of me.

A: Yes, we were both escaping monsters we'd helped create, but we didn't know each other's monsters except in a passing way. That made for a nice bond. Yet you seemed so full of shame about everything you'd been part of. I didn't hear you mention hardcore except to mock it for another twenty years.

S: I think you're confusing how I felt about my own output with how I felt about the genre. I get this a lot. Even when I was in Wrangler Brutes, I was frequently accused of somehow mocking hardcore by touring in a hardcore band. It was weird. From my perspective, I don't see how anyone could look at my deep level of immersion and think, "There goes a guy who hates underground music."

People don't know what to make of artists who don't like their own past art. For me, the right to regret mistakes is fundamental. This subgenre—underground, hardcore, whatever name we're using—is saturated in self-congratulations. There aren't many people in my position. I've always loved hardcore. I just don't love my own contributions to it.

A: That makes sense. But you're sarcastic both in person and in print. I've never heard you say you loved anything before.

S: My reputation for sarcasm has been hard to shed. An old Albany pal once called me to complain about not having been thanked on a record I released. At a certain point in the conversation, I realized he wasn't going to accept my heartfelt apology. He'd convinced himself that everything I said was sarcastic. It was like being trapped in a *Twilight Zone*. That was twenty years ago. I'm hoping I'll have made some progress on this front before another twenty years are up. I'm really not that sarcastic anymore. But I'm wondering if the subculture we're discussing is old enough that some of its sensibilities no longer translate. I've read blog posts trying to "explain" to Millennials why eighties punk bands wanted to offend people. Is this something you've encountered? Meaning, do you find yourself having to explain more and more of your past, or the larger past you were part of?[35]

A: I think of it as a challenge, but mostly a pleasurable one, because explaining is telling a story. But my audience isn't mostly Millennials, so a generation gap isn't the issue. I think it just takes a long time to understand people's motivations, including your own.

S: But I'm not talking about a generation gap—I'm talking about a shift in sensibility, one of those slight twists of zeitgeist that sneaks up on everyone all at once. For example, I spent a summer in the late eighties working at a small-town newspaper. One day, combing through their archives, I discovered that the paper had referred to DUIs as "tipsy driving" only ten years earlier. Some of the "tipsy driving" arrest notices came with funny little cartoons of cross-eyed drunks. I'd come of age in the world of MADD. Up until then, I'd assumed that drunk driving had always been considered one rung above pedophilia. But this was a misconception, an error based on a very recent change in sensibility.

A: I think it's silly to look at mainstream media as an accurate gauge of values from any particular time. I mean, how much do the TV shows and movies of the eighties and nineties reflect the values and aspirations you had then?

S: This is an interesting difference between me and you. I've always felt a deep sense of continuity between the mass media of my childhood and the underground media of my teens. Monty Python, The Muppets, Looney Tunes… all these zany bits of culture were mirrored by the wacky characters I read about in *Maximumrocknroll*. Band members wearing their own band T-shirts onstage has always reminded me of the old Ben Cooper Halloween costumes (the cheap plastic mask of the Hulk matched by a picture of the Hulk on the cheap plastic tunic). When I saw *Repo Man* at fourteen, the film perfectly bridged the realms of sci-fi and hardcore. I know you got into the underground at a much younger age than me. So are you saying that you completely forsook pop culture once you found punk?

A: Remember how you'd slag bands in *Dear Jesus*, including mine, who you'd never heard? I'm not even giving you grief—just saying that being proud of what you've steered clear of is a normal human trait. So is holding yourself a step above everyone else. For me, that came even before punk. What everyone else calls popular culture, we called "death culture" where I'm from. So I avoided Saturday Night Fever. I've still never seen MTV. It's a little ridiculous, but other people avoided drugs, and mainstream culture was like drugs to me. I never understood the appeal. It's not all garbage, but mostly.

S: Wait a minute, what band of yours did I slag? And how do you know I never heard them? Maybe it was terrible!

A: Actually, you bragged to me about slagging it without ever hearing it. And since I'm fairly sure you've never heard a record I've played on, it doesn't matter which band it was. But you hit the nail on the head with what you said about *MRR*. You could find an excess of personality there that rivaled animation's golden age or comedy from the UK, at a time when American culture was either bland or sickening.

S: God, I wish I could go back in time and pants that man who was me. Since we're discussing *MRR*, this feels like the right spot to revisit a conversation from a few years back. I mentioned I'd once had a plan to save that magazine, and you groaned and said you had one too. But neither of us divulged the details. Care to share yours?[36]

A: You first.

S: Well, I always admired the fact that Tim Yohannan published *MRR*'s finances every year. But when it became clear that the magazine would stubbornly refuse to improve in the years after his death, the yearly surplus became something frustrating. Even today, the magazine still obeys the will of Tim. But this set of guidelines is obviously interpretational, and on one of Tim's strongest stances, *MRR* completely disregarded its founder's playbook. As soon as the magazine adopted bar codes, his corpse started doing cartwheels in its casket.[37] There is no reason to continue the Tim Would Have Wanted It This Way game. Why not take the magazine in a bold new direction?

A: Tim was stubborn, but he wasn't adverse to change. Ever since he died, *Maximum*'s been like the old friend at the party who's a boor. It's judgmental. It never has anything nice to say. And no matter how much you give, it always wants more.

S: It was jarring when I visited the *MRR* house and realized the computers were the same ones I'd used the last time I'd visited, twenty years earlier. There wasn't even a copier. (A kindly volunteer donated her camera's memory card so I could photograph old columns, like a spy.) The set-up seemed needlessly masochistic. I have no idea if *MRR* still runs a surplus, but I do know they're sitting on two huge assets. They could digitize and sell off that massive record collection.[38] And they could digitize and sell their first hundred issues. Conservatively, either project could bring in $100,000. Imagine what could be done with that kind of capital.

They could hire freelancers, get new equipment, fund quality investigative journalism. Imagine ProPublica's AC Thompson writing *MRR* cover stories.[39]

A: I was on them for years to sell the records to a university or cultural institution that would allow them steady access. We're talking a *million* dollars, which was enough to put the down payment on a house and print the mag for years to come. Instead of bailing out the ship every month with benefits and funding campaigns, we should be looking at *MRR* and our other institutions the same way we look at ourselves: How can we have the longest, most fulfilling life, and what resources do we have to ensure that? Like my other old friends, *MRR* probably has what it takes to thrive without anyone's help, if only they would put their best foot forward and change.

But there's a larger issue here: Clubs like Gilman and ABC No Rio are our community centers. As such, they should meet the community's needs, which have changed considerably since we were teenagers. Probably they'd serve us better now as daycare and rehab centers. Flea markets. Funeral parlors.

MRR is supposed to be a community mouthpiece, but its content and format barely reflect what people actually care about. Even folks interested in the latest hardcore band from Burundi want reports that are passionate and informed.

S: This use of "we" and "us" gets to another major difference between you and me. I might have felt that kinship in high school, but by the mid-nineties I'm not sure I felt part of any "we" or "us," any more than I could feel that about people in a grocery store on any given day. Scenes are huge kinetic sculptures made out of people. Turnover is rapid. It seems doubtful there's ever been any two major urban shows with the exact same attendees at both, although statistically it must have happened.

I'm envious of anyone who can feel connected to a community over the long haul. It's caused me some serious grief over the years to not share this feeling. To me, the word "community" is something I've gotten burned on over and over again since childhood. Maybe this is too huge a question, but how do you see yourself as part of something so huge and unfixed, and constantly evolving?

A: Sooner or later it becomes a typesetting question, because you simply can't live with everything in quotes. It's annoying to read and even worse in person, constantly making bunny ears in the air like a crazy person. So far you've put qualifiers on punk, hardcore, the underground, explaining things, community, and now even us and we. Of course all these terms are loaded, but it's better to use them and hope that the complicated feelings are something we all share. At any rate, I try to include myself these days instead of feeling left out.

Funny you should mention the supermarket, though. That's where I feel a sense of community the most. I'm part of a members-only food co-op, which isn't only highly functional, its the sweetest place I know. It makes sense to aim for the same result from institutions like *MRR*, Gilman, and ABC No Rio, which we've put sweat equity into—and maybe even from punk itself. What's the alternative, anyway? Disappointment is crushing, but isolation is probably worse.

S: That seems too black and white. Isn't there any terrain between disappointment and isolation?

A: That's what everyone wants to know!

S: But this sweat equity argument gets to another question I've always meant to ask you. When I was sixteen and made my first fanzine, a collaboration with my best friend, I spent several months thinking we had invented something entirely new. Over the years, I've met other zine nerds who made the same mistake. So when you made your absolute first fanzine, were you aware of other fanzines? Or were you already plugged into this world?

A: I also started out collaborating with my best friend. We'd seen *Ripper* and *Creep*, which were two of the coolest magazines ever made, but there wasn't any question about imitating them, even if we'd wanted to. In a tiny way, by doing it our way, I think we did invent something new. Probably you did too. You may not realize that my coeditor was Jesse Michaels, who you did a split book with yourself not long ago. What became of the kid you did your first fanzine with?

S: He and I roomed together in college and eventually we drifted apart. It took me a long time, years, to figure out that I was completely capable of making a fanzine all by myself. Even then, I was always the guy on tour who tried to fill downtime by getting bandmates to make weird little one-off zines with me. It never worked.

A: I did end up making fanzines all by myself, which I kind of regret. I always thought someone would come along to replace Jesse, but it never happened. Those early collaborative relationships are crazy, because you don't know how to work with people at all. They can be amazing, but also spectacularly painful, and either way, they're foundational—you spend your life either avoiding that dynamic or trying to replicate it. Thankfully, me and Jesse are still friends. But I'm curious about your other collaborations. Can we talk about Adam and Neil?

S: All those Lifesblood guys hazed me by humiliating themselves. They'd pants each other and run around my co-ed dorm, hurl my food out the fifth-floor window, and follow me into crowded ATM foyers to loudly announce their plans for recircumcision ("It keeps growing back, guys!"). I was the straight man for their comedy troupe. Since I was a cringing ninny when I moved to NYC, this was probably a good thing.

A: So how did a comedy troupe turn into Born Against?

S: Only a year before we formed, Adam and I were both functionally apolitical. I followed the news carefully and owned a filing cabinet for clippings, but disliked "political" punk bands. He furiously protested, but only at shows of punk bands he thought had sold out. In hindsight, the Tompkins Square Park riot in the summer of 1988 probably accelerated our turns toward radicalization—the artistic version of radicalization—even though neither of us was actually present.

Once me and Adam clicked, we really clicked. There was a sense of mission I've never experienced since. It was an intense four-year partnership. Some parts no longer compute. For example, how were we able to collaborate so effortlessly on lyrics? It seems crazy now, like trying to write a diary with another person. I do remember we squabbled a lot. Sometimes there was shouting. Once, on tour, we both confessed that we'd dreamed about beating each other with pipes or baseball bats. At the time, I considered simmering mutual hostility the price of a successful partnership. I was too young to know any better. There is no way I'd ever collaborate like that again.

A: And with Neil?

S: My work with Neil substituted range for mission. We've labored together on dozens of projects—music, artwork, fanzines, shirt designs, short films, two different record labels—but none done with the intensity of those Adam collaborations.

I have a lot of respect for both those guys. Enough so that I'm willing to admit it in print, overriding my aversion to the backslapping self-congratulations that so permeate this world. They had to put up with a spectacular amount of my babyman baloney. I should probably get them both gift cards to Applebee's.

A: I love these stories. It's telling that you didn't talk about the music itself, which is the result of a band but not necessarily the point. Writing about music, as you're doing now, how do you reconcile the fact that the records and shows—the parts the public sees and hears—are just a tiny part of a band's life?

S: Well, I'm not a musician. The entire experience of being in a band has always been completely different for me. And tour got a lot less fun once I figured out I was spending twenty-three and a half hours a day to support thirty minutes of performance.

A: I never understood what bands were about until the people I'd played music with started dying. Then I was so grateful for the intensity we'd shared. Not the shows so much as the recording sessions, the fights, the all-night drives. Besides their lovers, no one had been that intimate with them, or sweated and screamed together in as many dark rooms. Now when I listen to the records we made, it's more telling than the Nixon tapes. It might as well be a recording of a conversation at the family dinner table growing up, or an argument with my girlfriend. It's that personal.

S: I'm grateful that none of my ex-bandmates have died yet. But that kind of passion was never part of my musical career. I never had cathartic moments. Instead it was constant crises of faith: in parking lots, dressing rooms, strangers' houses, onstage. So many moments where it was like a cartoon soap bubble popping over my head and I came out of a trance thinking, "Why am I doing this?"

Professional musicians are easy to mock for all the rules and restrictions placed on them by managers and labels, but it must be nice to have the through line of a paycheck, one unwavering motive, to propel them through the grind of touring. I do remember one instant—and only one—when I thought, "Hey! I'm the lead singer of a popular hardcore band! This is exciting!" February 12, 1992. Oakland. That was it.

A: I was there. That must have been right before your drummer impaled himself on the cymbal stand in an ill-advised acrobatic leap, and had to be taken to the hospital. Everyone in the audience was trying hard not to laugh.

S: Ouch. That was a serious injury! Although once he went into shock, our drummer seemed to find the whole thing just as funny as our loyal audience.

A: Can we talk about sentimentality in music? Obviously, it can be sickening. But it also takes guts to risk seeming cheesy, singing about something like love.

S: Knowing what you know about me, this feels like a set-up question. It takes a lot of guts to act on love. It takes zero guts to sing about it. Hitching your music to compulsory emotions— expressing feelings experienced by every human who has ever lived—is the cheapest of cheap shots. And I say this as someone whose best recorded track was a love song, although one written by a non-band member.

A: But those sappy sentiments seem to come with a wink and a nod, at least in the music I've been listening to lately. Like, "I want to slit my wrists, but instead I'm going to find one ray of hope, no matter how dim, and cling to it." As much as I like honest music, I think there's something noble about that denial, and the desire to see the bright side.

S: You know the hardcore group Uniform Choice? Their first LP finished with a track called "Silenced." It is nothing more than two men reading a Hallmark card. Literally. That level of pure cheese is how I hear all love songs. If I had to, I suppose I could come up with a half-dozen ones by bands I like. But still: gross.

A: But schmaltz is a real part of life. No one can deny how touching it is when your cat presents you with a dead mouse as a gift, even if it makes you sick. On me, the Bee Gees have the same effect. Besides, there's new wave playing at every wedding I go to, which makes me wonder if punks didn't fail at making the soundtrack to our own lives.

S: My beef is with the laziness. I like music that isn't lazy. In high school, I learned about Tom Waits (through *MRR!*) and completely fell in love with the storytelling craftsmanship of his *Rain Dogs* LP. Even then, the cornball sappiness of the track "Downtown Train" struck me as a clumsy fit with the rest of the record, the "TV Party" of the LP.

A: A novelty tune?

S: The wrong song on the right record. Different conversation. But at the risk of flipping this back on you, cop-style, what's the most aggressive music you listen to? I have a hard time picturing you enjoying the first Crumbsuckers LP.

A: I love hardcore, too—at least the early Bay Area version of it, like Society Dog and Social Unrest, music that's aggressive and vulnerable at the same time. Or maybe I'll listen to a thirty second blast of Midwestern thrash to gather strength to face the day.

Unfortunately, where I live is really loud, so noise is something I mostly try to avoid.

S: Aaaaaand this is the part where I thank you for saying the most old-mannish thing in a book I am the author of. This reminds me, have you ever heard of the "Reminiscence bump"? This is the idea that a disproportionate amount of your memories come from high school/college age, meaning, among other things, that your musical tastes get locked in from this age. I've noticed that the music I keep returning to is all the same stuff I listened to in eleventh and twelfth grade (early Dischord, Schoolly D, Slayer). Is this the case with you?

A: The music I like is mostly old, but a lot of it is new to me. Quintessential California records like Joni Mitchell's *Blue* or the last Mamas and Papas LP I've heard for the first time only recently, because I didn't grow up with music around. But I'm fine with having a handful of records that I listen to over and over. I'm a voracious reader but not a voracious listener.

I worry, though, about people putting too much emphasis on their formative years. They say it's impossible to make friends as an adult the way you did as a kid, but I haven't found that to be the case. I think it's that same laziness you spoke of.

S: Yeah, I'm the same way. Open as a reader, closed as a listener. I worry a lot about creeping laziness. Last month I got bored during a movie in Hollywood, so I left the theater and walked next door to Amoeba Records. But the endless rows of music disgusted me—it felt like the time my band visited a twenty-four-hour porno shop in Omaha and I wound up staring at the floor or ceiling in prudish distaste. I felt no connection to any of the records, or even genres. Only the books section interested me.

A: Bands are like families for me, so going to a porn store together is bound to be awkward. On the other hand, bands are used to being awkward in public. When my guitarist was in prison and the rest of us came to visit, we were more comfortable than the other families in the waiting room, since we were used to embarrassing ourselves onstage.

S: Certainly the comedy of it all is a hoot. I've seen so many insane onstage meltdowns, and participated in a few. I've heard so many outrageous justifications for irrational behavior, glimpsed so many simmering bandmate resentments exploding into rage over artistic direction, or perceived slights, or the Case Of The Missing $14. A hundred years ago, people had careers or families or military service. None of those human experiences are perfect, but at least they do a great job of providing motivation.

The healthiest definition I ever read was attributed to Tobi Vail from Bikini Kill: "A band is any song you ever played with anybody, even if only once." In that single sentence, one can view all sorts of new models for band life in the future. But in the here and now, musicians have to constantly justify what they do, to themselves and others. Since I'm no longer part of that mass suspension of belief, I can just relax and enjoy it as an amused bystander.

A: It's interesting that you quote a drummer, but all your collaborators were guitarists. I tend to see the world as a war between guitarists and drummers, with bassists as collateral damage and singers mostly just oblivious. The drummers in the audience would like to know your position on drummers, in case a battle breaks out.

S: But singers are almost always the face of any band. Which means we're the ones getting blamed for everyone else's behavior. Even now, I'm the guy who gets blamed and credited for everything

Born Against ever did, as if I'd driven myself from town to town, performing onstage with a kazoo, bass drum, and cymbals strapped between my knees.

A: Which would make drummers the ass of the band. We get it. We can read between the lines. But writing about bands besides your own, what interests you most—the intentions and conflicts? The records and art?

S: The only thing that doesn't interest me is the act of making music itself. It's not just that I don't know how to play any instruments. It's that even the applied science part of being in a band never made sense. I still can't name all the parts of a drum kit, even though I've carried them hundreds of times. I don't know how to operate a PA system. I have no idea what a "power chord" is. I've never heard any difference between analog and digital recordings. Musical notation might as well be Arabic.

A: Now you sound like a drummer yourself.

S: That ignorance made me the world's worst record label owner, and probably a pain to share a band with. But it gave me a better appreciation of everything surrounding the music— enough of an appreciation to fill a book, apparently.

THE TROUBLEMAKER

What Happens if you Just Continue on the Same Trajectory?

2008

ON A WEDNESDAY AFTERNOON last February, I shared a booth with a man named 26 inside the Travelers Club International Restaurant & Tuba Museum in Okemos, MI. We'd picked a spot far enough from the door to give us some respite from the winter blast, and dozens of African masks and beautiful battered tubas lined the walls above us. Police reports have listed 26 as five foot seven with a "thin" build. In person, it was a little hard to tell how thin he was. He wore a blue crocheted sweater, fraying and loose, and an over-sized baseball cap with the logo of the Weather Channel covered his scraggly hair, which was wild and wiry but not yet gray. He wears large rings on almost every finger and projects an amiable fragility.

The waitress seemed surprised and delighted to see him. "Oh, you have some new music since *Patricia?*" she asked in a Russian accent, referring to the solo album he named after the therapist he used to see in the 1990s, back when he was a regular at the restaurant.

"I've had a couple of records since *Patricia*," he said. "And I put one out just a few years ago under the name 26." She nodded, perhaps thinking he meant this as a band name, not his own. "Before that, I was in another band, with a bad word in the name." She smiled again. Earlier in our conversation, he'd winced repeating this bad word—26 no longer swears—and he seemed slightly relieved that she didn't force the subject.

Stereo speakers played NPR in the background, and when an update came on from the Lewis Libby trial, 26 quickly plugged his ears. Since March 20, 2004, he has refused all news of the outside world. "Technically, I don't even know who the president is," he said gleefully after the story was over. "I told one of my tenants not to tell me about anything in the news. Then he told me about this president that had died recently. I *specifically* told him not to tell me the news. He said, 'Oh, I thought it was okay if someone was dead.' I had a lot of problems with this tenant."

Thinking the president he was referring to was Gerald Ford, I mentioned that I would be taking a trip to the Gerald Ford Presidential Library in Grand Rapids later in the week. "No, it was the other president," he explained with a slight irritation, meaning Ronald Reagan, who'd passed away three years earlier. Our waitress' shift ended not long after we arrived, and she made him promise to bring her one of his newer CDs. On the other end of the restaurant, a large woman barreled in and screamed, "Where's my fucking money!" as she disappeared behind the counter.

"Oh," 26 murmured, rising from our table. "There's that word again."

•••

26, 54, WAS BORN Doc Corbin Dart outside Mason, MI, and has lived in the greater Lansing area all his life. His former first name is not short for anything, having been inherited from his grandfather, Doc Campbell Dart, who was himself named after a local Dr. Campbell.

His great-grandfather, Rollin C. Dart, founded the Dart National Bank, and his great-uncle Bill founded Dart Container, the world's largest manufacturer of Styrofoam cups.

Most people who know of Doc Dart do not know that he was well into adulthood before gaining notoriety. He started work at the Dart National Bank while still a teenager, beginning at the lowest position, collections, but on track to eventually become the fourth generation of bank president. In 1980, he returned to Michigan State University for his bachelor's in anthropology, married his girlfriend Angie two years later, and became a father the year after that.

His first passion was always music. Doc turned eleven the year The Beatles played the Ed Sullivan show and the band made a huge impact on him. From adolescence on, WABX and WKNR in Detroit served as slender lifelines (sometimes smothered by the signal strength of a local country station) to tectonic shifts in American culture. For young Doc, Bob Dylan and Jimi Hendrix had equal weight with the images of the anti-war movement he saw on TV, and the points where the war intersected his own life. Eighteen in 1971, he was issued a card for the last Vietnam draft lottery.

In the early 1970s, he played keyboard for local bands Kilgore Trout and Swell (to be said with a manic smile: "We're Swell!"). He bought records voraciously in East Lansing, and had a huge record collection by the mid-1970s. But by that time he'd also come to feel that his favorite bands had run out of steam, addled by drugs and withering under the malaise of the Me Decade. When Doc first heard the Sex Pistols in late 1977, he found a great continuity with the ferocity of his favorite sixties bands. More of this energy arrived in a deluge of new music: Talking Heads, Buzzcocks, The Stranglers, The Ramones, and especially Devo all had a huge impact on Doc. For years, he'd felt that the United States had gotten too apolitical after Vietnam, and the confrontational politics of punk rock invigorated him.

A new subculture bloomed in the early eighties that seemed to finally capture Doc's mood; the faster, more aggressive strain of punk rock calling itself "hardcore." Although its brightest stars hailed from the coasts, the Midwest produced its share of luminaries, covering a wide slice of the genre's diversity: teenage skaters The Necros hailed from small town Maumee, the ferocious Negative Approach came from Detroit, Lansing had the sadistic pranksters The Meatmen. At Club Doobie in Haslett, near Lake Lansing, Doc met Steve Shelley (later of Sonic Youth) and Scott Begerston, both members of a Joy Division tribute band Doc was fond of. Doc introduced Steve and Scott to his cousin Joe in 1981, with the idea of forming a band in which he could finally uncork his id. True to this concept, the new group called itself The Crucifucks.

Doc Dart was twenty-eight when the band started playing shows, but refers to himself during this period as a toddler. As a child, he'd been called Little Doc, to distinguish himself from his grandfather, and this nickname now became his alter ego. When Little Doc performed live he would frequently cut himself with razors or broken glass. Alcohol was often involved, and he did even more damage to himself diving off tall objects into the crowd. Because of their name, the band found itself locked out of most venues. They played Lansing as The Scribbles (named for Doc's old dog), and on the road would find themselves billed as "Crucifex," or "Cruise Effects," or "The Christmas Folks."

In April 1982, The Crucifucks were slated to play with The Meatmen at Bunch's Continental Cafe in East Lansing. Passing out flyers before the show, Doc continued off the sidewalk and into a restaurant, handing more flyers to bewildered diners as he walked through the building and out the restaurant's back door, where he was greeted by a police officer. The band didn't get to play that night, but Doc's mug shot became moderately iconic in the scene. That summer, The Meatmen got The Crucifucks on a much larger bill in Pontiac, MI, just outside Detroit, with San Francisco's prestigious Dead Kennedys headlining. The Dead Kennedys had been a band for four years at this point, and were bona fide celebrities in punk circles. They were also very similar to Doc's band in style, temperament, and confrontational theatrics.

Jello Biafra, lead singer of The Dead Kennedys, recalled this set. "Here was this singer with a really high voice and Lyndon Johnson ears and a great big grin tormenting every single person in the room. I mean, not all of Negative Approach and Necros fans were real bright. And the singer of this band had bored in on that and was just finding ways to needle them over and over and over again to the point where they were swinging at him or taking shots at him and yelling 'get off the stage,' and then he'd just leap on top of them! And somehow they'd miss and he'd get back on stage and annoy them some more." When he came through Michigan the next year, Jello brought The Crucifucks along to Cleveland, where he offered the band a record on his own label, Alternative Tentacles.

Without this intervention, The Crucifucks would probably have puttered along as a local band for a few years and disbanded. Instead, their 1984 debut album is a pinnacle of outraged and outrageous glee; a record that can be best described as *unreasonable*. The album's notoriety belongs to its vocalist. Doc's voice is so far beyond the pale of normal performance that it defies comparison. He squeals through several words at once, dripping with derision, at times channeling the quavering drama that Jello brought to his songs, at other points sounding like Walt Disney's Roger Rabbit. In "You Give Me The Creeps," Doc bleats, "Give me your money!

I don't have to make it!" In "Hinckley Had A Vision," he bawls, "I wanna take the president,"—here the band drops out and he continues a cappella—"chop off his head, and mail it to them in a garbage baaaaaaaaaag!" This last word is stretched out as the squall of a child having a meltdown in a toy store (perhaps because this act was expressed as desire, not intent, Doc never received Secret Service attention). I asked Biafra, a formidable record collector, if he'd ever encountered any vocalist who sounded quite like Doc. He hadn't.

•••

By the mid-eighties, the group had the dubious distinction of being one of the most extreme bands in a musical scene that was already pretty extreme to begin with. The punk subculture, having loudly dispensed with most hippie artifacts, retained the word "pig" to describe police, and in the early hardcore scene being anti-cop was one of the few issues everyone could agree on. Almost every band reflected this sentiment in their lyrics, from Black Flag (apolitical) to Dead Kennedys (wildly political) to Bad Brains (Rastafarian). But there was a distinct line between opposing police brutality and calling for the actual death of police officers, and Doc Dart was farther past this line than any of his contemporaries. In 1992, rapper Ice-T caused a national controversy with his song "Cop Killer." Only obscurity saved Doc's own "Cops For Fertilizer" from wider scrutiny.[40]

The second time the Dead Kennedys came through Lansing, The Crucifucks again opened. "Much to my own shock, the audience loved The Crucifucks," Biafra recalled. "And this was a *real* shock to Doc. He wasn't quite sure what to do. So finally he said something at the end about, 'the pointless spectacle that the hardcore scene is today.' And then of course the whole audience turned on him and began booing and throwing things and Doc was grinning ear to ear. He had to find a way to get at them, and he did."

•••

26 LIVES IN A suburban neighborhood of comfortable two-story houses and the occasional barn. The nearby streets are lined with well-shoveled driveways and a good selection of American flags— both the traditional house-mounted kind and the smaller yard flags that, in the president's second term, generally indicate support of Bush and/or the wars—as well as a smattering of peace signs. An anarchy symbol has been badly spray painted on the back of a traffic sign one block away.

His address was easy to find. Set back from the sidewalk, eight huge sheets of bright blue plywood had been nailed over the windows of his house. Hurled eggs had washed off with time, but there were still plenty of visible white streaks from the dozens of paint balls shot at the property. Two large sheets of tar paper covered several messages that had been painted near the front door. From the outside, the building looked abandoned.

Inside, a bright light shone upward on the floating staircase, spotlighting long, two-story front windows and the unpainted plywood underneath. In the living room, we had to step around a half dozen fifty pounds bags of bird and animal feed neatly arranged by the sliding glass doors leading to the backyard. Maps of Africa, India, and Lake Superior had been carefully placed around the room, and a poster of Princess Diana hung on the wall near the kitchen. The space seemed unused, but not dirty; the living room parlor reserved for the rare visitor. The incense was so thick that my jacket still smelled of our conversation hours after I'd left.

The layout of the backyard didn't quite conform to what I'd already seen online, but when I described peering down at the property a week earlier on Google Earth, I realized this may have been a violation of his news blackout. The rule was hard to abide by, partially because I constantly found myself tempted to test him. Driving through Okemos earlier in the day, we'd passed a flag lowered to half-mast, and I'd asked if he ever felt curious about what was going on in the world, prompting this strange exchange:

"I assume Cheney is president now."

"Well, I'm not going to tell you."

"Good."

In his living room, I produced an iPod to record our conversation. When I mentioned that it could hold hundreds of hours of interviews, he seemed incredulous.

26 frequently refers to himself as "a weirdo," and things he does not like (the first Crucifucks record, Rush Limbaugh, Buddhism) as "abominations." His conversation is sprinkled with Midwesternisms: "aw jeez," "gee whiz," "oh gosh," and the occasional flat "yah" I had previously associated with Minnesotans. When he offered me "some pop"—he keeps a refrigerator stocked with Faygo and little else—it took a moment to realize he didn't mean a joint (a grave mistake with the rabidly anti-pot 26).

When I tried to unearth the root of his anti-police attitudes, I was surprised to hear there had been no one defining incident in his history with the law. His first arrest in 1971 came as the result of social experimentation. "I didn't feel like I had a lot to be afraid of, but at the same time I was confused about the whole thing about rights," he told me. "And it was my understanding that you could say anything you wanted to say. I thought, 'I can say anything I want to say! And I can say it to the police! And I'm going to! So there!' And I wanted to see how that played out. I'd assumed that would play out fine in real life." He laughed. "But that's not the way life works."

Two more arrests came in the early seventies, one after he'd insulted an officer during a friend's arrest. In court he'd acted as his own attorney. "I was completely convinced that police officers lied under oath all the time. And now I can only point to my own experience in that regard. I can't assume that any more. My experience was all bad, *all* bad, but there could be a lot of reasons for that. I was just so saturated with hate. For police. That it was glimmering all over me. And they pick up on it right away. I couldn't have pretended I liked them. It was just a given that if I was anywhere around a police officer," he snapped his fingers, "they were going to pick up on that hate and they were going to take me in."

His four-and-a-half-year career at Dart National Bank during this period only hardened this radical bent. Rising through the ranks, he found his politics turning farther and farther left, even as he had to deal with the resentment of coworkers for the implied nepotism of his ascent. "I looked like an asswipe," 26 told me. "I had a beard and long hair. And I was depressed. I had no business being in a bank to begin with." Doc had been in charge of raising the American flag in front of the bank every morning and used to cross the lobby dragging it behind him on the floor. A long-standing dispute over his hair length spurred the final confrontation in 1976. The following year the bank denied him unemployment benefits and he went to court against his father.

By the 1980s, Doc was a known quantity to the Lansing police, especially after he started publishing the Lansing Police State Journal, a small fanzine filled with articles and photos relating to slain police officers. In the spring of 1985, Doc held an "Ozzy party" and for some reason a local band asked to play his porch. This was in a residential area, after midnight, and a severe departure from the party's theme (to play every record Ozzy Osbourne appeared on), but Doc agreed because he thought the authorities would give him one customary warning. Instead, a phalanx of squad cars converged on the house and police started arresting people. Doc ran back into his house, grabbed a beer and—in what he concedes was not a masterstroke—exited through the back door and returned to the lawn to watch the mayhem. Two policemen subdued him, beat him, and dramatically snapped his pinkie in front of horrified onlookers. He was charged with assaulting a police officer and lost the case to a judge he recognized as a friend of his father.

After his final arrest (for resisting arrest) in 1987, he was given two consecutive twenty-day sentences. His uncle Steve Dart, a prominent local attorney, arranged to have Doc released with a $1,000 fine and a promise to seek psychological counseling. His wife had earlier threatened to leave him if he'd ever gotten arrested again, and she made good on this threat after his arraignment, taking their four-year old son Evan and three-year old daughter Sarah. After his family left, Doc found himself alone in a messy house, drifting toward rock bottom, emerging for occasional beer runs wearing nothing but an oversized tie-dye shirt.

•••

To MOVE FROM FLOOR to floor in 26's house, one has to cross the small landing on the floating staircase, which requires ducking under the leaves of a seven-foot potted fig tree named Frank that, in lieu of sunlight, gets one high-wattage bulb for twelve hours a day. The naming of things not normally named—plants, wild animals, regions of the backyard—is generally the hallmark of a person whose world has been reduced to a house. Although he is not agoraphobic, 26 has achieved a high level of self-containment in his own quarters. He no longer rents out the spare room, and spends most of his time reading on his bed, or in the yard feeding the wildlife.

Seen from the outside, 26's days had at first appeared rather bleak. It didn't take long to realize that his private world with the animals, the endless soap opera of births and deaths and new arrivals and disappearances, took up much of his time and emotional energy. The raccoons in particular, 26 told me, are "a five to ten day story. That's how rich the story is." I'd looked forward to the feeding of the raccoons, but a ferocious cold snap had moved in on the entire Midwest that week, leaving temperatures, with wind chill, in the negative teens. When 26 gave me a quick tour of the backyard and back deck, we crossed dozens of tiny footprints. But the animals had gone elsewhere.

•••

In 1989, Doc Dart weighed running for Lansing's city council. The Crucifucks had disbanded not long after his family left, and the court-ordered counseling turned out to be a short-term godsend. Doc quit drinking, and opened a baseball card store called Little Doc's Cards in downtown Lansing (since childhood, Doc had been an ardent fan of the Detroit Tigers and, after their management made him "sick," the Chicago Cubs). The long hours and newfound clarity, however, only did so much to moderate his severe depression.

Despite his dark moods, running for public office had seemed worthwhile, and a natural extension of his contempt for the Lansing city council. Doc told only a few people of his intentions, but word somehow leaked back to his uncle. This uncle stopped by Doc's store one afternoon that spring for a "frank chat," the gist of which was that Doc should not embarrass the family by running for city council. Later, Doc realized that his feelings had been hurt. He thought through the message and decided that perhaps his uncle had meant it would be an embarrassment to run for such a lowly position. He decided to run for mayor of Lansing instead.

At first glance, a template for Doc's campaign seems obvious. Jello Biafra ran for mayor of San Francisco in 1979, finishing fourth out of ten. That campaign received wide publicity for his proposals to ban cars within the city and force businessmen to wear clown suits. Biafra and his supporters used the race for great spectacle, holding rallies with campaign signs like "Apocalypse Now, Vote Biafra" and "If He Doesn't Win...I'll Kill Myself."

Doc, however, decided to run as straight a campaign as possible. He'd recently read that Lansing had ranked fifth in rapes in the United States, just behind Flint, and made this the centerpiece of his campaign. Taking $400 slated for baseball card inventory, he put on his best suit and walked through every neighborhood in Lansing, pledging $30,000 of the mayor's $67,000 salary toward building a rape crisis center.

Children ridiculed him for campaigning in green tennis shoes. There were days when depression completely sidelined him, but he felt he had to push himself as much as possible. Doc decided that if the media unearthed his police record or his band, he was fully prepared to convert the run into another circus act. But the local paper and networks barely mentioned his past. I'd interviewed him for my fanzine a few years after this race, and even then he seemed slightly stunned that he'd been viewed as a serious candidate. "I could have been, like, David Duke," he'd told me in 1991. "I could've lead the KKK ten years ago and ninety-nine percent of the people would not have known. They knew I was a baseball card dealer."

The primary fell on August 9. Doc received just over five percent of the vote. The *Lansing State Journal* commented that the outcome was "to the surprise of no one—except, perhaps, Doc Dart in a moment of unbridled fantasy." ("There were a couple of times I thought I could win," 26 told me, laughing. "So, you know, they got it right.") August 29 was Doc's "Black Tuesday," a low point in his battle with depression. He describes this period in apocalyptic terms, and told me that it took a tremendous force of will to keep himself alive during the worst of his depression.

Doc's defeat removed all personality from the general election. Mayor Terry McKane and councilman Lou Adado had faced each other four years earlier, and both campaigns lacked passion. By October, the race was a dead heat. Realizing he had been handed a rare bit of leverage, Doc called each campaign to throw his 568 votes to whoever met his demands. Both candidates ignored him. He finally cornered Adado and McKane in October by calling into a public radio debate. While the show's host seemed receptive to Doc's anti-rape proposals, both candidates shrugged him off. Doc hung up, convinced his leverage had amounted to nothing. Two hours later, Mayor McKane stepped into his baseball card store and asked for Doc's endorsement. The mayor won reelection by 444 votes. The rape crisis center was built the next year, at Sparrow Hospital, just seven blocks from his store, and Doc served on the initial planning committee.

I'd spoken with the former mayor the week before meeting with 26, and Mr. McKane told me he had no memory of the dramatic baseball card shop endorsement, a matter of public record. When I relayed this to 26, he appeared disappointed, although the late-addition snub seemed in keeping with the general indifference that had greeted him in 1989. For their part, the *Lansing State Journal* never followed up on the big story in their midst: the singer of The Crucifucks had chosen the mayor of Michigan's capital city.

•••

IN 1992, ALTERNATIVE TENTACLES rereleased the first two Crucifucks albums on one CD. The back cover featured a photo of a police officer gunned down in the street. The picture first appeared on a poster for the Philadelphia Fraternal Order of Police, and had been sent to Doc years earlier by a fan. Unbeknownst to Doc, the officer in the photo, John Whalen, had merely posed, prone and bloody, as part of a public relations campaign. ("You wouldn't sacrifice your life for a million bucks," the poster read. "A Philadelphia police officer does it for a lot less. They need your support.")

Three years after its release, a friend of Officer Whalen walked into a Philadelphia Borders Books and discovered the CD. Whalen and the FOP filed civil suit against Borders, Alternative Tentacles, and The Crucifucks, perhaps the only time in American jurisprudence that a civil action has carried an obscenity in its title.[41] Doc was formally served notice in his baseball card store, but after Borders' dismissal from the case no one notified Alternative Tentacles, and in November 1996 the plaintiffs won a default judgment of $2.2 million. Although there was never much suspense about the lack of legal merit, the ruling suddenly put the record label in the awkward position of having to reverse a judgment that, if enforced, could vaporize their company.

Doc traveled to Philadelphia for an appeals hearing, but generally felt sidelined, forced by finances to piggyback on his label's legal team and once again operating in the shadow of Jello. Biafra had won his own high-stakes, high-visibility obscenity trial in 1986, and Doc resented the lack of exposure for his own trial. "Any time there was a lawsuit against the Dead Kennedys they soaked it for all the publicity it was worth," 26 told me.

The case was dismissed the next summer, on the grounds that Whalen could not be identified—an outstretched, bullet-riddled arm covers his face—and the FOP, not being a human being, had no right to privacy. 26 told me it was "a nice twist" that the FOP got the judgment first, to get them "all excited" only to have it yanked away. But he still felt deceived that the officer in the photo hadn't really been dead to begin with.

•••

DOC/26 HAS SPENT MUCH of his life operating as a near-caricature, the kind of character a right-wing talk-show host might invent. He has burned flags at concerts, mocked the deaths of specific police officers, and refers to himself as "pro-abortion," not "pro-choice." He also seems to hate leftists. At the infamous 1994 KKK rally in Lansing, Doc heckled the Klan, then heckled the police, then heckled the other hecklers. At one point in our conversation, he dismissed the Chicago Eight defendants for "making a mockery" of their 1969 trial. When I questioned him about the Crucifucks' song "Lights Over Baghdad"—which seems to express sympathies with mass-murderer Timothy McVeigh—he told me that this was his mindset in the eighties and nineties. "It all stems from my hatred of the United States government."

It is hard to imagine him breaking free of this trajectory had something larger not come to fill his life. Since 1999, much of his daily schedule has been consumed with what he calls his "mystical practices," although it was nearly impossible to pin down what this entailed, beyond extensive reading and breathing exercises. I found myself continually asking if I was interrupting his daily schedule. In our talks, he occasionally grew defensive, repeating that he wouldn't "apologize for his mystical practices," despite the fact that no one was asking him to do so. When I didn't understand certain points, the suggestion was more one of miscommunication than evasion; I was in his space, demanding answers for things he had long since given up explaining. "Mysticism is a huge subject," he finally told me, "and the semantics of it are complicated and very hard to communicate."

In his own environment, 26's physical demeanor is that of an intense loner, someone who is up to something deep within their own confines. As he spoke, I tried to figure out who he reminded me of. At certain points he grew quite animated, jabbing the air with an unlit cigarette or a Triscuit, and then his face would suddenly take on the hangdog intensity of actor Chris Cooper. At other times his voice dropped in pitch slightly and he resembled actor Ted Levine as Buffalo Bill, the recluse serial killer in *Silence Of The Lambs*. (A closer match was later offered by 26 himself: actor Jim Varney. "I think I could be the next 'Hey Vern' guy," he said, striking another manic grin.)

The name change came less as a result of the mysticism than a desire to distance himself from his old persona. In the 1990s he'd tried "Doc Corbin Dart" and his grandfather's shortened "D. C. Dart," but still felt that his name did not fit his personality. The number had come to him in a dream years earlier, but, as with his antagonism toward the police, there had been no defining event. 26 also pointed out that the number, like all pairings of two digits, appeared pretty much everywhere. "You get free advertising for your name all the time! Right? Am I right?"

"When I first started this mysticism thing," he told me, "a lot of my source material that was most important to me at the time involved men whose children had grown up, who separated themselves from their family deliberately, either to live in a cave or an ashram or something like that. You can't have *any* distractions... that includes family. So when I first started that, I put both of my children on notice that I may not be seeing them for a few years." Neither child approved this plan. "They both just piled it on." He smiled. "And it was really cool."

Evan Dart now lives a mile down the road from his father. At twenty-four, he is a soft spoken, handsome young man who looks vaguely punky in that way young people of the twenty-first century do even though they do not listen to punk rock (Evan favors electronic music). When we met in the living room, I was struck by the traces of young Doc's mug shot in Evan's face. 26 brought us each a can of Dr. Faygo and then dutifully made a point of going elsewhere while I talked with his son, as if he were following the protocols of a legal deposition.

I asked Evan if he thought his father was lonely. He said he didn't, but understood that the general atmosphere—the boarded up windows and lingering neighborhood hostility—were conducive to loneliness. Having gone to live with his mother as a young boy, he never fully learned of his dad's public persona until just a few years ago. We talked some about his father's history of depression, and I asked if the mysticism seemed to be helping. Evan grew quiet and said, "My God, yeah. I can't describe how much happier he is. I mean, it's his entire personality. When he threw all this other stuff out, he just changed completely."

We discussed some of the events leading up to the house being boarded. "It pains me to think about it, everything that happened here while I was gone. Like, if I had been here I could have been here for him. Because everybody was against him. I feel kind of guilty in that regard. Just so much happened while I was gone. To come home and have things be so different…it was difficult."

•••

ON SEPTEMBER 11, 2001, 26 still owned a television. He watched the horror unfold in New York and Washington for less than an hour before deciding on a course of action. On a large sheet of tar paper, he wrote "SEPT 11 JUSTICE IS SERVED" in white paint, hung this outside his house, and returned to the TV. Sometime that afternoon, a policeman came to the door. He politely told 26 that his neighbors were upset, and that although the police couldn't stop him from hanging signs on his property, they could not assure his complete protection. 26 reluctantly took the sign down. For the rest of the week he grew more and more enraged at coverage he found distorted and overblown, and as the country rallied and the national discourse inevitably swung toward war, he felt energized. That Saturday he started hanging more signs:

"DEMOCRACY: A MYTH"

"FREEDOM: A SUPERSTITION"

"BUSH: WHITE TRASH IMBECILE MAGGOT CORPORATE SLUT"

"PATRIOTISM REFLECTS A SECRET WISH TO BE SODOMIZED"

"US TERROR IN IRAQ MAKES SEPT 11 A TINY MIRROR IMAGE"

"US TROOPS TERRORIZE AS COWARDS FROM THE SKIES. THEY SHOULD BE IN BODY BAGS."

26's property faces a perpendicular street, so any car stopped at the traffic light would not have much to look at besides the front of his house. Along with his signs and several upside-down American flags, he also left his phone number in letters large enough to be read from the road. The first wave of messages were merely menacing, but as his signs gained local notoriety, his answering machine tape filled with death threats (many addressing him as "camel jockey"). 26 responded by recording serious political diatribes and cartoon-voiced skits for callers. I asked to hear some of the venom left on his four or five ninety-minute tapes from this period, and felt relieved when 26 denied the request; he'd never stopped using the answering machine for its original purpose, and still had personal messages saved in between the death threats.

On September 28, the nearby Chippewa Middle School held its annual Run-Walk Marathon, the school's only fundraiser. The entire student population ran or walked on a five-mile circuit through the neighborhood, including 26's street. A group of parents took up positions on the sidewalk in front of his property, apparently to shield passing schoolchildren. At some point he addressed the passing crowd with a warning to prepare for an anthrax attack. The police came, took a report and left. After this incident, the FBI started coming by his house to take photographs.

Or so 26 told me. This was the first point in our talks where I found myself dubious. It seemed hard to fathom that anyone in the United States could have made any kind of public statement using the word "anthrax," less than one week before the first anthrax attack, and not have disappeared into detention. "Some people call it intuition," 26 said. "Let's just say I got lucky."

Over the course of the next six months, he rotated seventy-five to one hundred signs, some thoroughly reasonable ("HUMAN LIFE IS NOT SACRED UNTIL ALL LIFE IS SACRED TO HUMANS"), others very much in the style of Little Doc ("NO CHOICE, ABORTION NOW, INFANTICIDE NOW"). He also added a plaster lawn statue of Jesus holding a pack of matches next to a gasoline container and an American flag. 26 seemed to relish the consternation he caused. "Oh! I had more fun just looking out my window and watching this old guy. I've never seen somebody so mad in my life! And that was still the old Doc. You know... I was just in seventh heaven watching people get so worked up. Because that was my purpose in life."

73

I pressed this point, because his situation seemed so stressfully alien. "I thrived on that stuff!" he asserted cheerfully. "That's the same as being in the Christmas Folks in the 1980s! Same stuff! I loved to be hated, at the time. Oh yeah!" But later in our conversation, he admitted that there had been a huge component of loneliness in his stand. To be in a band, even a heavily confrontational band, is to always be in the presence of two or three like-minded companions. His confrontation in 2001 was solo. The stress of being on the alert day after day took a toll.

The situation quickly snowballed. Strangers came to his front door to warn him that "something" was going to happen. After the inevitable rock came crashing through his window in the middle of the night, the repair man hired to install new glass tore down more signs and told him that the people on a neighboring street were going to "get" him. His homeowner's insurance was canceled.

Devil's Night, October 30, was hard on the house. Sometime that afternoon, 26 opened his front door and took a paintball to the chest. He'd come to feel that the cops no longer took his protection seriously. That night he wrote a charged letter to the police department in the style of Little Doc. "This control problem that is so typical of enforcement officers actually goes way back to their toilet training," he wrote on the second page. "But there are psychologists that can speak to this more eloquently than I." In a postscript, he added, "If someone is hurt or worse, I will be the one to go to prison, but it won't bring them back."

The next night, Halloween, someone pounded on the front door just before 9:00 p.m. Perhaps mindful of trick-or-treaters, 26 forgot to turn on the tape recorder kept by the stairs. He opened the door to find three uniformed police officers. The lead officer asked if he was on any kind of medication or if he was unstable, and said they had received his letter and had determined that he was

74

a danger to his neighbors. "All of a sudden the guy who's closest to the door puts his foot in front of my door, my door's open, I can't close it. They come walking right in. They say 'we're going to take you to the hospital and we're going to have you checked out and see if we can't get you committed. Because we think you're a danger to the community.' No warrant."

He didn't want to appear upset or manic, and did breathing exercises in his cell until he felt completely calm. The attending psychologist reviewed the letter he'd sent and said she felt the message was indeed manic, and possibly cause for concern. As for the implied violence, she said that if she hadn't driven past his house earlier in the week and seen the signs herself, she would have thought he was delusional. He was released with a warning to not make himself a martyr. The police paid for the taxi ride home, and 26 felt the cab driver acted "creepy" because he knew he wasn't going to get a tip. The obscurity that had once shielded The Crucifucks now put 26 at an extreme disadvantage.

•••

WHEN I LEFT THAT afternoon, 26 surprised me with a 3-inch thick stack of documents he'd obtained through the Freedom Of Information Act. Whatever doubts I'd had about the anthrax incident were put to rest by a series of faxes from the local police to the FBI. Most interesting were 26's letters to the police. In page after page of dense scribble, 26 pleaded, reasoned, insulted, and pontificated with the entity he had considered an enemy for most of his adult life. I was struck by the respectful tone of certain letters, but far more struck by the one constant in his communications with the police: a tone of deep surprise at his own predicament. I pressed this point when I saw him the next afternoon. What did he expect? Had he actually thought that events would have turned out differently? He told me this was a good question, and acknowledged that he has often had to learn the same lessons over and over again.

At the bottom of the pile, I'd found several of 26's public handbills. There was the flyer he'd left around town offering $20,000 "TO THE FIRST WOMAN WHO OFFERS HER NEWBORN SON TO BE SACRIFICED ON THE ALTER [sic] TO ATONE FOR THE SINS, RAPE AND BUTCHERY BY HER AMERICAN GOVERNMENT"; a flyer titled "The Hatred & Racism Of Christianism" [sic?] that he'd left on cars in the parking lot of a local Lutheran church; a copy of a letter addressed "dear neighbor" that he'd distributed along his street, chastising them for not welcoming him into the neighborhood, and signed by "26 The Messiah."

This also concerned me. 26 had been calling himself "the messiah" for years at this point. One of his longstanding house signs read, "VERILY I AM GREATER THAN YOUR MYTHICAL CHRIST FOR I AM REAL AND HERE AMONG YOU—26 THE MESSIAH." In a handwritten letter to a specific neighbor, he had concluded, "it is time for you and others to be aware of the following. My name is number 26. And I am The Messiah." I'd originally assumed this was satirical, but seeing the word in so many different documents gave me doubts.

"Before you get the wrong idea about me, the word 'messiah' is a Persian word," he told me. "I just want to clarify that I'm not on a Christ trip. That stuff is so silly and crude that I don't really want to be identified with it, other than... I probably liked, at the time, yanking the chain of the Christians." This didn't entirely make sense. Why, I asked, give ammunition to people he considered his enemies? He returned to his earlier themes of social experimentation. "It's all about boundaries... I didn't learn from all the experiments. I had to keep doing them over and over again."

As we spoke, the phone rang. The answering machine took the call and there was the slightest pause before the caller hung up. We returned to the death threats, and his dealings with the police. I mentioned the surprisingly respectful tone of most of his communications with the local department, both before and after Halloween, and asked if he'd finally come to respect the police. "I prefer their old fashioned and transparent dishonesty to the insidiously fluid dishonesty of all the other people I know," he told me formally, as if reading from a prepared statement.

Two deer approached the back yard at dusk. 26 produced a giant plastic bowl of animal feed, opened the patio door and said, "Hi sweetie." My view of the feeding was distorted by the heat streaming out through the gap in the sliding glass. He returned with corn dust on his sweatshirt, explaining that I'd just seen Little Deer Who Comes Close and Little Deer Who Comes Smashing Into The House.

As much as he clearly enjoyed feeding a few stragglers, the deer seemed a sad reminder of the final chapter of his siege. One morning in 2006, he stepped into his back yard and found a doe had been shot in the head and left for him as a warning. He covered up the signs out front as a signal to whoever was watching that he'd surrendered. "Eventually, I knew I had to get rid of this anger, and I had to approach things from a different perspective."

More sympathetic eyes had been watching his house as well. In the last year, several people have approached him to put his messages back up. His stock answer remains, "well, where were you when I had 'em up?" The idea of any outside support seemed frustrating to 26. "People say, 'I'll stand behind you'...but,"—he pointed into an imaginary distance far beyond his house—"they're way, way behind you."

In May 2006, a trustee for the Meridian Township came by the house. The trustee was an acquaintance of his, and a thorn in the side of the local authorities. The trustee told him that a new town ordinance regarding house signage and feeding wild animals had been introduced as a rebuff to 26. The trustee also told him that he'd managed to water the law down, and that he'd spoken with the ACLU, in case 26 decided to post more signs. "This is five years later after my signs, and I had called them. I have a history with the ACLU," 26 told me bitterly. "He says, 'they'll stand behind you. I already got their word…you can put up signs now. And they will defend you.' And I said, 'This is good. Now I'll put up signs attacking the first amendment.'" He laughed telling me this. "And he says, 'No. You cannot do that! This should be about peace! Or something like that!'"

•••

MIDDLE AGE IS HARD on radicals, but it is harder still on radicals for whom showmanship has been their primary form of activism. Hardcore's three wise men—Biafra, Fugazi's Ian Mackaye, and TV-star Henry Rollins—have all moved on to lofty artistic heights, but not one has sustained the anger of their earliest music. It's a nearly impossible thing to sustain. The man once known as Doc Dart has had to work hard to *not* sustain that anger.

Night had fallen and it was time to leave. In the daytime, there had been a coziness to this sanctum, a small environment where the recent horrors of Abu Ghraib, Beslan, Fallujah, and Katrina will never intrude. After dark, the house held a tone of menace. I thought of the hang-up caller, and my eyes were continually drawn to the thin sliver of unlit back yard I could see from the couch. The space seemed funereal but also expectant, the kind of house in which one would seek refuge from zombies. Showing me out, 26 seemed to feel that the plywood only made the house safer. "When the tornado comes, I'll be the one doing the snickering while they're doing the sniveling."

GERMS FILM REVIEW
Why This?

DISCLAIMER: HALFWAY INTO *WHAT We Do Is Secret*, Rodger Grossman's 2007 biopic of LA punk band the Germs, I had to use the john something fierce, so this review reflects a viewing gap. It is possible, however unlikely, that the five minutes I missed covered the vast range of subjects otherwise conspicuously lacking. Perhaps this segment addressed singer Darby Crash posing with a fake girlfriend in *The Decline Of Western Civilization*—Penelope Spheeris' flawless and starkly contrasting 1981 documentary of the early Los Angeles punk scene—supposedly to avoid gay-bashing by fellow band Fear. Or maybe the unseen segment examined the LA scene's descent into jock-fueled megabrawls. Perhaps there was time to examine the period's casual racism, or the scientology of Crash and his buddies. I wasn't present. It would be presumptuous of me to assume otherwise.[42]

When I did return to my seat, I discovered that the movie had taken a reckless new turn. A present day rock band (The Bronx, said the credits) portrayed 1980 Black Flag in unapologetically twenty-first century garb and presentation; they roared and stomp-danced and looked and sounded like every other post nü-metal KROQ flimflam that plays over the credits of a 2008 horror flick. It seemed a bold attempt to jumpstart a lost cause by reconfiguring the entire shitty premise midstream. For a few wonderful moments, I held out hope for a meatier, weirder, funnier, more postmodern movie to emerge triumphant from the first hour. Would it have been too much to ask for the late-inning substitutions of Jim Belushi as Darby Crash, Martin Lawrence as both Pat Smear and Rodney Bingenheimer, and an award-winning cameo by Cher as Penelope Spheeris? Realism is what we grapple with every morning in the bathroom mirror: it has no place in cinema.

Instead, the movie puttered and sputtered toward its hero's inevitable suicide. It's hard to recall any other (non-sequel) film so deeply overshadowed by another film. Shots and events from *Decline* were referenced with all the vigor of an *America's Most Wanted* reenactment. It was bad, but not funny bad. Local band The Mae Shi played The Screamers, and they seemed unhappy. So did many of the extras.

To be fair, no movie could survive a star like Shane West, better known as one of the interchangeable young doctors on TV's *E.R.* West filtered out the hapless, flabby, blotto pathos of *The Decline*'s Darby—in other words, all the interesting bits—and what we were left with was a sort of wise-alecky street poet. This alt-universe Germs frontman dropped preposterous thought bombs to his ecstatic buddies, who gushed lines like, "Darby, these lyrics are *genius!*"

In trying to recast Crash as a rock prophet in the Jim Morrison mold, the filmmakers ignored the obvious: The Germs weren't that interesting a band. Popular, diverse, groundbreaking, and influential, yes. But without the allure of suicide, their music would today flicker dimly alongside China White and The Urinals. At one point there was a brief glimpse of the actual Darby Crash, leering out from his iconic *Slash* magazine cover photo, and the cognitive dissonance gave the movie an unwelcome jolt.

It's a tad sad watching a bad movie about a historical figure who yearned for fame. It's sadder to see this movie in the only theater it played anywhere, on account of the fact that the bad movie never received national distribution and instead ran in one theater at a time throughout LA county. This situation can still be corrected. Shane West and the surviving Germs have reunited and are playing shows again. If that's not a great hook for a fictionalized making-of-What-We-Do-Is-Secret type drama, I really don't know what is. Jeremy Irons can star as the ghost of Darby. Start writing your congressperson. Make it happen.

ARTISTS

THE CASUAL DOTS

My Last Band

THIS FEELS LIKE THE right spot to pause and point up at the problem looming over this book. For 99 percent of humanity, music is a one-way mirror; you can see pop stars, but they can't see you. Underground music works differently. The mirrors here are see-through. Many of the bands I'm writing about I have a relationship with, either as distant acquaintance, close-range fan, booster, peer, or, occasionally, adversary. Trying to write around these backstories was always a challenge. So what if I just stopped trying?

•••

LET'S START WITH THE Casual Dots. The DC trio formed after the turn of the century, in an era when taste fragmentation meant any group of already accomplished musicians was a "supergroup." In the 1990s, guitarist and lead singer Christina Billotte was one third of Slant 6, a band associated with the Mount Pleasant, DC communal house known as The Embassy. Of all the bands I've gone out of my way to avoid live, Slant 6 is the most painful. In '94, I drove up to DC from Richmond with some friends to catch Cupid Car Club, the first of the post-Nation of Ulysses[43] bands and a fellow Embassy group. Slant 6 shared the bill, but I'd deemed them insufficiently cool and hung out on the sidewalk like a ding dong. It makes me sad, thinking of ding dong me, conspicuously milling around aimlessly, as if I had something, anything, cooler to do than watch this band.

Only later did I discover their joyous first LP, *Soda Pop Rip Off* (Dischord, 1994), which sounds like covers of the absolute best mid-sixties private press garage rock, expertly reworked into the kind of spooky punk that, in its exploratory prowess, sidesteps easy categorization. Slant 6 always struck me as a band stuck in the wrong era. Had their records come out a dozen years earlier, they would have fit nicely alongside the proto-hardcore of The Big Boys, or early Replacements, or the post-punk of The Raincoats or Bush Tetras, all bands who made music too unique to be imitated.

Before I knew her personally, I'd developed a precise and completely false image of Christina as a sort of tough-talking, gum-snapping, switchblade-wielding Pinky Tuscadero[44] type. This misconception came from her delivery on that LP (and maybe the jaunty pose she struck on the *Soda* cover photo). Also, I'm a lazy listener. I find something I like and I play it to death, and have a hard time mustering any curiosity behind the band backstories, and whatever little fictional backstories I've invented tend to solidify.

I met Kathi Wilcox, Casual Dots' other guitarist, when she played bass in Bikini Kill in the autumn of 1991. Although BK and my band, Born Against, had performed together earlier in the day in mid-state Massachusetts, I didn't actually introduce myself to her until later that afternoon, at a night show at Wesleyan University. And this introduction was less of a formal exchange of names than it was me bursting in on Kathi and Bikini Kill's drummer Tobi Vail as they were applying liquid eyeliner in the ladies' room and (according to Tobi's fanzine, *Jigsaw*[45]) screaming at both through a megaphone. In my defense, I was making my way across the campus yelling at everyone through a megaphone. I don't remember busting into bathrooms, but it has the general ring of something I would've done then to attract attention (which is the job of all hardcore vocalists, and a duty I took seriously).

Bikini Kill was one of the most polarizing bands I'd ever encountered. In the early 1990s, no one in my social circle liked them. With my male pals, the issue was "musicianship," despite a) Bikini Kill not lacking it, and b) fans of the most hapless fumbling chuggings of the shittiest outer borough all-male New York hardcore bands obviously not being concerned with it. All my female friends (mostly New Yorkers) also distanced themselves from this new entity called Riot Grrrl, the underground uprising now associated with third-wave feminism (and which Bikini Kill were the most visible band associated with). Their reasons were far more complex than the boys' dismissals, and are not things I'm qualified to speak about with any authority. My suspicion now is the same as it was then; I'm guessing my female pals resented being asked their opinions on all things related to Riot Grrrl and, by proxy, Bikini Kill.

I intersected both from a weird angle. Only two years earlier, a college class on feminism—plain old Feminism 101—had hit me with the force of a religious conversion. Probing the range and depth of my own blind spots was such a jolt that it felt like a drop into science fiction. Privilege lubes life for those it favors; ignorance can be a smooth ride. In the space of a few weeks, I "discovered" a new reality hiding in plain sight, a world of threats and humiliations that seemed tailor-made for the performative anger of the very music I'd championed.

And yet I was skeptical of Bikini Kill for a long time. Their meteoric rise rubbed me the wrong way, and when I try to dissect my emotions now, I keep looping back to the same unsettling conclusion: professional jealousy. On the surface, it seems hard to have professional jealousy when my "profession" was fronting my own polarizing and money-hemorrhaging punk band. But I think there was a time when I liked being important in a national network of tiny scenes. When someone else came along and did what I was doing, with far more success and relevancy, it seriously rattled me. Although I kept this skepticism to myself.

Six months after both bands met, Born Against snagged a bill with Bikini Kill and MDC[46] in DC. Sometime between the booking and the show, my bandmate Adam wrote a one-page for his brother's fanzine. These one-page pieces were the opposite of the "one-sheets" used in the music and entertainment industry to publicize new merchandise. These sometimes bizarre screeds were meant to function as position papers, showing where our band stood on important issues of the day (it's a hard thing to place in context, and not something I knew of any other bands doing). This particular rant went after Riot Grrrl in an angry, scattershot fashion.

Although I didn't know that Adam was using Bikini Kill's lyrics against them, I disagreed with the content and demanded that he not sign my name to it (meaning, the name of my record label, which served as a catch-all umbrella for everything he and I and the band did). But the piece ran as was, Bikini Kill cancelled because, I heard (wrongly), they no longer wanted to share a stage with us, and Adam and I got into a loud argument over whether or not we should care about what "cool" people thought of us. I remember playing the show with a background feeling that, once again, I'd screwed something up.

At the time it registered as one more bit of lost control on my part, in keeping with a period in my life when I seemed to abdicate control of my actions in ways that didn't quite make sense. Later, when I learned how physically challenging Bikini Kill's tours had been made by a constant barrage of misogyny and near-assaults—conditions far closer to the menace of early Black Flag tours than anything my band would face—I felt bad that I had, in some small way, contributed to the overall atmosphere of dread and danger they'd had to wade through[47]. I felt a shade worse when I realized that I actually liked their music, most of which I'd dismissed the first time around.

Two years later, when I was unpopular and bandless, drummer Tobi Vail reached out to me, we started corresponding, and I essentially remet the band in '95. I never knew why Bikini Kill gave me a second shot. After a certain point, it felt weird to ask. The ugly zine incident kind of seemed like a strange joke to them. Certainly they had no idea how much their friendship meant, coming on the heels of my expulsion from the New York scene I had been one of the most visible faces of. Through my correspondences and then seeing them live again, I figured out the roles within the band, that guitarist Billy Karen was the zany one, the Harpo Marx of the group, which would make Kathleen and Tobi the Groucho and Chico and Kathi the Zeppo—meaning, the hardworking, dependable member of every good quartet[48].

Casual Dots' drummer Steve Dore also shared that Wesleyan bill the night I met Kathi. But I must have met him a few months earlier, when we'd played in Willimantic, in the basement of a lawyer's house. Steve's band Maude, being kind of pop punk, did not float my boat. But they were such an impressionably upbeat bunch of young fellers, just the kind of weird guys you hope to meet in a little nook of Connecticut (The Belgium of New England, according to Steve). Steve and his pals seemed to validate one of the big ideas behind band touring, the idea that you could create access to a potentially infinite supply of new friends and comrades and interesting people, simply by driving around playing bowling alleys and barn lofts and the basements of lawyers.

•••

CASUAL DOTS ALSO SOUND stuck in the wrong era. They could almost be the lost garage group whose dusty records were discovered, decades later, by Slant 6. Their two covers (1960s "Bumble Bee" by LaVern Baker and 1961's "I'll Dry My Tears" by Etta James) fit into their one and only LP (Kill Rock Stars, 2004) as snugly as Tetris blocks. The album follows a tidy little bell curve, peaking in the middle with "Hooded," a hypnotic conversation between guitars I must have heard hundreds of times. I would do terrible things to have a voice as sweetly authoritative as Christina Billotte.

And that's all I have to say about their songs. The twenty-first century, with its badly curated festivals and American Idol aspirations, has tricked us into believing that music is a communal experience. It's not. Consciousness is a solitary phenomenon, and the emotions we experience from music are just one private part of our solo selves. The Casual Dots were the last band I really loved, the last band I desired to see live. For you to fully understand why, you'd probably need to be me. But I'm glad that they were my last band, for they were a classy and good thing.

DIE KREUZEN

The Yawning Maw

THE JULY 11, 1977, issue of *Time* magazine looks like a coffee table prop from *Death Wish*. On its cover, yellow letters blurt YOUTH CRIME over a trio of advancing hooligans—black, white, and brown—with sharp knives and desperate faces. Adding to the menace, a little graphic in the upper right corner shows the tail of an aircraft over the words THE B-1 BOMBS.[49]

In the house where I grew up there was a junk room. My parents had bought a gutted Italianate brownstone for $3,000 and hadn't had enough money to complete the renovation, so this space stayed as it was for years, with chipped plaster walls and window frames that whistled in the wind. In this room, there was a rickety bookshelf full of magazines. I used to creep into the foreboding space and sneak a peek at this particular magazine. As a kid, I had no idea that the magazine cover meant "bombs" in the sense of fiscal failure. All I knew was the cover seemed to advertise a warplane that flew around blasting cities into rubble, leaving the multiethnic scavengers to pick off survivors.

Inside, hidden among articles on war, gangs, and Son of Sam, I kept returning to a two-page spread labeled "Anthems of the Blank Generation." The text came with seven photos, each of which I would study like a Talmudic scholar. I was fascinated by Soo [sic] Catwoman, The Weirdos, and a picture of "Chicago Punkers" done up like *Rocky Horror Picture Show* groupies. One photo showed The Dead Boys' pale Stiv Bators, laying on a stage, screaming into a mic with his eyes closed. It looked like someone having a very public seizure. The photo scandalized me.

But this wasn't as scary as the adjacent picture of an even paler Lee Ritter of The Infliktors [sic], posing onstage in a sweat-stained belly shirt, ribs visible, looking like a Dachau prisoner performing in some nightmare cabaret for SS officers. And this photo wasn't nearly as terrifying as the one, just above, of Johnny Rotten mugging for the camera. In the blotchy offset of seventies printing, Rotten's pasty skin was almost the same color as the whites of his eyes, so that he appeared to have two black rat pupils staring back at me. A hypodermic syringe hung from the lapel of his puce jacket, a visual that filled me with an obsessive dread. *What was in the syringe? What if he tripped? What if the needle went into one of his rat eyes?*

And none of these photos were as scary, as circuit-trippingly wrong, as the picture labeled "parachute costume with raw meat." This wasn't a person, just a person-shaped shroud; an audience member fully draped in an actual parachute, cords drawn in, hoodie-style, to completely cover the stranger's face. No skin was visible. Sausage-colored rubber gloves hid the hands. Horrifically, chunks of raw meat dangled from several loose strings. As a thing to see as a kid, this was bad. The abomination resembled one of the wriggling, sheet-wrapped corpses from that harrowing basement scene in the original *Dawn of the Dead*.[50]

In childhood, each of us has to assign meaning to those bits of the adult world that don't make sense. We begin our lives struggling to grasp the mysteries of adulthood, then spend the rest of our lives struggling to access those raw emotions of childhood. The two periods of life peer back at each other. It's easy to forget how sacred all those childhood terrors felt. When I was twelve, I caught Fear's appearance on *Saturday Night Live*, and the quick glimpses of chaos reminded me of all those violently abstract nightmares from the dawn of my consciousness. I assumed that actual punk records would do the same.

So when I finally borrowed the Sex Pistols LP from a friend in high school, the request had a slightly illicit feeling (similar to when I later purchased *The Turner Diaries* at a Virginia gun show). I was shocked to find that the music itself was not illicit. It was just plain old rock and roll. Parachute Meat Person did not listen to this record down in the basement.

•••

MILWAUKEE BAND DIE KREUZEN didn't start out terrifying. Their first EP, 1982's *Cows and Beer*, came during the initial explosion of American hardcore bands, when competition was low and disincentives to playing harsh music were high. The record is a well-made prototype (and thus a collector's gem), but not particularly scary. Or unique. Their singer, Dan Kubinski, sounds young, and strained, and he screams with the very familiar outraged certainty of a teenage boy who suddenly finds himself in a man's body.

The title played on the boredom of the Midwest, but the cover art showed something else, a strangely solemn Flanders Field type scene, with rusty barbed wire circling a graveyard cross (the band's name is meant to mean "the crosses" in German). Richard Kohl is the artist, and this neat crosshatched illustration began a collaboration with Die Kreuzen that has now lasted thirty-five years.

Kohl drew the cover image for the band's self-titled debut album, released on Touch & Go two years later. The yellow and black hatchwork shows huge skeleton creatures in some sort of industrial landscape. These monsters resemble Indonesian shadow puppets, or the hyper-doodle chicken-scratch asylum art of Rudimentary Peni's Nick Blinko. When I first saw it, this cover reminded me of the artwork on the Bantam Book Club paperback edition of Ray Bradbury's *The Martian Chronicles*, as drawn by British fantasy illustrator Ian Miller (and surely influenced by the intense religious engravings of Albrecht Dürer, almost five hundred years earlier).

The Martian Chronicles scared me. It's a stealthy book, presenting itself as hokey sci-fi, then opening the trap door into horror.

This album doesn't have any trap doors. It is the trap door.

•••

THE FIRST THING TO know about their first album is that the order is wrong. This feels done to keep the listener off-kilter from the outset. Side one is clearly side two, starting with the processed feedback that opens "Pain." The reedy squeals sound like insect noises from another planet. Even in its ferocity, there is something troublingly *insect*-like about the entire LP. At times the bass scurries, scuttling like a bug in the underbrush. There is a relentlessness far deeper than just the physical speed of the music (twenty-one songs in under half an hour). The urgency is emotional, like the feeling of running from something in a nightmare.

When listened to correctly, the album ends with "All White," the only slow track. From an all-white room—"walls, ceilings, and floors"—Kubinski shrieks to be let out.[51] It's like Charlotte Perkins Gilman's *The Yellow Wallpaper*; even minus the terrible social undertow of the female protagonist, this song is just as devastating as the story. And the story is rough.

Here are some other things you should know about this record:

—Blood.

—Run.

—The yawning maw behind Jim Jones' sunglasses.

—The terrifying first paragraph of Shirley Jackson's *The Haunting of Hill House*.

—The horror of hugeness, the massive shadow Saturn casts on its own rings.

—Vocals like a scarecrow screaming at you from across the cornfield at night…why did you anger the scarecrow?

—The knowledge that a "Blood Cleanse" could be a supplement, smoothie, or a barbaric ritual of the post-apocalypse.

—Parachute Meat Person standing in the back of your closet, barely visible behind all the dangling shirts and coats you will never wear again.

What would it have been like to record this album? What would it have been like, running through your morning routines—bathroom, breakfast, driving to the studio—all the while knowing that you were helping construct this wormhole into an obscene universe?

•••

SIX OF THE SONGS had appeared earlier on *Cows and Beer*. The implication seems clear enough. *What if they just kept rerecording the same handful of songs, each time making the music exponentially scarier? What if their next album drove listeners frothing-at-the-mouth, pants-around-the ankles insane, and the album after THAT had to be stored in some kind of lead-lined underground vault?*

Instead, the band leveled up by changing one big variable. Their next LP, 1986's *October File* slows everything down, and they stalled at the tempo of a ho-hum indie band, more or less, for the next thirty years. "The primary reason that our sound changed," bassist Keith Brammer told an Australian interviewer in 2001, "was that we never, ever wanted to do the same thing twice." (In 2016, Kubinski formed The Crosses to perform the first Die Kreuzen LP in its entirety.)

None of which matters. As with all artists, an infinite number of mediocre works don't cancel out one great work. And an endless, ever-expanding ocean of disappointing bands and records can't cancel out this one singular album.

"This exists, too," a twenty-three-year old Steve Albini gushed about the album in a Chicago fanzine. "And that's enough."

DISCHARGE

Flying Piles of Meat

IN THE SPRING OF 1977, a fledgling punk band from the British West Midlands recorded an utter pile of shit and called it a demo. Although punk was itself a newborn, Discharge managed to craft one of the genre's first works of derivative art. London was 170 miles away and the Sex Pistols were a fresh novelty, and yet the demo pulls off a precisely studied and wondrously incompetent impersonation of the raucous new rock stars. The recording's first song, "I Don't Care," uses the same riff for chorus and verse. "I don't care about the human race," the singer Tezz asserts, trilling the R's in a shameless imitation of Johnny Rotten's cockney-mocking-the-aristocracy accent. The song ends with the recreation of the vocal snarl in *Anarchy In The UK*, which had charted in the UK only a year earlier. Four tracks in, the band rages against acne.

Nine years later, Discharge was a Hollywood-style hair-metal act with Axl Rose falsettos. And somewhere in between, they transformed into the musical equivalent of World War Two.

•••

THE DEMO HAD FAILED to impress Mike Stone, owner of a local record store. He had no way of knowing that, in the two years since its recording, Tezz had moved to drums, seventeen-year-old roadie Kelvin Morris—Cal—had taken over as front man, and that one of those unexplainable transformations of human chemistry and artistic alchemy had transpired to produce something vastly more potent than the sum of its parts. In late '79, on a tip, Stone decided to catch the band's first outing with the new lineup. This close to the initial punk explosion, audiences were still hungry for antics, and Discharge obliged by flinging slaughterhouse guts off the stage. When Stone walked into a sold-out church hall, a flying pile of cow guts landed at his feet with a wet splat.

Thus was born a collaboration that produced some of the fiercest anti-war art of the twentieth century. Stone was launching a new record label, Clay (Stoke is a pottery town; the menacing nuclear reactors of the company logo are actually pictographs of Stoke's iconic bottle kilns). Discharge's first record, 1980s *The Realities of War* EP, was also Clay's first record. In four short songs, the band's new incarnation presented a fresh and ferocious direction for protest musicians.

Cal often yells in one note. There's nearly no melody to his vocals, so he leans heavily into the delivery. He sounds like a plausibly angry man. He looked like it too, playing shirtless and enraged, abs flexed mid-scream, too truly angry for a metal singer, too beefcake for a Johnny Rotten clone. Although the band spiked their hair and jackets, the vocals plug into another stereotype of eighties Britain; the Righteous and Grubby Hunk. Without setting out to, the band had invented a wide-open new genre of ferocious rock; music more aggressive than the new wave of British heavy metal and somehow angrier than the Sex Pistols.

As voice, lyricist, and designer, Cal drove this new direction, a rebuttal of the nihilism of entry-level punk and metal. Where the band once sang about not caring about the human race, Cal offered a full-throated defense of humanity. The band adopted "anti-war" as their one line of attack. Throughout this part of their career, Discharge weathered criticism for being a single-issue novelty act. Most UK punk bands made full use of the wide canvas offered by Thatcher's Britain; the desperation and unemployment, the garbage strikes and rising racism. Discharge stuck largely to one lane. By keeping it deadly simple, the band bypassed one of the biggest problems facing all protest music; there's always someone to the left of you.

A band without a shred of humor or hope probably sounds like a bad time. So it's important to remember how vital this was. By 1981, the second coming of the cold war was in full bloom, but it arrived on the far side of the sixties and was thus stripped of any illusions of survivability. "Duck and cover" had been revealed as a quaint relic of a distant decade. And yet even discussing the possibility of nuclear annihilation was a deeply partisan issue.[52]

Up until this point, nearly all artistic responses to nuclear terror skewed to the wimpy side of the emotional spectrum. It wasn't all shaking-tambourines-at-the-war-machine acoustic guitar posturing— the full spread of oafish behavior now known as Hippie Bullshit—but almost all anti-war art veered toward fear, despair, and dignified protest. The Sex Pistols fired anger as buckshot. Discharge used a high-powered rifle. They were the first artists to sustain this attack, and the first to both sing about and sound like a nuclear holocaust.

After one bad interview with *Sounds*, the band shied away from press. Breaking with the norm of first wave UK punk bands and US hardcore bands, Discharge had no flamboyant personalities, no Captain Sensible-style goofballs, no Joe Strummer-style working-class intellectuals. The band let the music speak for them. This left young and impressionable listeners, like me, with the impression that they were messengers for an idea so huge and so abstract that it fell outside the scope of the human imagination: the simple reality that humanity could end at any time.

•••

DISCHARGE IS KNOWN FOR its iconic record covers, so it should be noted that the band constantly experimented with graphics. *The Realities of War 7"* EP showcased minimalism with an iconic photo of a studded leather jacket with the band's off-kilter logo at the bottom. *Fight Back*, the band's second EP, is a high-contrast blur of a live shot, and *Decontrol* showcased a sloppy photomontage of the band in action, arrayed in ripped segments, like a bad yearbook page. *Never Again* featured a blown-out version of John Heartfield's 1939's anti-fascist photomontage "Peace and Fascism." This singular image of a dove impaled on a bayonet became the band's best-known graphic.

The *Why* 12" of 1981 extended this imagery to its awful conclusion. The cover consisted of three terrible photos of real-life atrocities: violated cadavers from the Rape of Nanking, a child's glassy-eyed corpse in a field, and one harrowing photo of a Polish girl, wailing over a sister who had been machine-gunned by the Luftwaffe moments earlier. The pornography of this cover seemed to take a cue from the Viennese Actionists, a tiny band of 1960s performance artists who staged their own shock theater (animal carcasses, body fluids, public orgies in piles of guts that made Discharge's early antics pale in comparison[53]). In their own vile way, the Actionists made art addressing wartime atrocity. There is a connecting thread here, with just a few small differences. Unlike confrontational shock art, Discharge's use of shock carried no risk. And unlike performance art, album art is made to sell albums.

This one record cover opened the door for more hardcore bands—bands of far lesser ability and vision—to appropriate other photos of atrocity.[54] The resulting mini-genre probably made *Why* look that much better. After all, if you're going to include photos of atrocities, your music at least better live up to the imagery. One could view Discharge's first forty-eight songs, everything from 1980 through 1985, as one self-contained artistic unit, like Picasso's *Guernica*, or Dalton Trumbo's *Johnny Got His Gun*; a singular work of anti-war art that future generations (assuming, the teenage Discharge fan in me asserts, there are any future generations) will hold in supreme esteem.

That's one interpretation. Here's another. The Polish girl on the cover of *Why* may well have survived the war. If not, someone from her family might have survived. The odds are small but real that one of them could have found this record and recognized the photo, a picture showing one person's death and another person's most agonizing moment. Could any possible justification cover this scenario?

•••

THERE WAS ANOTHER SUBTLE form of experimentation afoot with Cal's vocals. On *Realities of War*, still getting his bearings, he doubles vocal tracks without harmonizing (which sounds, you know, not great). By *Why* he's positively blotto with rage, a raggedy hermit stumbling out of his cave to shriek pure indignation at a fallen humanity. On *Decontrol* he fully emerges as the righteous man, howling with uncontained fury. As of 1982, the band had no logical musical precedents. Their second LP, *Hear Nothing, See Nothing, Say Nothing* leaves a perfect time-capsule document of Discharge at their otherworldly best.

But no band is static. On *Warning: Her Majesty's Government Can Seriously Damage Your Health* (featuring a high-school art pencil drawing of a knife-wielding Maggie Thatcher) and then *The Price of Silence* single Cal starts singing. His lack of range seems smartly self-imposed. I first heard these songs as part of their LP compilation, *Never Again* (same cover as the EP) and I didn't know enough to read anything into the vocal discontinuity. On 1984's *The More I See*, Cal drags the word "war" into several notes, and it does nothing to dilute from the *Apocalypse Now* gravity of the track, the solo that always makes me think of explosions and burning palm trees and gunships swooping over rice paddies.

Fans only slightly older than me sensed trouble. For those invested in the band's career, the smoother vocals of these tracks hinted at compromise (a dispute mirrored two years later with the Cro-Mags' *Age of Quarrel*, perhaps the only record to match *Hear Nothing...*in sheer emotional firepower[55]). The 1985 *Ignorance* 7"gave a stronger preview of where the band was heading, with its hints of a smoother rock sound, and the cover photos of band members with slicked-back hair and sunglasses, the cool-guy vampire look done so much better by Sisters of Mercy. Worse, Cal sounds phoned in, strained, and off.

Still, it's hard to imagine any of the band's fans being prepared for Discharge's 1986 album, *Grave New World*. Gone are the screams and howls, replaced by a shrill, reverb-drenched falsetto and the kind of migraine-blunt bar rock that might soundtrack a lesser Chuck Norris flick. To promote this abomination, they'd shot what is surely the most infamous press photo in all of hardcore. In the picture, the band members reveal themselves in their full rocker glory, back-lit with preposterous coiffures. Cal crouches on one knee in a sleeveless black shirt, threatening to bust into a U2 song at any second.

It is a tasty little irony that Discharge's dismissal of punk resulted in the most "punk" band tour ever. Black Flag faced cops and Bikini Kill faced fuckers, but both bands had fans in every port. Discharge faced eighteen North American concerts of unrelenting audience hostility. It's hard to overstate the *hatred* that greeted this band in its glammy-man phase. Rumors from the tour are cinematic. In Cleveland, Cal got punched out on stage. In North Carolina, the band needed a police escort to leave the club. At an infamous show at the Ritz in New York, the audience hurled full glasses of beer, then random chunks of garbage, and then, because these still seemed insufficient expressions of disgust, members of the Bad Brains(!) hurled full bags of trash off the balcony and on to the stage (in some versions of this story, they dragged trash cans onstage). Presumably the band developed thick skins. By San Francisco, two weeks in, Cal was taunting the audience with a preening falsetto of "State Control."

•••

DESPITE THIS FAILED FUMBLE at selling out, Discharge's shadow grew longer and longer.[56] Starting with their tour of Scandinavia in 1982, the band spawned clones, first dozens, now, probably in the low three-digits.[57] These Discharge worshippers fall somewhere between tribute and imitation, each loyal to something called "D-beat." Tezz credits Motorhead's drummer Philthy Animal for inspiring the beat (a hometown nod; Lemmy Kilmister hailed from Stoke), a cymbal-bass-snare combo I don't pretend to understand and frankly don't think many others understand either.[58] In the years since, "D-beat" has come to mean something wider than a style of percussion. Now it's more a full package: music, lyrics, merchandise, lifestyle.

Discharge wasn't just a connecting channel from both metal and punk to hardcore, but also the source of many smaller tributary sub-subgenres. *Hear Nothing See Nothing Say Nothing* spawned grindcore, thrash, thrash metal, black metal, crust punk, and presumably other seedy little subgenres and sub-subgenres, each competing in its own way to be the most extreme. This influence worked in the other direction as well. Metallica, Anthrax, and Sepultura have each manhandled Discharge's songs. As I write this, new musicians, somewhere, are struggling with their own interpretations.

The band eventually recovered from *Grave New World*, returned to the more commercially viable apocalypse thrash, fired and rehired Cal, and eventually parted ways with him for good in 2003. Since *Grave New World*, the band has released eight albums of thunderously mediocre hardcore, three more nations became nuclear states, and the world of hyperbole dreamed up in the earliest records has largely come true. In 1980, someone screaming, "It's so fucking sick" about the arms race would have been a lonely voice of sanity. Now everyone is screaming it, every day, on countless social media platforms. The world has become a Discharge record.

•••

IN 2016, I DROVE past the Glass House, Pomona's dependable midsize venue, and saw Discharge was playing. I muttered "yuck" at the line of black-clad youngsters snaking down the block in the rear view mirror. Then I remembered they'd been my favorite band for thirty years.

Why is life dumb?

THE FLYING LIZARDS

Six Magic Little Words

As A TEENAGER, I accepted the idea that the best days of everything had come and gone. I'd just missed hardcore's heyday, and the original punk scene five years earlier, and the sixties before that. In my twenties, I became aware of another sort of loss; the creeping homogeneity that lurks near the edges of all good art. "Arty" is an epithet in the realm of hardcore. And sometimes artiness is a liability, especially when used in the attempt to conceal creative bankruptcy. What interested me was the pursuit and execution of excellence through artiness.[59]

Hardcore owes its existence to punk, and punk owes its existence to the arty. Many of the artists I gravitated toward still had one foot in the realms of the absurd: Gary Panter, Saccharine Trust, Teenage Jesus & The Jerks, The Plugz, *Sick Teen* fanzine, Suburban Lawns, Geza X, George Petros' *Exit*, early Devo and Meat Puppets, and Raymond Pettibon.[60] The growing literality of hardcore disturbed me, as did the slow-burn realization that my own hardcore band may have contributed, ever so slightly, to the narrowing of a strange and beautiful art form.

And sometimes "arty"-as-an-insult marks the birth of something great. New art forms are often considered self-indulgent. Both Monty Python and Fugazi overcame initial periods of audience confusion.[61] Sometimes new things need to build to mass acceptance.

•••

THE FLYING LIZARDS GOT their mass acceptance in one spasm. The band lives on the rim of popular memory for their postmodern take of "Money (That's What I Want)" sung by Motown hit-maker Barrett Strong in 1959, and popularized by The Beatles four years later. It's a quirky, funny cover, with space alien instrumentation, cheeky robotic vocals (singer Deborah Evans, using her "posh voice"), and an extraterrestrial take on disco jagged enough to count as social commentary.

Since its release in 1979, the song has appeared on a staggering 144 compilations,[62] from Ronco and K-Tel one-hit wonder collections, to soundtracks, to dozens upon dozens of compilations celebrating cover songs, synthesizers, both new wave and punk, and both the 1970s and the 1980s. The band had the fortunate/unfortunate timing to have released the cover just before the Me decade turned into the Greed Decade. The sarcasm of "Money" could be easily dismissed by a generation of suspender-wearing stockbroker sociopaths.

This was all the more impressive because The Flying Lizards aren't a band. The group is the creation of David Cunningham, the London-based composer and producer who has made a career of creating experimental music, usually with a rotating cast of hired guns. Their first LP, *The Flying Lizards*, exists on an accessibility scale with Laurie Anderson (whimsically cerebral) on one end, the slicker Lizzie Mercier Descloux stuff (accessibly quirky) in the middle, and Tom Tom Club (universally danceable) on the other side.

Although each track occupies very different spots on this continuum. Several of the songs ("Her Story," "Russia") were club-friendly; more New York, more mutated, and, somehow, more disco than NY's own Mutant Disco scene. There are three covers ("Money," Eddie Cochran's "Summertime Blues," and an old German showtune, "Der Song von Mandelay"), and several tracks ("Trouble," "The Flood") that sound like scores from a forgotten East European science fiction film.

Suddenly, at the end of the LP, we're back in the here and now with "The Window." Writer Vivien Goldman sings, and her delivery is a perfect counterpoint to Evans on *Money*; insistent yet warm, like a voice you'd hear floating over a fence on a summer day. It's the bright vocal melody style of Young Marble Giants, but the words are dark with menace:

Can you hear him bang on the window?
He's throwing things at the window
I don't want to let him in
I wish he wasn't twice my size

Melody Maker dismissed the track as "a woman's song," calling it "mundane enough...boyfriend wants in, bangs on window, girl ponders." (Had the track come out ten years later, it could've been dismissed—in the reductive crappiness of rock journalism—as "a feminist response" to The Rollins Band's "There's a Man Outside."[63])

•••

ON A TRIP TO London in 2018, I tracked down Cunningham's email, explained I was writing a book with a chapter on TFL, and asked if he'd care to meet up and chat. He agreed, then added, "a whole chapter? Seems a lot." Can I take a moment here to acknowledge how refreshing I found those six magic little words? To find someone with no interest in curating a legacy? To find one person, somewhere, utterly uninterested in participating in the endless self-congratulations backslap marathon of underground music?

We met the next day at his studio in Spitalfields. Cunningham, a cordial chap with an Irish lilt, still wore the expression I'd seen in photos and film from forty years earlier, a poker face that occasionally, in slight, quick flashes, betrays the slyest of wry humor. We sat down next to his home studio, a modest space but for the half-dozen open computer screens. I took pains to be upfront about the band's second LP, *Fourth Wall* (Virgin, 1981).

"Just so you know, I've never really sat down and listened to it. I'm saving it for later in life. I mention this up front, in case it comes up later and I seem disrespectful for not being familiar with the material."

"Disrespectful?" Cunningham seemed astonished at the idea.[64]

The night before, I'd read most (all?) of the TFL press from the late seventies and early eighties. I opened by attempting to resolve the key riddle of The Lizards, Cunningham's chronic self-deprecation.[65] In interview after interview, he referred to his skills as a musician as "very bad" (*Melody Maker*), "a joke" (*Smash Hits*), "adventurous through complete ignorance" (*Rolling Stone*). When I asked how many instruments he was proficient in, he said, "I'm not. I'd be sub-grade one on any instrument." Cunningham seemed far more comfortable as a producer, someone assembling sounds so expertly that he willed his own band into existence.

The press played up the "DIY" angle with The Flying Lizards. Depending on which article one reads, the recording for "Money" cost something between thirteen and forty dollars (the price of the tape), and it sounded like something that could plausibly have been recorded by a genius in a basement. Some of the in-studio experimentation produced sounds that were inherently absurd.

In this heyday, the media portrayed The Flying Lizards as a sort-of punk band, one without flashy public personas or live shows or even recognizable motives. This idea—that The Flying Lizards were briefly a valid punk band—fascinates me.[66] It wasn't just proximity. Cunningham's world intersected with the budding punk scene(s) over and over again. In 1976, he scrubbed blood off the walls of an abandoned meat locker in Brixton, then bleached and painted and helped equip the space into a usable recording studio. This was Cold Storage, a hub for Cunningham's core group. Over the course of a few short years, the studio attracted some of the best and brightest from this embryonic art form. The Raincoats practiced there, Young Marble Giants recorded there, Laura Logic of X-Ray Spex helped upgrade the studio. Xerox artist Laurie Rae Chamberlain worked upstairs.[67] And the space had Cunningham.

"What punk allowed was for me to release records," he told me. "'Summertime Blues,' the first Flying Lizards single, was actually made in 1976. It didn't come out until 1978. Because punk needed to happen. Record companies didn't take that kind of weird stuff seriously."

That first LP sounded overtly British in a way that quickly became associated with UK punk.[68] And yet the band resembled no other. Neither did their peers: Pop Group,[69] This Heat, and The Slits (Viv Albertine plays guitar on the first LP), all groups that were reclassified "postpunk" at the exact cultural moment "punk" contracted into one narrow definition. "They didn't sound like anybody else," Cunningham said of his colleagues. "No one even attempted to copy them. Which is probably a tribute, I think."

We were veering toward a bad truth, a thing well known but seldom questioned: the period of punk's limitlessness was far too brief. From my vantage point, it looked like a shared dream. People in different cities reached similar artistic conclusions at the same time, like Joseph Swan and Thomas Edison both inventing the light bulb in 1879. Except this was a thousand light bulbs all going off at once, in New York, and London, and Detroit, and Los Angeles. In this brief, unnamed interval (pre-postpunk?), somewhere between 1975 and 1978, the pool of talent was so small that everyone bumped into each other. In Berlin, Iggy Pop introduced the Devo demo to David Bowie.

Cunningham agreed. "The vibe around punk, when it started, wasn't that kind of 4/4 guitar thrashing thing. It was much, much more open. It seemed that anything was possible. For a short time. I've always thought it was a much broader church than the way it got pinned down."

I was a kid when this happened; I was into *Star Wars*.[70] My longing for those magical few years is historical. Would this question be a bummer for someone who actually experienced the possibilities only to watch that moment vanish?

I pivoted to something related. The Cold Storage scene is remembered as one of several early relations of punk. There were others. Devo was a successful one-band branch, NY's brief No Wave scene less so. Although these other branches flowered in wildly different directions, they started with similar inputs: fine art (Warhol for Devo, Fluxus for Cunningham), a handful of outsider rock groups, the drama of the outside world. There was one through line: anger.

Anger is entirely absent from The Flying Lizards. In the song "TV" there is a preposterous guitar solo that brings to mind the cruel mockery of Philo Cramers guitar work in Fear. But TFL doesn't feel cruel. None of Cunningham's work does. It was a lost, distant cousin of punk, one in which subversion had been successfully separated from anger.

"Maybe I just don't see music being the place for it," he said. "I don't remember John Cage saying anything negative." He thought for a moment, then added, "I've been listening to Ute Lemper doing 'Songs for Eternity.' It's songs written in the concentration camps in Germany and performed there. Music from the ghettos in Germany during the Second World War. When I heard about this, I thought, 'gee, this is going to be so depressing.' It's the exact opposite. What's extraordinary is those songs are full of life. And rebellion. Theres no moaning. They're delirious tangoes.

"I've always thought Throbbing Gristle were kind of negative in that way. They present a completely black future. I always found it disappointing. Human beings can invent much worse things than Throbbing Gristle. So in a sense it didn't accomplish much for me. What I remember of the punk thing was, it was *funny*. In a slapstick kind of way."

•••

BEFORE DEPARTING, I INDULGED myself one personal question. For years, the Flying Lizards felt like my own personal thing, the one group I didn't have to share. This despite those 144(ish) compilations, or the soundtracks, or the fact that Barack Obama was once a fan. Now I was face-to-face with the man behind the curtain. So what band filled that role in his life? He appeared to give my question serious thought.

"Well, it's not like they're exactly obscure, but...Neu, the German group. For a long time, it felt like I was the only person who knew about them."

This was a good answer. Similar emotional neighborhood, far out but not so far out that I didn't also know of and also enjoy them. Only after we'd made our goodbyes and I was back out on the street did it hit me: life now had one fewer mystery.

FORT THUNDER

Time to Knock Down all the Buildings and Eat the Inhabitants

I LEARNED OF FORT Thunder the night Dan from Landed lit himself on fire. This was at the Met in downtown Providence, RI, in 1997. Local band Landed opened the show strong when their singer, Dan St. Jacques, emerged from backstage in flames. When I say "in flames," I should be clear that I mean engulfed in a fireball from the waist up. In the video, I'm shocked that the flames lasted less than ten seconds. Shirtless and smoldering, Dan performed a full set of belligerent, indecipherable songs before setting out for the hospital.

For some reason I never learned, locals hated the club. The next act, Forcefield—who sound like exasperated robots failing to communicate an important message—started up a motorcycle outside the nearest window, through which they'd run a hose, through which they funneled the exhaust into a huge cone aimed at the audience. The third band, Dropdead, played what had all the makings of a "normal" hardcore set. Until the last song, when the guitarist jumped offstage, squirted a line of lighter fluid to the back wall, and lit it in an apparent attempt to burn the club down. Then it was my band's turn to play.

After what must have been the biggest anticlimax in the history of New England underground music, I remember milling around the departing audience in something like shock. Dan returned from the hospital. He was swaddled in bandages, grinning as burn ointment dribbled off each earlobe. I have met many Elmer Fudds and very few Bugs Bunnies. Dan was a Bugs. The only things missing were the balloon drop and a dramatically unfurled banner reading WELCOME TO PROVIDENCE. I moved there the next year.

•••

THIS PROVIDENCE SCENE CENTERED around Fort Thunder, a 7,000-square foot warehouse in the downtrodden Olneyville neighborhood. Roughly half the space was open for shows and events. The other side of the space was a warren of rooms: living areas, practice space, silkscreen studio, bike repair station, communal kitchen. I vaguely remember wandering its corridors and stumbling into a library. The interior changed, grew, *mutated*, from day to day.[71]

On most visits, exploring like a cat, I'd find myself studying some new patch of architecture and trying to sort out what exactly I was looking at. Objects—toys, dolls, beads, masks, cereal boxes— so covered walls and ceilings that you could no longer see the original structure. The effect seemed organic, like walking through a rainforest made of colorful plastic.

Roommates (twenty-four, I once read) were invited to join on a homesteader basis; find space, build a room. The front door sometimes went without a lock, and strangers could and did wander in and make themselves at home. The place could generate its own rumors and internal urban folklore, some of which, because of the opaque layout, could be neither disproved nor verified. Brian Chippendale once debunked the idea that a gang of local kids used a nook, deep inside Fort Thunder, as their hangout. But how would he know for sure?

Chippendale was one of two cofounders with informal authority inside the space. Brian printed his own wallpaper and sometimes drew with both hands at once. He used rubberstamp letters that had to be painstakingly set by tweezers, like early movable type. It was a labor-heavy aesthetic as monastic as the Letraset lyric sheets I'd labored over for years.[72] Brian also drummed for Lightning Bolt, and I've read him describe his own "micro-beats" as parallels to both the comics (stunning, dense) and construction (daily, endless) of Fort Thunder. Chippendale once explained the act of decorating his interiors as an attempt to make his comics physical.

As much as I admire Brian's art, I found the work of his cofounder Mat Brinkman hypnotic. Brinkman's comics and posters opened onto worlds where life is cheap and strange. It was the stuff of kids' adventures: blobs, goblins, ghosts, giants, demons, dragons, kachinas, skeletons, parasites, cloud people, hierarchies of guards, soldiers, warriors, and underlings, subterranean caverns and chasms and sewers made of slimy cobblestones, as if this was the gritty, dangerous reality that Minecraft was later based on. Sometimes the print was so small the letters smeared together, which was a shame, because of great dialogue like, "time to knock down all the buildings and eat the inhabitants," and "my head is full of micro-men!" and "my tentacles suck!"

That small scene grappled, not entirely privately, with the specter of success. They faced the disruption of professional acceptance on three fronts, in music, comics, and fine art. In 2002, the Whitney Biennial included an exhibition by Forcefield (not a band, but a "collective" that included Brinkman). Given a seventeen-foot-high space as a blank canvas, Forcefield created a walk-in diorama of life-sized creature-mannequins, a display in the vein of the historical armor exhibition across town at the Metropolitan Museum of Fine Art, if we could see what such an exhibit would look like a thousand years from now. Serious old ladies scribbled *force field* in their little notebooks. I was never sure how the rest of the community felt about several of their own making it this far in the big leagues (conflicted, I suspect), but from my vantage point I found the exhibition inspiring. And I never use that word.

•••

When I intersected this scene in the late 1990s, Fort Thunder was halfway through its six-year run. My bandmate and business partner Neil lived in Providence, and I'd received a warm welcome from Ben McOsker, owner of Load Records, a company I wanted my own label to be more like (except for the part where Ben, nude, fellated himself on the cover of a Landed 7"). He seemed conspicuously gracious about another record label moving to town. In hindsight, this was clearly the high point of my two-decade immersion in the wackadoo underground, and I wish I had approached the space with the attention I now know it demanded.

Providence, with its convicted felon mayor and creepy recorded bird tweets (reverberating through a vacant downtown at night), offered some of this strange beauty. Rhode Island School of Design dumped a lot of fresh talent into a relatively small city. In the year I lived there, I detected a clear difference between the Brown University students, who wore turtlenecks and cared about their futures, and the RISD students, who dressed like futuristic scavengers and cared about the life-sized Sasquatch they were building out of, you guessed it, turtlenecks. Fort Thunder ushered in an era where some of RISD's graduating talent stayed within city limits.

Fort Thunder offered glimpses of possible distant futures. Alien characters roaming through alien bazaars buying alien consumer goods. An explorable dark dream. Halloween parades of parachute meat people. In Pasadena, decades later, I viewed a museum display of New Guinea ceremonial masks two centuries old and instinctually thought, *Fort Thunder rip off.*

•••

PUNK VENUES FIGHT JERKS with rules. Rules have many guises. At CBGB matinees it was Dennis, "the voice of God" on the PA, berating young men into staying offstage. Gilman Street had membership terms. In German squats, it was long screeds angrily taped to walls (including demands that all men piss sitting). At a squat in Sydney, I once marveled at the pharmaceutical small print covering a wall with precisely worded Dos and Don'ts.

Fort Thunder didn't have jerks. Why would they have rules? I once attended a wrestling match where giant insects battled a human Pepto Bismol bottle. The audience seemed split between papier-mâché monsters and dweebie weirdos that had wandered in off the street. At the end of the wrestling match, a one-story scaffold holding a dozen people collapsed. I'd been on the other side of the room and heard the crash before I caught the horrified expressions.[73] I knew the backstory: at a (pre-Landed) Krang show, elsewhere in Providence, a few years earlier, an audience member had fallen out a third story window and died. The absence of rules always struck me as a direct defiance of this danger. Everyone knew the risks of living a life of adventure. They chose to not cede any freedom to this risk.

Sometime during the year I lived in Providence, Neil took me to The Station, a rock club a dozen miles from Fort Thunder. He needed Blue Oyster Cult tickets. It was that grim time of the day when nightclubs are open for business but still hours from any live music, and the only other people present were employees. I don't like that bar smell—the mix of smoke and beer and airborne sadness that never fully fades—so I waited in the hallway and inspected promo photos of hair metal bands. I had a hard time wrapping my mind around the truth that all these photos of ridiculous, stoic rockers could actually be real, that they had actually been placed on these walls without irony. Repeat exposure to Fort Thunder had warped my sensibilities.

It was in this hallway that thirty-one corpses were found, stacked like cordwood, after the club burned down in 2003. The fire was many awful things all at once, but it also retroactively made Fort Thunder seem willfully negligent.[74] The space did take basic fire precautions (sprinklers, extinguishers, second-story windows that could be leapt from). But the mazes of room were clearly deathtraps. In contrast, The Station was ground floor and had four clearly marked exits. And yet 100 people died the worst deaths anyone can die.[75]

•••

THE OUTSIDE ART WORLD was easier to resist than the outside realty world. Turn of the century Rhode Island saw the sharpest rise in home prices in America. The sweat equity of two dozen artists, it turned out, was no stronger than the papier-mâché animals that lined the walls. Fort Thunder occupied space it did not own. In Chippendale's words, "one asshole sold it to another asshole." It was the same lesson in obscene greed being taught all over the country. The city demolished the building in 2001 to make way for a shopping mall in which all the businesses immediately failed.

Fort Thunder never got to fail. It was never allowed to gain enough cultural gravity to draw the inevitable drunks and fuckers that are as much a part of the DIY show circuit ecosystem as beetles and maggots in an old growth forest. Its core group of in-house fanzines (*Teratoid Heights, Paper Rodeo*) has left a distinct impression on a generation of high-visibility artists. You see traces of Fort Thunder even now, in the DNA of Cartoon Network's *Adventure Time*. It lives in The Dirty Goofball, a Millennial-and-younger lifestyle that seems to be slowly replacing The Hipster. I visit it every year, at the annual LA Art Book Festival, held in the 55,000-square-foot Geffen Contemporary at MOCA, a space large enough to comfortably hold seven Fort Thunders.

On the last day I would ever live on the East Coast, I brought my couch to Fort Thunder. It was a nice piece of furniture. I wanted it to go to a good home. A show was underway, so Neil and I lugged the thing into a dark corner and left it there undetected. Almost. On the way out, an old acquaintance materialized, told us his solo act was headlining, and that he'd be covering a song by my and Neil's band. I didn't want to seem rude, so as we stepped out into the parking lot, I assured him we'd be back later that night.

I never saw the Fort again.

THE GOSSIP

Saxophonist Wanted

IN THE SECOND SUMMER of the second Iraq War, I found myself emceeing for an ironic pro-war hardcore band. My duties were simple. Before each set I was to slip into my Uncle Sam costume, charge onstage, and denounce the audience's atheism, doping, free-love depravity, and general dearth of patriotism. It wasn't always an easy tour. In Berkeley and San Francisco, groping drunks blocked my way, astonished that they'd finally found the entire United States of America in one easy-to-manhandle persona. *"You,"* they would hiss, tugging at my fake whiskers.

In Sacramento, it appeared we'd found our crowd. People weathered my zingers with good humor. The ironic pro-war hardcore band received polite laughter at their ironic appeals to invade Syria, Iran, North Korea, and France. The audience seemed to be in on the joke, which made the night's moment of disconnect that much more jarring. The ironic pro-war band introduced an ironic pro-life song—"You DO know it's murder, right?!"—and a terrible silence descended over the crowd. Too late, I thought of writing SATIRE on a cardboard sign and holding it aloft. It struck me that I had simply not noticed the many large, angry, shaved-headed ladies in attendance. The feeling of impending skinhead brutality recalled the worst of the last century's CBGB matinees.

The Gossip headlined. This was their audience, and when the band took the stage all was well. In person as on record, singer Beth Ditto is the star of the show. She could have followed a botched cockfight and still made for an enjoyable evening. I have read Ditto's voice compared to that of Etta James, Janis Joplin, Peggy Lee, Bessie Smith, and Ann Wilson. The voice is sultry, brash, *loud*. It implores, commands, that we cease doing its owner wrong. For those of us who have dabbled in live vocals, the Voice is a source of gnawing jealousy. When combined with her stage persona—pro-queer, pro-fat, all swagger—that voice is a freakish superpower.

I've read praise of Ditto as a backhanded swipe at her band mates. That is not implied here. Their sound, labeled "blues-punk" by those lacking firmer reference points, would feel manufactured in the hands of a lesser group. The band's tours with the White Stripes and Sleater-Kinney seem evidence not so much of luck as meritocracy. The band's much-mentioned move from small-town Arkansas to Olympia, Washington, would be viewed as opportunism if not for the raw talent of all three members—Ditto, guitarist Brace Paine, and drummer Kathy Mendonca (since replaced by Shoplifting's Hannah Blilie).

The Gossip faced a chronic problem of female-fronted bands; critics (mostly male) assigning motives and omitting or distorting politics. Most Gossip reviews I have read dissect the band's lyrics to the point of unfunny bummerdom. Yes, divorced from their songs, Ditto's sentiments can come off as cornball. Without the muscle of music, whose lyrics do look good on paper? I've heard an equal amount of grumbling from friends (mostly female) that the band's brand of feminism is "pedestrian" and "redundant." This is the bane of the talented band: unfair expectations from both directions. It is this writer's opinion that only one critique holds up. For a band with such a fat-positive message, the Gossip sure has a thin sound. The addition of a guitarist, bassist, keyboardist, or sax attack would all be wonderful things.

Writing the words "fat-positive" is another unfunny bummer. The phrase makes me feel the way I did that night in Sacramento, after the show, loitering in my patriotic Halloween duds, and unsure who I had and had not offended. It's great that "fat" is making the same verbal trek to respectability as "queer." As a hetero white dude who occasionally dresses up as our nation's father, I can work with either confusing bit of semantics. But I've seen the band play twice now, and both times I felt like a creepy intruder. They are the kind of band that can change the life of a sixteen-year-old, that can bestow confidence upon the insecure. Where does that leave those of us who have way too much confidence?

GREEN DAY

Giraffe, Unicycle, etc.

ON THE SUBJECT OF Green Day, I behaved myself for a long time. When the band exploded like a pandemic in 1994, I shut my trap. My pals shut their traps as well. For any of us involved in punk bands to publicly disavow the world's largest punk band would have come off as a massive sour grapes hissy fit.[76] For years, I'd railed against "selling out." Green Day's rise exposed the performance-art futility of this crusade. It's odd to remember now, but concerts on their *Dookie* tour—supporting a major-label debut that would eventually go diamond—literally involved protestors, grown adults, waving anti-major label picket signs as if they were involved in some sort of labor dispute.[77] The spectacle of so many people high on outrage was an epiphany.[78] I no longer wanted to be that kind of person.

And if I'm being honest, it was more fun to sit back and drink in the dark humor of this particular band emerging from this particular scene. My pals and I experienced a potent combo of shock, mirth, and disgust that provided months of entertainment. You know that feeling you get when a giraffe in leopard-print panties comes roaring down the street on a unicycle? Same deal here, only more so.

···

GREEN DAY'S NAME WILL be forever linked with 924 Gilman Street, the Berkeley, CA, communal punk club the media loves to name check. In a quarter century of badly written blurbs, reviews, and profiles, Gilman Street is Green Day's "old stomping grounds," where the band "cut their teeth," and "honed their chops," and "spent their salad days." The club's membership rules have been bootlegged and sold as T-shirts at Green Day concerts in London's O2 Arena.

How do we inhabit a reality where Gilman Street—one of the most vibrant punk scenes in American history—can be reduced to a footnote in the biography of Green Day? By the time I intersected this world in early 1991, Gilman Street had been in full swing for half a decade, long enough to build an entire mythology. The Gilman crowd was like a comedy with too many rich characters. There was the intense, brooding Tim from Op Ivy, the enigmatic Neurosis guys, and Jake, frontman of Filth, whose terrifying barbarian shrieks were a badge of honor for every band he heckled. My tireless friend Ken Sanderson of Prank Records, whom I'd met when he still lived in small-town Alabama, brought his saloon-keeper courtesy to the big-city hustle and bustle of the Bay. Then there were all the holdout celebrities from the early days of the Bay Area punk rock scene, all those Jello Biafra sightings, or the time my bandmate Adam walked in on Dave Dictor—singer of Millions of Dead Cops and thus an icon of American folklore—sitting stark naked on a Gilman toilet.

Coming from the East Coast, my interactions with this scene always gave me culture shock. In their song "Fuk New York" [sic], the band Blatz insulted, by name, many of the entities that had long terrified me.[79] In an almost exact contrast to NYC scene characters, all the local nicknames (Eggplant, Lint, Jesse Luscious) were

121

upbeat, goofy pseudonyms. The East Bay was, in many ways, an alternate New York hardcore scene, one where the goons had not won but were always storming the gates, perpetually threatening a fragile democracy from the sidelines.

Gilman was but one branch of this democracy. There was Mordam (a cooperative posing as a wholesale record distributor[80]), Blacklist (a nonprofit posing as a retail record distributor), and Epicenter (a social center posing as a record store). The 1960s social services/counterculture history of the Bay Area scene gave the region an air of exceptionalism. It also made everything subject to the paradox of rules; the more organized people get, the more structures are needed to make that organization hold, and the more rules are required to keep the project stable.

I once sat in on a meeting at Epicenter, when one of the longtime volunteers was pushing to make her position a paid one. As a kid, I'd spent six years in two different hippie schools, and everything about that Epicenter discussion—the simmering resentments, the grinding procedural tedium—smacked of the Endless Meeting, a classic goof of the organized left.[81] That experience gave me the uncomfortable conclusion that the Bay Area scene offered a sort of glass ceiling, the arresting sense that this was as high as one could go in the underground, a scene zenith that had come at the cost of organization and rules and, despite everyone's best efforts, hierarchy.

Really, it was two ceilings. The Bay Area was famously puritanical ("overly scrupulous" is how Lookout Records founder Larry Livermore[82] once politely framed it) on issues of authenticity. So there was a limit to how far bands could rise outside the underground framework before receiving severe backlash. And in the pre-Internet world, this backlash had far more bandwidth, and thus carried far more weight than it would now.

•••

BLACKLIST, GILMAN, EPICENTER, AND Mordam each started as spokes. The hub of the wheel was *Maximumrocknroll*. Born in 1977 as a KPFA radio show, in 1982 the entity evolved into a pulpy newsprint fanzine that would come to be known as *MRR*. From the start, *MRR* defined itself through several unusual style choices. Readers were encouraged to submit "scene reports" that mapped out the living maze of underground punk, a moving target that mutated and metastasized on a monthly basis. From the onset, a decision was made to keep the record reviews concise.[83] This bypassed the threat of the nauseatingly narcissistic rock journalism that defined most music writing. It also deprived the fanzine of any good music journalism, or much of a singular voice outside the columns. The zine took on the low-frills, utilitarian feel of the Sears catalog that would double as a month of outhouse paper in old-timey times (although not really; the smeary newsprint left inky smudges on fingers, and anything else its pages grazed).

By the time I'd become aware of the magazine, only three years after its founding, *MRR* had already entered the rarified realm of the *New York Times*; it was an institution, one influential enough to set norms within its field. With such authority comes intense criticism. I'd first come onto their radar with a lengthy anti-*MRR* rant in my high school fanzine. Two years later I was a columnist.

It's hard to overstate the magazine's unique status. The first time I made the pilgrimage to the *MRR* house, I remember smiling uncontrollably when I stepped into their front office. My traveling companion (whose invite had gained me access) caught my expression and said, "Yeah. It's all real." The memory is a weird one. Emotions don't match visuals. I've seen so many "cool" offices in the decades since that it is difficult to remember what an anomaly it was, in 1989, to see a professional space dedicated to this esoteric society I'd championed.[84] Certainly there was nothing else like their basement record library, a plush, carpeted lounge with more punk and hardcore records than I'd assumed existed. I once found myself alone in the space, registering that same giddy delight I later felt when I first logged into Napster.

When the Gulf War hit, there was a surreal week when I and my bandmate Adam seriously considered, in the event of a draft, moving to Oakland, "going underground," and living like the A-Team (the logistics are fuzzy; would we have played shows under a fake band name?). That detail now has the feel of other bits of my band life—*I was so young and wacky and seriously mentally ill back then!*—that mask how scary that tiny war was to a generation that had grown up in peacetime. But this daffy plan was also a testament to the high regard in which we held the Bay Area punk scene and their organizational structures.

Nearly every aspect of the scene flowed back to *MRR*, meaning every aspect of this scene flowed back to *MRR*'s founder Tim Yohannan. When I met Tim, he was younger than I am now, but did a reasonable impression of a wise elder from another era. A full generation older than me, Tim had the graying, overgrown crew cut of a retiree and dark, deep-set eyes that, from certain angles, made him appear done-up like a 1930s Hollywood vampire. Part of the magazine's mythology was this bridge to an older era, as its core creators—Tim, Jeff Bale, and a few other sixties holdouts, middle-aged men in fedoras I'd seen once or twice hanging out at weekly marathons of the board game Risk—had ties to the radical politics of the sixties (although I was never sure exactly what these had been).

My relationship with Tim occasionally threatened to veer into protégé/mentor.[85] He was a good sport about my Angry Young Man posturing, while I ignored all his quirks that I would've berated less connected scene people for. Tim ate meat like a ghoul, and yet one night I, a proselytizing vegetarian, made the mistake of taking him up on an offer to eat out (he ate out every night). He brought me and a few other young acolytes to some seedy steak joint with moose heads on the walls, and one meager iceberg lettuce salad on a menu that otherwise offered a wide selection of steaks and guts. Tim combined this diet with heavy smoking, so it wasn't entirely a surprise to hear he'd gotten lymphatic cancer in his early fifties.

The last time I talked with Tim, I'd called to complain. As part of an April Fools prank, he'd reprinted one of my old columns without asking. The prank issue was, and presumably still is, an annual thing at *MRR* (one year, I'd gotten to write his fake resignation), and the only funny part was that someone fell for the gag every year[86]. We had already drifted apart, so I was pissed that he ran a bad piece of writing without permission, and more pissed still that I, inevitably, had become the butt of their annual hoax issue, and even more pissed than that at Tim for making me one of the countless people bitching and moaning about his fanzine.

After a good twenty minutes of my venting, he offered an uncharacteristic apology. The conversation started drifting when he added, almost as an afterthought, "if you're concerned about having a bad rapport with me, you really shouldn't be, because I'm in hospice, and I'm going to be dead in six months." I responded, with exaggerated iciness, "you might have said so twenty minutes ago and not wasted my time." We both laughed like it was the end of a *Scooby Doo* episode. Two weeks later he was dead.[87]

•••

TIM HAD BEEN SICK for a while, long enough that a half-year earlier Green Day had released a track on its fifth LP, *Nimrod*, called "Platypus (I Hate You)." The lyrics aren't included, but guitarist and lead singer Billie Joe Armstrong enunciates well enough, so one verse is clear as a bell:

I heard you're sick
Sucked on that cancer stick
A throbbing tumor and a radiation high
Shit out of luck
And now your time is up
It brings me pleasure just to know you're going to die

Ponder this. By 1998, Green Day was well into a multi-multi-platinum career (as of this writing, the only thing standing between them and the 100 million sales mark is a full-scale nuclear war). To record *Nimrod* unencumbered by earthly distractions, the band sequestered themselves for four months at the Sunset Marquis Hotel in West Hollywood, where a junior suite goes for $695 a night and the 1,800 Square-foot Luxury Spa would take all the floor space inside 924 Gilman. And yet, even in the midst of all this success—an unending avalanche of luxury denied even Nirvana—the band was so upset *at things an old man wrote about them in his fanzine* that they could stay silent no more. They simply must speak their truth!

The song was Tim's crowning prank, a stupendous sendoff. That they couldn't even wait the last few months for him to die is a testament to Tim's knack for burrowing under people's skin. This was surely the greatest triumph ever achieved by any fanzine anywhere. To seal Tim's victory, in 2011 Billie Joe confirmed online that the song was indeed about Yohannan.

•••

A FEW MONTHS AFTER Armstrong's post, I found myself with some time to kill in the lobby of a cheap Israeli motel. In a corner of the room, a TV played a block of Green Day videos. Maybe because

I was in a foreign land (and couldn't browse through my phone) I pulled up a chair and watched one song, then another, and another. I'd been aware, obviously, of their continued existence. I'd distantly registered that they'd kept making records and had produced a Broadway rock opera. I knew that the demographic that adored them was several orders of magnitude larger than the core of old fans who despised them.

Now I understood how much I'd willfully overlooked. While I'd spent the last seventeen years ignoring this band, this band had not ignored me. They'd been hard at work making my life more difficult. I'd been hearing their songs for years, as the background music for my life in public. Their music had tormented me in supermarkets, and airport terminals, and doctors' offices. I felt like the TV detective who finds one perp behind a string of crimes.

In the seventeen years since I'd paid attention to them, Green Day had somehow morphed into something immense and terrible, a mewling behemoth that embodied the worst aspects of pop music: the preposterous pomposity of nineties alt-plop, the cock rock awfulness of eighties arena schlock, the preening sincerity of seventies singer-songwriter ballads. Worse, they'd done so with the tenacity of a cockroach, refusing to die, or even peak. They could have decades—a long, lucrative Vegas career—ahead of them.

•••

IN 2017, GREEN DAY produced *Turn It Around: The Story of East Bay Punk*. It's a remarkable documentary, one directly benefiting from the band's lonely reign in the center of an odd Venn diagram, the point where the vibrant but fragile undergrowth of Gilman Street meets the sterile but hearty overhead of American popular music. Guys from Guns N' Roses and Metallica share time with members of Soup and Tribe 8. The film dismisses the seedy bits of Gilman (and there were many, including corpse theft and murder) and simply highlights the rare beauty of this thing.

The film triggered a flood of conflicting emotions, some of which were hard to gauge. I'd forgotten how much that scene intimidated me, even though its top export—pop-punk, in all shades of competence—was so grossly unappealing that I couldn't always tell Gilman bands apart. I'd forgotten how much I'd envied the faith of the Gilman regulars. I've never achieved the suspension of disbelief required to be part of the long-haul gruntwork required to sustain something like Gilman Street. I'm too lazy, too cynical, and, above all, don't know how to bypass my deep and enduring distrust of all communities.

It's a hell of a twist. I've spent half my life resenting this band's intrusion into my psyche, resenting the civilization that forces me—through its grocery stores and bank lobbies and airport terminals—to listen to the punk band I don't want to listen to. And now I must envy and deeply admire their faith in the underground as well? How the hell is *that* fair?

MISSING FOUNDATION

Your House Is Mine

ANYONE LIVING IN THE bottom of Manhattan in the late 1980s is probably familiar with an eerie bit of graffiti that, for a few years, seemed to earmark every other building on the Lower East Side. This Pynchonesque insignia (an inverted martini over a three pronged tally) often accompanied equally cryptic slogans: "Your House Is Mine," "1988 = 1933," "The Party's Over." In both design and placement, the logo seemed less like the cartoony tags of graffiti gangs than the cryptic markings utilities crews leave each other. These markings *meant* something.

Having moved to New York in mid-1987, it took me an embarrassing six months to learn that the symbol's author was industrial band Missing Foundation. MF claimed the logo as a tool of "property devaluation," in a campaign to halt the high downtown rents creeping out toward both rivers. It's unknown if the tagging ever hindered a single real estate deal; would a true or even prospective New Yorker balk at a spot of spray paint? But as guerilla marketing, it was magic, the kind emulated by thousands of corporate "street teams" in the years since. For two or three years, Missing Foundation was the scariest band in the city. Their early shows occurred in vacant lots, powered by generators, and abandoned, Viet Cong style, at the first whiff of police. In January 1988, the band trashed CBGB, setting fire to its stage and destroying some or most of its sound system.[88] Actual damage, in dollar amounts, has been lost to rumor. As dealers of confusion, Missing Foundation were hard to beat.

As musicians, however, MF have been handicapped by all that has come since. The songs could be called "Neubautenish," if one (like me) doesn't know much or care about German band Einstürzende Neubauten. Two decades ago, the use of oil drums and found percussion seemed somehow bold. In the new millennia, their music comes filtered through Burning Man and Venice Beach drum circles and the trash can showtunes of *Stomp*. Although some of their shtick was born of necessity—frontman Pete Missing allegedly used a megaphone because no club would trust him with a mic—it takes some mental footwork to remember that this genre once felt subversive.

Also, their songs need context. New York in 1988 was still the wounded metropolis of Mayor Ed Koch. This was the grimy Manhattan of *Death Wish* and *The Warriors*, its subway cars vandalized, its streets full of perverts and vigilantes and burning station wagons. Missing Foundation sounded like that city. When the band played Tompkins Square Park on August 6, 1988, they preceded a riot. It would be incorrect to say "caused a riot," although the NYPD ruthlessly pursued them as scapegoats. After the local CBS affiliate accused the band of Satanic cultism in a bizarre three-part(!) series, Pete Missing found himself tailed by the FBI.

That I only learned of the riot from the *Wall Street Journal* (on a flight to Albuquerque), made the band ten times scarier. I'd never seen Missing Foundation live. When I returned to New York, I avoided their concerts with the same diligence I'd shown as a tenth grader evading punk shows. The following summer arrived heavy with anticipation for the Lower East Side. "The next riot" seemed a strangely forgone conclusion. I spent most of that year working at a health food store whose glass front faced First Avenue. Although my store was equidistant from the park and ninth precinct headquarters, and thus on the exact opposite side of the park, we were treated to an almost weekly display of police cruisers and urban assault vehicles taking the bend down St. Marks Place, racing toward some minor disturbance in Tompkins Square, as if they'd gone the long route as a sheer display of military might.

The Riot of '89 never came to pass, but the tone of conflict seeped into the neighboring music scenes. The early nineties punk circuit ran concurrent to the squatter world, an underground of grubby adults that smelled of heroism and bullshit in equal parts. The squatters seemed interchangeable to me, but something important to mankind was always transpiring in one of their buildings three blocks over. And they were organized, and talented. Where my crowd had fanzines, theirs had local newspaper *The Shadow*, and *World War Three Illustrated*, the arts magazine founded by Peter Kuper, (later of *MAD Magazine*) and Seth Tobacman (whose cartoons brilliantly channeled the depression-era woodcuts of Lynd Ward and smooth geometry of *NY Times* illustrator David Suter).

•••

THREE YEARS AFTER THE riot, Born Against toured Europe. Our unpleasant promoter terminated contact one week in, and the band arrived at venues without any idea who we'd be sharing the bill with. In Karlsruhe, in southwest Germany, we arrived to find Missing Foundation. I remember being surprised by their lack of menace. The only intimidating member of their entourage was roadie Sid, the former singer of Italian hardcore band CCM, known for slicing himself onstage with broken glass.[89] After some polite negotiations, it was agreed that Missing Foundation should headline.

Bands performed at one end of an arched, torch-lit vault in a squat basement. While loading equipment down dimly lit, ancient stairwells, two members of their party conferred in stage whispers about the night's explosives. I'm still not sure if this was done for our benefit, or as a prank at our expense. When it came time for MF's set, they sealed themselves into the space with a sheet of plywood. After a long wait, Sid removed this with great drama— the stone from Lazarus's tomb—to reveal the band members frozen in place for five impressively awkward minutes. In the hands of almost any other band, the moment would have been bad art. Their set was loud, enjoyable, and not memorable for violence or explosions. The only sour note came later, when Sid threatened our young squatter hosts with decapitation if Missing Foundation weren't paid another twenty Deutschmarks. In the morning, both bands parted cordially. I never saw them again.

As we now know, 1988 did not equal 1933. Koch eventually begat Giuliani, but Giuliani also begat Bloomberg. And although the city has undergone some improbable changes, it still doesn't much resemble Nazi Berlin. In 1990, the band mystified their fans by signing a deal with Restless Records (falsely rumored, in those final days before online fact-checking, to be owned by Capitol/ EMI[90]). I only heard one defense offered by Pete Missing, and it came to me secondhand, and was thus (at the time) unverifiable; "People say we sold out. *But what did we sell out to?*"

NO TREND

911 as Laugh Track

THE MYTHOLOGY OF No Trend—in their time as a disorienting and malevolent 1980s hardcore band—has grown entwined with their relationship with the DC hardcore scene, meaning entwined with the mythology of Dischord Records.[91] I grew up scrutinizing early Dischord releases. I debated the minutia and rumors of its bands and artists for years. I critiqued records I found lacking, and defended the label from accusations of elitism.[92]

In the lore of Dischord's DC, 1985 begat "Revolution Summer," a period of renewal in which many of the original hardcore punks wrested back control of their scene from the skins, dicks, and turkeys who had so thoroughly wrecked shows with violence. They did this by making music that was complicated, and far harder to provide a soundtrack for jerks fighting. This period's biggest bands—Rites of Spring, Beefeater, Embrace—were Dischord artists, and their impact on this subculture was profound. Like Berkeley's Gilman Street club, Revolution Summer presented a model for others to follow in their quests to create sustainable artistic atmospheres.

There was a downside. With this shift came the drum circles, and the speechifying, and the college freshman political awakenings.

The DC/Dischord scene always took itself seriously, not just with their ethics and art, but as a mass persona (starting with its founding premise: "take us seriously even though we're teens"). Revolution Summer brought this seriousness to full maturity. Although I liked (not loved) the Revolution Summer bands, it all looked a tad too close to hippie times for my tastes.

This tonal shift is glaring in *Salad Days*, the 2014 documentary on the DC hardcore scene of the 1980s. Opening with Bad Brains and Minor Threat, the first hour of this documentary crackles with vitality. At the halfway point, the film abruptly transforms from *Raiders Of The Lost Ark* into *My Dinner With Andre*. It's the Ben & Jerry's that becomes potato salad in your mouth, the Chuck E. Cheese that turns into an H&R Block at the stroke of midnight. It's simply no longer fun. It's no one's fault, not the interviewees, and certainly not the filmmakers. The culprit is called 1985. And for as exciting as 1985 DC was to those inside it, it paled when placed next to 1982 DC for all of us on the outside.

The lore of both Dischord and Revolution Summer loomed large enough to generate sub-lore, including the myth of the DC outsider band. There weren't many of these groups, so each was off-brand in its own unique way. There was the ethereal weirdo pop of 9353; and the arty, not-necessarily-fun Nuclear Crayons; and the alienating blorty funk of the Wicked Witch 7". None of these bands seemed completely outside the label's artistic wheelhouse—Void were prominent Dischord outliers[93]—leading to the impression that access to the Dischord label could be granted through schmoozing (and if so, so what?).

No Trend, the ultimate DC outsiders, are now remembered as the antagonists of the Dischord scene and, somewhat anachronistically, Revolution Summer. Hailing from Montgomery County, Maryland, far beyond the beltway, the band is now remembered in one of two ways: 1) composing one side of a triangle that included Butthole Surfers and Flipper; the talented anti-hardcore hardcore bands, and 2) open hostility to DC punk and Dischord. Both reputations feel imposed retroactively.[94]

It's a shame that this is what they are remembered for. What they should be remembered for is their unrelenting misanthropy. Unlike Flipper (who played the searing, anti-war "Sacrifice") and Butthole Surfers (who eventually proved they did care quite a bit about money), early No Trend records give the sharp impression that there's nothing and no one worth saving. I saw the band as part of a different triangle, one keyed to my own young adult fears: Die Kreuzen (fear of the unknown), Discharge (fear of annihilation), and No Trend (fear of insanity).

The type of insanity exposed by the band's first LP, *Too Many Humans* (No Trend Records, 1983), springs from unrelenting disgust. It's one of the most disgusted hardcore records I've ever heard. It's also, somehow, the most desolate. In the second song, "Blow Dry," the guitar squeal sounds like one of those rusty spinning wheels that creaks around in the dark playgrounds of horror movies. The reverb makes the vocalist Jeff Mentges sound like a crazy man hollering at cars under an overpass. It is only when you drive past and catch what this man is yelling that you slightly shiver:

Acid rain is falling
Watch the humans crawling
Mud huts made of concrete
Cattle tracks in city streets

The album is full of proper nouns howled with such total disdain that their datedness barely registers: *Adidas shirt, Trans Am, Nielson ratings, Joanie Loves Chachi*. Some of the lyrics from this period seem cribbed from those anonymous, fascinating rants one sometimes sees stapled to telephone poles in major cities.

The LP is an indictment. If space aliens started destroying everyone and you were all, "why are you destroying us?" their answer could consist of nothing but this album, played in its entirety, and it would be a just and valid reply. Barring such an extinction-level calamity, *Too Many Humans* will be the secret theme song of the twenty-first century.

•••

SUCH SPITE IS, I suspect, unsustainable. On 1987's *Tritonian Nash-Vegas Polyester Complex* (Touch & Go), singer Jeff Mentges actually does an Elvis drawl, one of those things that, even then, merited a double-take for sheer cheesiness. But the record is at least recognizably bad, the same kind of retreat into sludgy camp being practiced in other scenes by other bands who had also perhaps run out of things to say.

In contrast, No Trend's full-bore stab at career advancement was impressively unique. Their posthumous 2001 LP, *More* (Morphius Archives, 2001), reminds me of Guns N' Roses *Chinese Democracy*, or the Winchester Mystery House, or Francis Ford Coppola's *One From The Heart*; each is a work of art that grew too large for its maker to constrain. *More* features ska, prog, free jazz, jingles, theme songs, double-time hoedowns with backup singers and a full horn section, and swelling, *Hair* soundtrack jam sessions that lead nowhere.

As impressively awful as it was, this LP had no bearing on the earlier work. Artists are remembered by their best work, not their worst. Black Flag fans generally ignore their last few LPs. Bob Dylan fans ignore his three born-again Christian albums. Beloved LPs with imperfect lyrics get remembered for their best lines.

Despite their time as mocking nihilists, the band was capable of great profundity, not so much depth as complete bottomlessness.

Depression was a staple topic for hardcore bands, yet hardcore is one of the least apt formats to tackle the subject. Black Flag's "Depression" is a giant, triumphant blast—the opposite of what depression feels like.[95] In contrast, No Trend's "For The Fun of it All" actually resembles depression; the indecision, the paralysis, even the jangly, slightly seasick riffs that don't really go anywhere, like the bluntness of unending emotional pain.

Whenever I hear this song, it transports me back to a specific night in mid-1990s Richmond, Virginia. I was in the bus station. I had to go somewhere, but was utterly unable to force myself to physically board the bus. As I stood there, sobbing and slobbering all over myself for reasons I didn't understand, paralyzed by the doubt of depression, I decided to search the station for a sign from God. My eye landed on TV monitors, and I saw that the comings and goings of the busses had been replaced with a string of gibberish. I had a flash of insight that at the time felt utterly real: we live trapped in the attics of our own brains, and when we call 911 there's nothing but an audience laughing on the other end of the line. Life is a journey to oblivion. No Trend were right.

7 SECONDS

Narcing On The Fuck Givers

NEVADA'S 7 SECONDS MAY have been the first hardcore band, although the honor comes with an asterisk; the band called themselves hardcore as in "hardcore new wave," a genre pairing that never came close to existing, but which has tantalizing alternate universe possibilities. The band formed three weeks too late to get grandfathered into the 1970s. That anyone could fit "new wave" and "hardcore" together without ridicule speaks to the uncharted rawness of the early Skeeno Scene (Reno, Sparks, Tahoe).

Apparently no one had settled on the exact role of skinheads in this new subgenre either.[96] The cover of the band's first 7", *Skins Brains and Guts* (Alternative Tentacles, 1982) features a bald, angry young man (original vocalist Dim Menace) glaring into the camera and making a fist for the viewer. His knuckles read SOCIETY and a large numeral seven has been drawn and circled on the back of his fist. It looks like a confusing ad for a small town news channel.

Debut cover aside, the band soon found a balance between hokey and jokey. The punks of 1980 Nevada would have had physical safety issues in public, but 7 Seconds responded with a Little Rascals-style, put-up-your-dukes scrappiness. Singer Kevin

Seconds sang "I Hate Sports," but also wore jock-style eyeblack for live shows. The band's upbeat, sing-songy choruses sometimes felt like a put-on. Skeeno punks assembled The Crew (immortalized on 1984's *The Crew* LP), which I understood to be the kind of safety in numbers that vulnerable people need in a region isolated by the vast distances of the American west. It was all done with the vague do-gooder vibe of shaggy Jesus freak caravans from a generation earlier.

This vibe came to define the band. Vicious Scam cassettes, the band's original tape label, became Positive Force, both a record label and, later, a sort of national do-gooder franchise with intriguing durability (the DC chapter exemplified DC's Revolution Summer, and survives to this day).[97] The band assumed the brand-new mantle of a "positive" hardcore group. Of the dozens of lyrics I could present for your inspection, the one that has always stuck with me is the chorus to 1984's "In Your Face";

Use your head
Be Aware
Give a Fuck[98]

The band 7 Seconds adopted creeds from several groups— Discharge's defense of humanity (minus the rage), straightedge[99] from Minor Threat (minus the outrage), and the Positive Mental Attitude of Bad Brains (minus the resistance to the humiliations of white supremacy). All that virtue made the final product a tad squishy, a bit too similar to the hippie subculture that punks saw themselves vanquishing. Perhaps to defuse this critique, the band announced (in the song "Clenched Fist, Black Eyes") that they were "the new kids," "succeeding where the hippies failed."[100] In their exuberance, 7 Seconds offered a gallant alternative to the Asshole Guy hardcore band template (or a Goofus alternative to Up With People, depending on your perspective).[101]

Vocalist Kevin Seconds was my first micro-celebrity, the first Hey-There's-That-Guy guy I saw up close at a show. Accessibility is one of hardcore's biggest selling points, which means someone like me could, with a bit of patience and perseverance, encounter all their favorite musicians in person. This also meant I've always awarded Kevin Seconds a baked-in prestige, regardless of what I thought of his musical evolution (or the awkward time, in Albany, when the band had the audience sit during their set).

•••

It also seemed like the band had plenty of self-awareness about their status. *Walk Together, Rock Together*, the group's second LP, feels cocky. Ian MacKaye guests, Troy Mowat smacks cowbells, and Kevin raps, making Debbie Harry's freestyle on "Rapture" sound like Ol' Dirty Bastard.

In 1986, the band discovered U2. Touring that summer for their third album, *New Wind*, they found they had accumulated enough goodwill for at least half of the original audience to hear them out. And if you liked 7 Seconds, *New Wind* wasn't unlistenable. It was merely bland in a way that felt nakedly unoriginal, both in mediocrity and trajectory. Many of the original hardcore bands attempted to soar away from their hardcore larval stage. A few rare groups (Beastie Boys, The Replacements) actually pulled it off. However, 7 Seconds was not one of those groups.

Boldly, 7 Seconds advertised this B-list status with their logo, a sort of pictographic bronze star the band awarded themselves. Although they started strong. The era of early hardcore band symbols produced some stunning graphic design, and the first 7 Seconds logo—a clean circle and square cross combo—could rival any band emblem. Unfortunately, white supremacists also used this logo (the "Odin's Cross" decried by the ADL and outlawed in

Germany), so at some point the band merged this with the circle 7 on Dims hand, creating a sort of duct-tape hybrid of both things at once. Teenage me used to draw these things obsessively, and something about their new logo eluded me. It wasn't fun to draw.[102]

From *New Wind* on, the band seemed to bleed both relevance and respect. When Jawbreaker signed to Geffin in 1995, the backlash was scandalous and prolonged. I don't recall anyone saying anything when 7 Seconds signed to Sony a year later. No one cared.

•••

I NARCED ON POSITIVE Force Records in high school. I'd sent the company three dollars for the *Nuke Your Dink* 7" Nevada Hardcore Sampler compilation, and after a one-year delay in mail order I got impatient and sicced the Better Business Bureau on them.[103] It was not one of my finest moments. In my defense, three dollars was a lot of cash in 1986. I didn't yet understand that problems can indeed occur at one's pressing plant. I received paperwork from Positive Force and the BBB, and the record eventually arrived with the explanation that they'd had other one-year backlogs. Both companies were exceedingly polite.

The summer after this unfortunate exchange, I booked a 7 Seconds show at the Albany Hibernians Hall. This was a big responsibility, and despite the beer demands of their rider (I was eighteen), I felt like I'd pulled the gig off without any major snafus. Except one: the band never showed. A phone message gave me the odd excuse that bassist Steve Youth had a tooth ache. There was almost a pun in that, but not enough to placate 150 distressed show-goers.

Later that month, leaving Albany as a confident, competent young man headed for college, I stuffed all my worldly possessions into a passenger van and made my goodbyes in front of my mom's house. Somehow the hard-won Nevada Hardcore Sampler floated to the back of one of the piles and got smooshed up next to the window. After my mom hugged me farewell, she looked up and said, *"'Nuke Your Dink'?"* and the thought occurred to me that perhaps those weren't the best three words with which to start one's new life as an adult.

•••

IF IT ISN'T CLEAR, I always liked 7 Seconds. Their early records are fun listens in the same way that summer of '82 blockbusters are fun movies. Despite their corniness, it seemed like they filled an important role in that very early hardcore world. They were the nice guys, the people who gave a fuck about the world. If that influenced things I later found artistically shady—more on that later—then oh well.

But they did make me feel bad about my mortality. The band really dug in on the Boys Adventure thing: Steve Youth, "Young Till I Die," grown men singing "Diehard Youth" in a chorus…as the years wore on, the planned obsolescence of it all was a bummer.[104] As I was writing this book, 7 Seconds broke up. They almost made it to their fortieth anniversary. What would it be like to perform in a band for forty years? To never get the chance to forget your own lyrics? The idea sounds like existential horror to me, but I get that some people are able to make it work like a good marriage. Kevin Seconds' announcement of the breakup was clearly written with grief.

•••

IN 2010, I LANDED on a spoken word bill with Seconds at Chapman University in Orange county.[105] I've met enough of these original hardcore personalities to know I should assign a low value to first impressions. People aren't always "on," and punk and hardcore celebrities—operating without the vigilance of actual celebrity—usually aren't even aware of the impact they make on those they meet. Whatever Seconds' demeanor, I'd already decided to give him a pass and enjoy myself.

But Kevin was disarmingly cordial. I opened the show by publicly presenting him with a twenty-five dollar Applebee's gift certificate as a peace offering for the unfortunate *Nuke Your Dink* incident (he had no memory of this), did my set, and took a seat in the tiered lecture hall. A mutual pal filled the middle slot, leaving me enough time to ponder my mix of emotions. Was it actual expectation? Wasn't this how I'd felt back in Albany, waiting for 7 Seconds?

Even now, I struggle to explain Kevin Seconds' set. He simply stood there and told stories, and it took a few of these stories to realize that his humility wasn't contrived, or a comedy bit, or any sort of impediment to the flow. And for those of us familiar with his work, the stories were all red meat: shows from '82, young Glenn Danzig, playing a prison. Did he have notes? I don't remember. What I do remember is that a tale of early eighties ultraviolence threatened to choke him up. In the rapt silence of the audience, I remembered how scary and awful some of that violence got, that these weren't just funny memories of adventure, but also scalding memories of trauma.[106]

Afterward, over dinner, my pals and I attempted to debrief on what, exactly, we'd just witnessed. Kevin's assurances that he'd almost never done "this sort of thing" before seemed ludicrous. How could a spoken word novice soar so effortlessly? It felt as if we'd somehow been hustled.

Only on the drive home did I get it. Kevin Seconds did what so many hardcore bands had sung about. In the language of a thousand 7 Seconds-influenced bands, he'd "stayed true to himself." I've known people who took this idea as literally as possible, guys (and they're always guys) who locked in their young man personas as a way to calcify at an early age, to stick to the comfortable confines of music and experiences and emotions they could share with a small handful of trusted, likeminded pals. I'd always assumed this was a liability.

Kevin Seconds sure made this look like an asset. He gave every appearance of being the engaged, cheerfully humble guy I'd encountered twenty-five years earlier. All he needed was the eye black. I thought back to the me of 1985, how utterly different that person was from the adult me. I'd always assumed that was a good thing. But what if I'd just been a great person to start with?

SSD

Pro Footsie League

WHEN I TELL YOU that Society System Decontrol is my catbox band, I need you to understand: this band is so important to me that I listen to them whenever I clean my house's catbox. Meaning, this band is so important to me that I needed to weave them into my everyday routine. I suspect I've never owned a dog because of their music.

SSD were the first insider band I gained knowledge of. Listening to tapes of their records (already rarities in 1986) offered me a first glint of secret info, one that seemed to transcend the normal quest for teenage acceptance and verge close to forbidden knowledge. Later in my life, the bands Can, Chrome, and Magma each occupied this position—the cool band only cool people knew about—although none ever came close to SSD's oomph. When I saw Nirvana's Krist Novoselic in an SSD shirt on MTV, I remember cheering at the TV set, even with the knowledge that this secret thing was clearly no longer secret.

Society System Decontrol were a central pillar of the early 1980s Boston hardcore scene. The cover for their flawless debut LP, *The Kids Will Have Their Say* (1982, X-Claim) showcases

Boston's central symbol of state authority. In the original photo by photographer Phil In Phlash, a bunch of bros jog up the steps of the Massachusetts State House on a sunny morning. Visionary designer Bridget Burpee solved the missing drama of this picture with one bold stroke: she removed the sky. In the retouched version, the building looks floodlit against a starless void. Something terrible has happened, and now grown men storm the halls of power during an emergency session in the dead of night.

Writing about the music of SSD is tricky. For one thing, their performance—songs that swoop and crash with all the gusts and torrents of a violent ocean squall—balances their production—visceral but gritty, like a distant radio station (you compensate by playing it loud). Then there are all the layers that came after, both the hardcore punk they pioneered and the straightedge hardcore they hyped. It's a lot of heavy emotional shit to sort out.

A few particulars. Springa the singer had a great flinty scream and seemed to grasp the vocalist's role as actor. Toward the end of "Police Beat," an oddly touching anti-cop dirge, he yells "police" like a crime happened in the recording studio and he needs an officer. Chris Foley drums with such aggressively confident precision that certain songs sound martial, channeling that fife and snare scrappiness of the Revolutionary War. I am incapable of hearing the first ten seconds of "Fight Them" (repeated, on the same record, as "The End") without getting goose bumps. Their second release, Get It Away (X-Claim, 1983), is just as good as the first.

As with most early American hardcore bands, pictures are key to the deal. These guys made great photos. Everyone is young and fit and knows how to leap. The band's guitarist Al Barile played with an exertive physicality many have since aped. One famous(?) photo by Glen E. Friedman shows Barile leaping into space, leg outstretched like he's simply decided to fly over everyone's head and out the front door and off into the night.

•••

THE YOUNG MEN STORMING the capital building on that LP cover were the Boston Crew, which included members of Negative FX and DYS,[107] who were both very good but saddled with the yoke of not being SSD. The Boston Crew had its own fashions. Onstage, men wore athletic shirts (sleeveless tee or sports jersey), sneakers, or boots (by season?) and the occasional sweatband (head or wrist). Women didn't exist. The rabid straightedge stuff merged with the male bonding stuff, which merged with the confusing jock-not-jock thing. The music made all the weird parts worth it to me, but those weird parts were always clearly marked.

Neither of those first two records offered any clues of what was to come. *How We Rock* (Modern Method) of 1984 goes metal. The LP's best track, "On The Road" is a whole bunch of guitar solos with bits of song in between. The next album, *Break It Up* (Homestead), completes the transformation, somehow managing to make eighties party rock appropriate for teen funerals. To their fans, the metal albums exposed the band as slithery strivers. It's hard to imagine their new music won them a fanbase in the hair metal community. After *Break It Up,* the band broke up.

In 1992, Boston's Taang Records released *Power,* a compilation album mixing songs from all stages of the band's career, blistering hardcore and cheesebag metal in a seemingly random assortment on one disc. This LP came at a point in my life when I was starting to value the rights of the artist over the rights of the audience, so I loved it. I loved the idea of such a ferocious band intentionally sabotaging their slick rerelease with some of the most belligerently uncool tunes from their catalog.[108] Not long after it came out,

I talked with an acquaintance whose holy zeal for all things hardcore made me feel like a rookie.[109]

"That new SSD album is hilarious," I said. He looked at me with what seemed like genuine contempt.

"There is *nothing* funny about that record." It was as if I had said something racist.

•••

SPEAKING OF RACISM: BOSTON. I always assessed Boston bands on a sliding scale that factored in the ugly busing desegregation battles of the 1970s. For as long as I've been alive, the city has had a serious racial tolerance problem. In SSD's case, one misheard lyric prompted discussions. In "Jock Itch," a fifty-second assault on the athletic frat bros they suspiciously resembled, there is the line,

Anyone different is a commie to you
Anyone black is a n*gger to you

Although they weren't using America's dirtiest word in an exactly ironic way, the anti-racist intent seems clear.[110] My friends and I, however, heard "anyone" as "every," which seemed like an eloquent expression of that lumpy Archie Bunker racism where there are always "good ones" to be found among the swarthy hordes. (If that sounds confusing, in *The Kids*...title track, one line protests "atomic bombs on helpless Japs").

For their first two albums, SSD was SS Decontrol, and on flyers the band used the jagged lightning bolts of the Nazi Schutzstaffel (KISS used similar letters in their logo, which they altered for their West German releases). They were pretty explicit about not being Nazis, so I figured that the SS lettering was merely a tough front, like biker helmets designed to resemble German army gear. As a kid raised with *Star Wars* stormtroopers, I understood that not all Nazi imagery was necessarily out of bounds.

The half-life of the overt Nazi imagery from Sex Pistols era was perhaps longer than most thought. Other bands used those lightning bolts (Sweden's Crude SS, the proto-punk London SS, the feminist Basque punk band Las Vulpess) in a manner that, I suspect, was almost an homage to those mid-seventies shock tactics, and not even meant to serve as actual shock tactics themselves. A lot of bands played footsie with racist imagery without doing the basic math on how this would make them look to outsiders.

Although, the Boston Crew played footsie at a professional level. Example: I've long revered The Last Rights 7", featuring vocalist Choke (of Negative FX), as the greatest East Coast hardcore record ever recorded. And I say this as someone who deeply loves all the greats. BUT ALSO: the band made a special edition cover featuring a photo of Hitler, and which was recorded, according to its back cover, "in the ovens of Auschwitz." Although this record was a collector's item, it was never a secret.

Choke was the first person I ever interviewed for a fanzine. After answering my questions politely, my zine partner and I asked if he had anything else about himself he'd like to include. "Yeah," he laughed. "Tell 'em, Choke's a racist, and he hates n*ggers!" We both laughed because we were teens and he was a grown-ass man and we clearly didn't "sound black," so surely it was in jest and everyone was cool. In the printed interview, I just left the quote out.[111]

Sometime later that year, fellow Bostonians (but staunchly non-straightedge) Gang Green played Albany. Singer Chris Doherty introduced the band by mumbling a joke with a one-word punchline: "n*gger." The crowd booed in shock. Albany was a polite scene, and a largely white scene. Most of us had never experienced anything like this before. At some point in the first or second song, my friend Billy the skinhead, one of the largest men in the room, mounted the stage and just stood there, his middle finger jutting two feet from the singer's face. Eventually the band apologized for their "racialist" humor, finished their set, and slinked off. They seemed surprised by the bad reaction. Had the joke landed in Beantown?

•••

THIS WAS ALL A long time ago. People change. I accept that. I'm one of them. In 1988, I had a vintage varsity jacket on which a pal screened the band name in its half-abbreviation, SS Decontrol.[112] Although the S's weren't lightning bolts, they were still the largest visual element. Wearing this jacket, I walked into a Bowery deli. The odds are decent I was also wearing the same design on a T-shirt. If I wasn't above playing footsie with Nazi imagery (and I was in college; I must've known I was doing this), then why would I be above advertising one of my favorite bands with two pieces of clothing?

"SS," the man behind the counter mumbled. He looked middle-aged, vaguely east European.

"Different SS," I stammered, with that cringe-worthy smile that I used to get when utterly flustered.

"I know SS." He said. "They kill my family."

If you are this guy, and you've stumbled on this book somewhere and are reading this now, please know that I was young and high on hormones and had not quite yet worked out the mechanics of being a decent human. I've never been quite sure who was more at fault here, you—with your jump-to-the-worst-possible-conclusion assumptions—or me—with my playing-footsie-with-playing-footsie fashion sense (and seriously: I must have known that something like this was bound to happen). But I have taken pains, in the years since, to be sure that whenever I wear an SSD shirt, that shirt damned well better read SSD.

THRONES

Doing Time in the Can of the Mind

I ONCE SHARED A bill with Thrones—the one-man band of mighty, bearded bassist Joe Preston—at the only all-ages club in Anchorage, Alaska. In a city so isolated that any musical event was an excuse to congregate, the show drew two hundred kids. Many of them were actual kids, children, subject to a strict 10:30 p.m. curfew in a town where the sun didn't set. The Thrones set was so forcefully odd, so defiantly, triumphantly singular, that I was taken aback by the warm reception. It's not often that weirdo bands get their due.

After our set, a stranger told me there was "a scary Eskimo bar" next door. I investigated, finding that it was indeed a very scary bar, and that the clientele were almost entirely native Alaskan, and that no one smiled. The low-ceilinged, windowless room seemed to absorb light, so that it suddenly felt like the time it actually was. A cover band played The Chantays' "Pipeline" and a frowning, unhealthy-looking middle-aged woman roamed the floor with a keytar as if she were doomed to this one room for all eternity.

I noticed a dark tableau in an unlit alcove toward the back of the room. As I cautiously approached, I could just make out two mannequins, one with a bugs bunny head, its arm forever up the skirt of a scantily clad lady mannequin. I thought the bar's baffling decor would have been just as appropriate a venue for the Thrones set I'd just witnessed. Then again, I'd only known Joe for seventy-two hours at that point.[113]

•••

I'D FIRST LEARNED OF Joe Preston from an interview in the fanzine *Joe Preston's Legs*. The zine's name was a play on Joe's own fanzine, *Matt Lukins Legs*, named in honor of the original bassist of the Melvins. The Melvins were a big deal in 1991, both because of the grunge explosion, and because they were a fantastic band. I'd heard he'd become the new bass player for the Melvins, and I'd found inspiration in his story from afar. For some reason, I'd registered Joe's victory as a win for all us Regular Guys. From his interview, one quote stayed with me:

> "I was programming 'Mississippi Queen' on my drum machine in the front room and I heard some sort of commotion, it's really weird, I heard it and I looked out the window and Kurdt and Dave…coming around the corner, and they must've been whooping and hollering, like they were really excited and they had this note and they were like 'Joe Joe Joe, Buzz called, you're in the Melvins.' And I was kind of really overwhelmed and struck dumb for a number of days."

At the time I had no idea who "Kurdt and Dave" were.[114] I just thought it was an oddly poignant quote about achieving one's dreams. When I'd heard he'd been fired from the Melvins a year later, the news had made me strangely sad.

Joe intersected Melvins at an opportune point in the band's history. During his brief tenure, the band released three 12" solo EPs, each a faithful parody/homage to the Kiss solo records. *Joe*

Preston (the record, not the man) sounds like the first Thrones release. On "Bricklebrit," the drum machine is intentionally artificial, as cold and unprocessed as the earliest new wave bands. It was a hallmark of Thrones tracks to come.

Joe originally saw Thrones as a two-piece, but his chosen drummer didn't mesh and he didn't want to dictate style to someone not on the same wavelength. He started working more with drum machines (the Alesis HR-16 and Roland MC-505), linking more and more "doodads" to these machines until his own equipment boxed him into going solo. Performing live with the double-neck Ibanez bass/guitar combo he bought from one of the Godheadsilo guys, Thrones the live act came across as something larger and more powerful than most one-person bands, more *Project Grizzly*[115] than street busker.

Over the years, Thrones became the nucleus for a much larger career. Joe has played in at least twenty other bands, some of them—High On Fire, Harvey Milk, The Need, Sunn O)))—acclaimed, nationally touring acts. He roadied for Unwound, Blonde Redhead, Bikini Kill, and Nirvana.[116] When I asked how many tours he'd been on, Joe replied, "probably forty to fifty–plus" (for some perspective, I only did seventeen tours in fifteen years, and it felt exhausting).

Oddly, Joe thought he'd met me long before we actually met. A few years earlier, a stranger had interviewed him in Buffalo for my fanzine. I have no idea who this was. I didn't have freelancers. When we did meet up, I found a kindred spirit on a parallel trajectory. Like me, Joe had done time in the can of the mind. Both of us had been marked by the kind of depression and loneliness that can seriously derail a life. And we were both in the process of learning that being an "ex-member" of a popular band rarely translates into large audiences. It just meant that every flyer from then on would serve as a minor jab of frustration.

Having toured together thrice, we shared long stretches of that strange dilated-reality inhabited by all touring musicians. It's one of the few benefits to life on the road; your personal sense of time expands, so that each day feels far longer than the average routine of an average life. And you witness an abundance of strange life experiences through the sheer act of being constantly in motion throughout roadside America. He and I accumulated stories.

There was the time I threatened to punch Joe in my sleep. And the time I tried to cheer Joe up by buying and badly attempting to smoke a pack of cigarettes in front of him. And the morning, in suburban Utah, when I found Joe standing in the middle of the street, rumpled and groggy. He'd slept in the van—van duty—and seemed bewildered.

"Which house did you guys sleep in?" he demanded. I pointed to the house I'd clearly just emerged from.

"Well, I just pissed in the corner of the basement in *that* house," he announced, pointing at the wrong house, apparently angry at its owners for having so deceived him.

I'm less interested in recalling those shared tales than I am in hearing of stories from the solo tours. How does solo touring even work? When a bungee hook slapped Joe's eyeball in San Diego, who was there to get him to a hospital? When a man propositioned Joe in a Florida park and then returned to yell "faggot" out his car window, who was with Joe to revel in the absurdity? And when Joe drove 3,000 miles with a mannequin named Steve (a roommate's possession too large to ship), who was there to say *stop, this is weird, and unhealthy*? Besides Steve?

•••

THIS LONELINESS INFORMS ALL Thrones songs, although Joe seems able to turn the isolation knob up and down at will. Some reviewers call his music "experimental metal." On certain tracks, like "MANMTN," one can hear the Melvins influences that propelled Joe back when he was an uber-fan and not an ex-member. His track "Coal Sack" is both a blorpy blort and the greatest Cro-Mags song never written. It was vaguely irritating that he'd managed to write and perform a better hardcore song than I'd ever be involved in. Despite my pleas, Joe would never tell me the lyrics. When has anyone ever been in a position to harangue the author of one of their favorite songs for the lyrics?

"Experimental" sometimes overwhelms "metal," and it is here that the solitude gets boosted high in the mix. On 2000's *Sperm Whale* (Kill Rock Stars), the cover's whale-attacks-whalers scene—an especially intense papercut by Olympia artist Nikki McClure—sets up the sixth track, "Ephraim." It's a lovely, lonely, percussion-free lamentation in the vein of that earlier Melvins solo EP. But is he Ahab, or the whale?

Then there was his cover of the Roberto Fia version of Luis Bacalov's *Django*, a 1966 spaghetti-western triumph, sung in Italian, with a chorus of wailing angels that deeply moved me the dozen or so times I saw it performed live. In the middle, there's a gorgeous, out-of-the-blue guitar solo. I once saw Joe completely eat it on this solo, yell "shit!" in front of a baffled audience, and still somehow nail the emotional heft of the original.

Many of his slowest songs convey a solemnity, a piousness, that seems very nineteenth-century, the kind of piety once practiced in small congregations surrounded by bear-filled forests. On 2005's *Day Late, Dollar Short* compilation LP (Southern Lord), there is "Obolus," a nine-minute track invoking the soaring cathedral of nature, both its vast majesty and the fearsome, religious wonder of it all. The song makes my cat flex his ears back and glare at the wall. What does that cat hear that I don't? I realized I could call the songwriter and ask.

Sweet Christ, was the answer a letdown. Apparently Joe uses something called "distortion" on his bass guitar. He also uses things like "synths" and "samples." I felt like someone trying to reverse-engineer Coca-Cola by mixing up all the ingredients listed on the side of the can. The unique chemistry of four-piece bands is hard enough to crack. One-person bands are impenetrable.

Although HBO's *Game of Thrones* surely messed up Joe's online presence,[117] Thrones have been Thrones long enough that Joe has entered that rarified realm of beloved performer.[118] I have seen audiences treat him with a reverence completely detached from any performance. The *NY Times* once described Joe as "phlegmatic," which made me realize I had no idea how a Thrones performance would read to someone who didn't know him personally. Which version do other people see? Jolly Joe? Pensive Joe? Walter Matthau Crabby Joe? Bluto from *Popeye* Angry Joe? Stone Head From *Zardoz* About To End Everything And Everyone Joe?

Then again, which version of Joe do I see? Touring isn't marriage. You spend long blocks of time cooped up with someone, and you get opportunities to see your bandmates at their worst and occasional best. But ultimately, you spend only a tiny sliver of your life alongside these people.

There was a night, years ago, when the two of us were the only ones awake in his van, driving across a vast expanse of darkness. I was sitting in the passenger seat, bored but not tired. My mind wandered, and I remembered that Joe had once roadied for Nirvana. It struck me that he must have had this same kind of moment with Kurt Cobain, quiet, late-night interludes between two people staring out at the endless highway.

I remember spending some time composing my question. When I finally worked up the nerve to ask what that would have been like—I don't remember my exact words—he chuckled in the half-light of the dashboard, and finally said, "oh, I don't know." It was a Joe answer to a Non-Joe question, and I winced in the dark. But then I remembered we'd known each other long enough to count each other as friends, and that most friendships involved exactly these kinds of weird slips, and if I gave him enough time, he'd hopefully say something just as embarrassing around me.

YOUTH OF TODAY

Wrong End of the Tube

HERE'S ANOTHER MYSTERY FROM my teen years. Why did I wait a year to go to shows? I knew about hardcore in ninth grade, and championed it in tenth. But I didn't take that first step of admission, going to shows, until eleventh grade. Why? When I lived in Burlington, Vermont, in 1983, I'd seen flyers for local band Nation of Hate. I remember being fascinated and slightly repelled by the grainy photos of blurry people rushing across stages. When I moved back to Albany the next year, I came across a photo of Black Flag in the city's weekly, and I would study this picture, the grown men screaming in the audience just behind the long-haired singer. I knew that I should join these men, but their ardor terrified me. It took a year to work up the nerve.

My first show took place at a Knights of Pythias lodge, kin to the VFWs, Knights of Columbus, Modern Woodmen of America, The Benevolent and Protective Order of Elks, and American Legions whose basements hosted shows across the US. I remember walking in on local band Fit For Abuse,[119] and the cognitive dissonance of seeing a slam pit for the first time.[120] The music was so loud it registered as physical trauma. I left to find a napkin to stuff in my ears, but also so that I could collect myself. I sensed that this was probably going to be a big part of my life, but I wasn't sure yet that I liked or even recognized it.

The touring California bands Ill Repute and Scared Straight both cancelled, so the Connecticut band Youth of Today became the headliner for the night. This was only YOT's second show, but they'd sprang from a vibrant scene in Connecticut, one with links to Albany, which offered New England bands a direction for jaunts besides New York or Boston. As happened frequently with hardcore, the band had put sufficient thought into their thing to spring forth fully formed. In this case, their thing wasn't a costume or even a specific sound. It was ideological, more or less: "straightedge," as defined by Minor Threat just a few years earlier, but with most of the hard emotional edges sanded off.

A switch occurred right around the time I started going to shows. In the early 1980s, the Albany punk scene—realm of plucky, oddball bands like Capitle [sic],[121] The Plague, and The Verge—had been heavily influenced by smart, arty Boston bands like Mission of Burma and The Proletariat. But by the middle of the decade, staleness was in the air. On the national stage, many of the original, blue chip hardcore bands had either broken up or gone bad. Heavy metal had stank the joint up, virtuoso guitar solos embraced, hair grown out.

In '85, the East Coast scenes began to gravitate toward the grittier, angrier sound of New York hardcore. In DC, the esteemed Dischord Records crowd—the previous sphere of influence for Albany-sized scenes across the East Coast—mounted a forceful rebuke with their own wave of smart, arty bands. But the rest of the coast was shifting toward a far more aggressive version of hardcore, one more explicitly celebrating the confidence of young white American men. This was more than a coastal shift, but one that would soon conquer the country; "New York" as a level of testosterone if not yet a precise geographic sound. Albany, being only two hours from Manhattan, was an early adopter of this shift.[122]

Youth of Today's first EP, *Can't Close My Eyes* (originally on Kevin Seconds' Positive Force Records), doesn't exactly sound like it's trying to be a New York record. This EP would've fit alongside 7"s by Neon Christ, or Peace Corpse, meaning records that were cool to own, but not so much fun to listen to. It's the badly recorded exuberance of young guys, eager to jump and holler and waggle their astonishing physiques at passers-by (and singer Ray Cappo and guitarist John Porcelly were *remarkable* physical specimens). Only the vocals make the music a slightly memorable listen, and then only because Ray growls in the general key of cartoon cereal salesman Tony The Tiger.

This was the first record I'd bought from a band I'd actually seen live, so I listened to it a lot. Despite my own youth and lack of musical references, the chorus to their self-named anthem jumped out as something deeply iffy;

> *Physically strong*
> *Morally straight*
> *Positive Youth*
> *We're the Youth of Today!*

This was a slightly reworked Boy Scout motto (Cappo wore a Boy Scout uniform the day he met Porcelly) used in the service of something strange and sinister and not yet fully recognizable. At the time, the distinct tinges of fascism didn't register. It just seemed creepy. Over the years, that creepiness never dissipated. It's like the relative who made a pass at you last Thanksgiving, something you can't quite let go of.

Ten months later, Youth Of Today opened for Grievous Bodily Harm at the Washington Avenue VFW. GBH were an exotic joke in

1986, a pack of central casting UK punk rockers with little appeal to a small, clean-cut American hardcore scene. When Cappo took the stage, he mocked GBH's alleged $750 guarantee with a rant about "fucking rock stars." It was boilerplate hardcore guy stage banter,[123] and not particularly bold talk in front of a sympathetic audience, especially an audience that didn't include GBH (I remember them cancelling). Then he continued, taking an entirely new line of attack.

"Punk rock, and that bullshit in '77, was twisted. And I'm glad to see it's over," Cappo huffed, working himself up with the showy bluster of all good frontmen. "I'm glad to see hardcore move in a positive creative direction," he added, launching, screaming, into their theme song.

Ray's rant was probably confusing to some in the audience. This was the era of The Bad TV Punk. ABC Afterschool Specials set the tone, with a barrage of cheesy dramas too smug for teens and too dumb for adults. And TV punk episodes were dumber still. *CHiPs* had featured the fictional band Pain, whose singer (done up in Adam-Ant-via-Darby-Crash war paint) croons their hit "I Dig Pain" as cops bust up the mosh pit like an open-air prohibition speakeasy. *Quincy* mounted a more frontal assault against the fictional band Mayhem, and music that, in Jack Klugman's anguished plea for sanity, "said life is cheap, and murder and suicide is okay!"

Having this *Reefer Madness*-style self-satire come from the frontman of a hardcore punk band was a new development. Five months later, Phil Donahue would unwittingly parrot Cappo's rant on his own shallow dive into the evils of hardcore punk. "Life is meaningless," the silver-haired fuddy concluded, with obtusely extrapolated sarcasm, to groans from the studio. Later in the episode, Cappo himself stood up in Donahue's audience and gave a spirited defense of hardcore punk from the exact kind of attack he himself was delivering onstage. It didn't make a lot of sense.

•••

THERE WAS NO WAY to know it then, but the band had pulled off a canny move. By marrying the athletic fraternity of SSD (their obvious muses) to the pushy positivity of 7 Seconds (their elder mentors), Youth of Today had stumbled into a marketing bonanza.

Earlier hardcore bands saw themselves as a further wave of punk bands. Youth of Today were the first popular hardcore band to break continuity, to denounce punks as loudly and forcefully as punks had denounced hippies. Other hardcore bands would soon take up the charge (within a few years, Slapshot would sell "Punk's Dead, You're Next" shirts). YOT could claim to be something new, a punk band that renounced everything about punk but the music. Taking a cue from the 7 Seconds' *The Crew* and the Boston Crew storming SSD's first LP cover, Youth of Today spawned the Youth Crew.

Over the course of just a few months, the Youth Crew assimilated Albany audiences. The ratio of boys to girls swelled, and many of these boys had a conspicuously clean-cut uniform. The Youth Crew wore particular brands (Champion, Nike, Swatch). Punky hairdos and ripped clothes were out, thick, heavy sweatshirts and varsity jackets were in. This well-groomed aesthetic extended to the graphic design of this new scene, a new world where flyers and records and shirts and stickers all triumphed the same collegiate font.[124]

Up to this point, identifying with punk and/or hardcore carried a price, socially if not physically. You dressed as a hostile in a hostile society, and you assumed the burden of resistance. I looked pretty tame throughout high school,[125] but strangers twice threatened me, once with a baseball bat. The Youth Crew's new dress code provided a means of gliding through life without threat of confrontation.

This was a shift. That there was an approved uniform (and that the pushers of this uniformity were neither coy nor ashamed) had big consequences.[126] Until YOT, conservatism thrived in the germy corners of punk scenes. When it popped up in public, it took the forms of extremists, usually skinheads, people whose shitty behavior forced a fight or flight response. The Youth Crew ushered in true conservatism, the norms and boundaries of William F. Buckley's America. It wasn't just that everyone started dressing like normals. This new scene fostered normal thinking. Hard politics were out. Fuzzy platitudes were in. Bands looked the same, sounded the same, and sang about the same very limited range of experiences and emotions.

YOT relocated to New York right around the same time I did (autumn '87). There was no announcement, no grand debut. At some point, the band, like me, just decided they were going to be New Yorkers. But I've never understood how the New York scene came to accept the interlopers. Five years after the notoriously drug-addled CBGB punk scene had fallen apart, an equally drug-addled hardcore scene moved in. And where the first crowd favored heroin-haze decadence, their replacements preferred PCP-fueled ultraviolence. So how did the clean-cut fashions of Americas wealthiest state fit into the hardcore scene of America's most poverty-wracked metropolis? How did the polite children of Connecticut, The Belgium of New England, infiltrate the NYC of 1980s, a city with neighborhoods that still resembled Berlin in 1945?

Even with the mystery of New York's acceptance, all of this feels inevitable. If Youth of Today hadn't existed, the Youth Crew would've had a different name and zip code. Every social swing creates its own backlash, and when those tidal forces play out on compressed timelines, it's nearly impossible to recognize what's happening in real time. I knew several of the Youth Crew main players, one well, and always had the impression they were just a bunch of regular guys who got swept up in something large and forceful and, from the inside, tremendous fun.[127] (It's a bit harder to give Ray Cappo a Mulligan; as someone who built a cult of personality, then harnessed this following in the service of a bona fide cult—the Krishnas scored bigly with Cappo as recruiter—he forces the question: when does tackiness become villainy?

•••

A CONSENSUS MARKS HARDCORE'S heyday from 1981 to 1986, although different benchmarks gauge the end. The death of The Minutemen's D. Boon, the end of Black Flag, or Dead Kennedys, any one of dozens of different anecdotes about fights, or club closures, or unfun metal albums. Here's my theory. The end of hardcore, as an evolving artistic force, was subjective. It ended at different moments for different people. Specifically, it ended the moment any given listener realized that the name Youth Of Today wasn't ironic. YOT sprang from a vibrant scene of cheerful, ridiculously named hardcore bands: Crippled Youth, Vatican Commandos, Violent Children. In their wake, they left an expanding subculture of young man bands whose stern names—Up Front, Wide Awake, Chain Of Strength—signaled a new, zero-tolerance policy for satire.

Of course, it was the end of more than just hardcore's evolution. In the space of a single decade, punk had willed itself into existence and then mutated into its own inverse. Picture a tube. At one end are the innovators—the demented Weimar cabaret of the Bromley contingent, the early New York and Los Angeles and Detroit scenes, the crowds of cheery, campy, vibrant proto-punks arriving for shows in lingerie and top hats and, yes, parachute meat costumes. At the other end of the tube are their cultural offspring; an ocean of identical, clean-cut white boys and men, decked out in varsity jackets and sowing a few wild oats before heading off to college or the work force.

There's a pattern. One market correction (punk fixing the falsity of rock) causes a smaller correction (hardcore fixing the falsity of punk), which causes its own, even smaller correction (the Youth Crew offering the fun of hardcore with none of the risk). The music would continue, and still continues now. But from here on out, it would be a closed system, one more infinitely expandable artistic echo chamber, reacting solely to its own brief but deep past.

PROBLEMS

THE DEBATE

Oops

ONE MORNING IN EARLY 1990, my father called me into his living room, produced an accordion folder of financial statements, and told me I would soon be rich. I hadn't grown up wealthy, but my grandfather had partnered in a prestigious Midwestern law firm, and a small bit of his capital had trickled down into a trust in my name. Left to accrue, this trust had done spectacularly well during my first two decades. I'd been kept ignorant of the secret loot. Now I was approaching my twenty-first birthday. There was no longer any way to keep it from me.

My dad lived just outside Albany, NY, so I had a long bus ride back to Manhattan to ponder the news. I was in my third year of a liberal arts degree at The New School For Social Research. Although my current reality hadn't panned out—a broken heart and several inept professors had soured me on college—I had no idea what I wanted to do with my life. The trust fund didn't fit into my existing world view. My life centered around hardcore.

Back in Albany, I'd produced fanzines and booked bands every other week. In New York, I made larger fanzines and saw bands every other night. I'd started a record label and saved enough from my job at a health food store to pay for half of a split-EP release. *Maximumrocknroll* took me on as a columnist. In a city brimming with new opportunities, I'd gone as far as possible in one very limited and familiar sphere of activity.

The Albany hardcore scene had provided an entirely safe sandbox for my creative pursuits. My pals and I shared a scene phone list, and shows ended with trips to Chuck E. Cheese. One night, everyone played a huge game of Duck, Duck, Goose on my best friend's lawn. Not only had I never seen a fight at an Albany hardcore show, the entire concept of fights at hardcore shows was alien.

New York City hardcore shows seemed to be all fight. In a scene that revolved around weekly CBGB matinees, violence—endemic, hallucinatory—informed every part of the experience. Audiences reenacted bands' brutal lyrics. A typical NY show featured beatings, theatrical showdowns, and/or random assaults. More than once, I'd seen people moshing while swinging heavy chains. And this wasn't only in Manhattan. Rumors filtered through the scene of far more brutal outer borough shows where young men where maimed, or blinded.

Three years earlier, I'd had a strange insight into this older New York scene. Not long after moving to the city, I'd traveled with friends to the Anthrax club in Norwalk, Connecticut, to see the band Dag Nasty. Their guitarist, Brian Baker, had played bass in the revered Minor Threat. Dag Nasty held the title of the Washington, DC scene's flagship band in the mid-eighties interim between Minor Threat and Fugazi. In the closed circuit of East Coast hardcore, they were celebrities.

Earlier, I and my Albany friends had ingratiated ourselves into their circle, and we prided ourselves on hanging out with the band in their meager backstage area. Sometime during the night,

I noticed Baker cozying up to a young woman. I registered her identity and who I thought her boyfriend was, but didn't think much of this observation beyond a sharp, secret pride that I was cool enough to have insider info.

Two days later, Dag Nasty came to New York. The CBGB Sunday matinee was a pilgrimage for music fans and psychotics alike. For one afternoon a week, the famous club had two theaters: the actual stage, inside, and the more violent stage of the sidewalk out front. This stretch of pavement never seemed entirely safe to linger on, and yet that was precisely what I (and everyone else) did between bands' sets. As Brian Baker crisscrossed from club to van and back again, I spotted members of the local band Sick Of It All milling ominously.

Fronted by singer Lou Koller and his brother, guitarist Pete Koller, SOIA flaunted a working class machismo whose cartoony packaging (their motto, "It's Clobberin' Time" came from *Fantastic Four* comics) in no way detracted from their real-world toughness. Pete seemed unhappy with Brian Baker. From thirty feet away, I observed the action with a sickening schoolyard certainty. In seemingly slow motion, Pete approached Brian. From my vantage point, I could see the heat of his words, the hostile gestures. Brian twisted out of an arm hold and speedwalked back toward the club. As he retreated, Koller barked, "where are you going, GIRL!" as if this was the worst insult he could summon. "Come back, you GIRL!"

The trouncing was total. A founding father of American hardcore had been humiliated in front of the Independence Hall of American punk. Through a haze of bystander adrenaline, I pledged a solemn vow: never, ever make the Koller brothers angry at me.

•••

I WASN'T IMMUNE FROM the city's aggression. In college, my fanzines and writing took a sharp turn toward antagonistically leftist politics, and my politics took an even sharper turn to encompass all the minutiae of the hardcore sub-subculture. I'd made the classic mistake of self-styled radicals throughout the ages; I'd conflated the global with the extremely local. I hated tyrants, racists, "sellouts," and major record labels with equal force.

By 1989, I'd finally found a suitable outlet in Born Against, the hardcore band I cofounded and fronted.[128] The rhythm section quit after five shows, but guitarist Adam Nathanson and I had soldiered on, united in our principles. Adam and I formed a tight alliance. We both passionately believed that hardcore punk had strayed from its vibrant roots (although not deep roots: the golden age we emulated was less than a decade old). He and I despised what we saw as the commercialization and conservatism of the New York scene during Reagan's second term. Heavy metal record labels courted flag-waving nationalists, and a vocal minority encouraged gay bashing and white supremacy.[129] For us, the scene was a contrarian's paradise.[130]

I, however, confined my outraged sniping to fanzines. Adam believed in direct confrontation. Inspired by *State Of Fury*, the fanzine of musician and author Abraham Rodriguez, Adam produced *War Prayer*, a funny, scathing one-sheet screed against scene hypocrisy, which he would distribute on the sidewalk outside venues. In 1988, he'd flyered a showcase of popular hardcore bands at the Ritz. Friends had predicted a severe beating if he went through with it, but his protest only generated indifference. Adam thought of himself as a lone truth-teller, the Diogenes of NYHC. To his baffled audience, he was just another street kook.

Making our relationship one shade more complicated, Adam lived with my ex-girlfriend, Christina. Christina and I had dated for a year in high school. The relationship had been far more intense for me, serving as both my first serious romance and an entrée into a much larger world of film and music. I'd been devastated when she'd left for a Midwest college one year ahead of me. But we'd stayed in close contact, and she'd wound up transferring into NYU housing across the street from my freshman dorm. When I learned about the money, Christina had been the first person I'd called.

Adam and Christina and I benefited from a shift at the turn of the decade. Fights finally forced CBGB to suspend hardcore shows just a few months before an entirely new scene emerged at ABC No Rio, a dilapidated social center seven blocks away. The downtrodden Dominican neighborhood of bodegas and botanicas was at least as rough as the Bowery (I once watched shirtless men fight in the street with chains, as if the city itself was one vast mosh pit). At ABC, however, the outside violence inspired indoor camaraderie. In the space of just a few months, outcasts from the larger scene all found each other.

This new community quickly developed an aesthetic that could best be called Confrontationally Puerile. Drawing penises on show flyers or fanzine covers was an effective way to banish the thugs of the larger, tougher scene. It also established a milieu of confrontation. The new venue essentially played punk scene to the punk scene itself.

ABC No Rio came at an opportune time in my life. The New School housed me in a six-foot by ten-foot room in the Thirty-Fourth street YMCA, one cell in a honeycomb of urban squalor and desperation. I was depressed, isolated, aimless.[131] Outside of expanding my record label, I had no particular dreams or aspirations that this windfall could help me fulfill.

The YMCA sat two blocks from Macy's iconic Herald Square department store. Sometime in the days or weeks after learning of the trust, I toured Macy's many floors, dazzled by the opulence of objects I would soon be able to afford. I decided I'd buy a $4,000 canopy bed designed in a faux Chinese imperial style, complete with track lighting and mahogany dragons. Exiting into the reality of street level Manhattan, the choice felt hollow, more like a dare than a decision.

•••

IN EARLY SPRING, I met with my dad to review paperwork for the upcoming handover. In a jumble of statements from Niagara Mohawk, Northern States Power Co., and various mutual funds, my eye caught one word: Exxon. The Exxon Valdez oil spill had occurred only a year earlier, and any further association with this word seemed morally invalid. I knew nothing of shareholder activism, and didn't grasp how to go about transferring cash to ethical investments. One halfhearted review of socially responsible equity funds didn't pass my crudely basic standards.

I had no real interest in sorting any of this out. As a freshman, I'd worked for one day on Wall Street, tallying shareholder proxy votes. Instead of using the job as an opportunity to learn about finance, I'd excused myself for the bathroom and dashed out the front door. Financial literacy itself felt morally suspect. I ordered my holdings liquefied.

In late April, I spent the afternoon of my twenty-first birthday at a Born Against show in Tompkins Square Park. The park was a magnet for squatters and those who dressed like squatters. Rain cancelled the concert before we could play, and I remember standing on the bandshell, gazing out on the dreary, trash-strewn plaza and its raggedy inhabitants, registering that I was officially rich.

A strange suspense settled over the next month. It felt rude to inquire about the money, or even mention it to my dad. When my semester ended, I moved into a cheap punchline of an apartment in New Brunswick with Adam and Christina. The front door opened into their bedroom. To get to the bathroom, anyone would have to pass through my bedroom. A doorless kitchen separated the two areas. Macy's faux Chinese bed would not have fit in either room. Although I'd already settled into a strange sibling relationship with both, I'm still not sure why it seemed like a good idea to live in a de facto dorm room with my ex-girlfriend and her fit, handsome new boyfriend.

The money suspense continued for six weeks. On June 13, I had $1.79 in my checking account. On June 14, I had $111,508.35. That afternoon, I made the first of many, many daily $400 withdrawals and treated a few friends to a shopping spree at the Princeton Record Exchange. I'd entered the life of a trust fund brat.

The next day, we drove to Connecticut for another show at the Anthrax. This time, we drove up for Shelter, a Hare Krishna hardcore band newly formed by Ray Cappo. Cappo had fronted the wildly influential Youth Of Today, a Connecticut band that had relocated to New York City. We ABC No Rio regulars found Hare Krishna offensive, an affront to the antireligious roots of eighties hardcore. This was selective outrage—Bad Brains and Cro-Mags were deeply religious bands—but it was true that Shelter represented a friendlier, far more proselytizing branch of Hare Krishna.

In a group vindication of Adam's flyering actions, a dozen ABC No Rio regulars drove up to Connecticut and essentially picketed the concert. If that sounds alien now, there wasn't much more context for it in 1990. One flyer simply read "fuck Religion" in block letters. Another featured the Krishna logo next to a swastika, denouncing both as symbols of "hate, separation, and elitism." We'd pulled off the odd trick of making members of a cult the more rational ones in an argument.

Several devotees complained, "you wouldn't have flyered a Cro-Mags show." This was true. Shelter sprang from a newer iteration of the New York hardcore scene, one that had insinuated itself into Manhattan from Connecticut and Long Island. These carpetbagger bands and their straightedge fashions—varsity jackets, nice haircuts, collegiate fonts—represented a cleaner (meaning "more marketable" to me and my friends) version of NY hardcore. Although a few of their fans called us "faggots," the band members themselves gave the protest a disconcertingly respectful hearing. Our action wasn't particularly dangerous.

The Cro-Mags were part of an older, native, scarier New York scene, one more aligned with the subculture of skinheads than straightedge. Although Cro-Mags were also a Krishna band, they emphatically embraced violence. Overtly homophobic, vaguely fascistic, with chiseled, snarling personalities straight out of central casting, Cro-Mags weren't a band any sane person would antagonize. The same could be said about many of the older NYHC bands.[132]

Adam had mercilessly attacked the newer scene for its seeming elitism and toxic superficiality. He hadn't critiqued any of the old guard bands, partially because he'd still been friends with some of their members. But in the aftermath of the Shelter protest, our group felt emboldened. In the hyperviolent CBGB scene, we'd each been isolated. Now we discovered a degree of strength in numbers. Voicing our opinions about anything seemed suddenly doable.

Much of this group's hostility increasingly focused on In Effect Records. Formed the year earlier as an imprint of Relativity Records, In Effect neatly distilled every complaint Adam had been voicing for years. The label offered slickly packaged albums by large, metal-tinged bands like Agnostic Front, Killing Time, and Prong. Many of the releases bore a label logo that read HARDER

THAN YOU. It was as if a caricature invented by Adam had sprung into reality, fully formed.

In 1989, In Effect released *Blood, Sweat, and No Tears*, the debut LP by Sick Of It All. The cover and insert sleeve featured a collage of crowd shots featuring many of the people who'd tormented all of us at CBGB. Most galling to us, the lyric sheet censored the word "shit." As Adam and I grew more and more vocal about bands and labels we didn't like, this album became a lightning rod, both for us and for the likeminded community we were the most visible members of. And as we grew more antagonistic, a sense of resignation set in. I was allowing myself to drift toward confrontation, against the very people I'd never wanted to confront, with a sense of inevitability that felt somehow out of my control.

A week after the huge deposit, I stopped at an ATM and discovered there'd been another payment, this time for $105,022. For a brief period, my cash supply seemed both infinite and ominous. I hadn't earned this money. I intuited that I just might not have this much money for the rest of my life. I developed a plan. I'd use this wealth to get my helicopter license and become a professional pilot. Although that too seemed more like a dare than something I'd actually do.

•••

IN THE FIRST WEEK of July, the Koller brothers came looking for us. They'd swung by an ABC No Rio show while we'd been at a recording session and roughed up a few of the regulars. One friend, pushed to the pavement, quickly gathered himself and fled. Adam was outraged, but not at Sick Of It All; he felt our pal should have stood his ground.

Sometime later that week, a third party told us that Pete Koller wanted to debate us on college radio. In my memory, the set-up had an implicit tone: Debate Or Else (Adam later told me he didn't recall any threat). It also seemed a strange concession. Sick Of It All were already a hugely popular band. Born Against hadn't yet released any records. Not only were SOIA handing us a giant publicity boost, they were doing so in terms that felt highly advantageous to our side. A debate seemed like the perfect opportunity to validate Adam's credo of direct confrontation in public.

In hindsight, this seems laughably naive. But I'd already handled one minor run-in with this older, scarier NYHC scene. A few years earlier, I'd printed something mildly disparaging about Murphy's Law, a jingoistic pro-drug hardcore band who'd managed to tour with the Beastie Boys. After hearing that singer Jimmy Gestapo had threatened me onstage, I got his number and called him to clear the air. Still a teenager, I'd been terribly impressed with my own ability to defuse a potential beating with some adult conversation (we ended the chat by sharing put-downs of Ray Cappo).

Less than a month after the move to New Brunswick, our lives took another detour. Adam had been working for the Rutgers University recycling program. One of his coworkers left abruptly, and Adam agreed to store the man's remaining belongings at our place. The coworker may or may not have been homeless; his garbage bag of possessions looked and smelled like garbage, and, when left outside, had been mistaken for garbage and hauled away. The coworker returned, demanded his bag, and forced Adam to drive to the dump. After turning up empty handed, he informed us that the bag held something of great value—money, cocaine, at one point diamonds—and that a local drug gang was coming to kill us. The three of us gathered whatever we could fit in Adam's car and fled.

I'll never know if the threat was real, but this act of seeming self-preservation was, in retrospect, the beginning of three years of what Adam dubbed "out-of-whackness." Decades later, he told me that his bouts of depression went into a spiral after fleeing New Brunswick. Our lives no longer followed regular rhythms. My bank account could buffer us from threats, but over the course of the band, the money provided risks and opportunities that were hard to make sense of. His thrift contrasted my wealth. On tour, we ate cheaply and slept on floors. At home, I often covered the rent for our new, comfortable apartment on a quiet block of Weehawken.

•••

In July, Adam and I found ourselves in the WNYU studio, seated across a conference table from two very angry Koller brothers. There was a tense prelude before we went on air, and the dark comedy of that moment is something I've tried to capture on paper in the many years since. *How did you wind up here, Sam? What is the path that led you to this particular room, with these particular people glaring at you? You did okay on your SATs, never touched drugs, never got anyone pregnant. And yet here you are.*

Each party brought a third. We'd included our friend Charles Maggio, singer of the Jersey metalcore band Rorschach, whose masterful first album would lend my record label instant credibility a year later. Sick Of It All brought Steve Martin, head of In Effect Records. Steve had played guitar on two Agnostic Front records, and had an interest in the debate beyond defending his company's honor. He'd already engaged Adam, among others, through a nasty exchange of letters. His tone could toggle between articulate frustration and condescending spite from sentence to sentence.

An ON THE AIR sign lit up. We opened by questioning their self-censorship, neatly highlighting the divide between the two camps. SOIA had no reason to care about Robert Mapplethorpe, the NEA Four, or any of the other first amendment battles of the day. This wasn't, I realized, going to be a polite Greek Agora airing of opinions. In Effect packaged records for sale in mall chain stores; their motives were rational and clearly stated. Our deeper point—that more hardcore records in malls meant more meatheads at shows—contained such a logical flaw that Adam and Charles and I didn't bother mentioning it. We'd already won our own violence-free scene. We had nothing to gain from the debate, except the presumption of not getting beaten up at a later date. Our entire premise (and presence) was flawed.

My memories of the discussion itself are hazy. I recall Lou growing heated that I'd made fun of his jacket, and one of us asking "What's wrong with girls" to a chorus of mocking, manly groans. Mostly I just remember a sensation of slow-motion panic I'd experienced only once before, four years earlier, during a high school performance of Tom Stoppard's *The Real Inspector Hound*. I'd blanked out before an auditorium of parents, while my castmate whispered that he was going to punch me as soon as the curtain came down. It was the stressful weirdness of bad dreams that no bad dream ever really prepares you for.

Since their persona (working-class guys) was genuine, and our shtick (outraged truth-tellers) was acquired, we'd needlessly handicapped ourselves from the start. The debate ended with one of the brothers crashing a chair aside in a manner that made for good radio. We'd prepped for the event by bringing fanzines with highlighted passages. But no one had given any thought to our physical safety. Exiting the building seemed problematic (and added another touch of comedy: did we all share an angry elevator ride, or did everyone regroup in the lobby and continue the argument there?). On the pavement outside, there were some sour words between the two groups, like drunks ejected from a bar. But besides one of our pals getting shoved, the clock had not struck clobbering time. Had this sort-of-triumph translated on-air?

At the next ABC No Rio show, I was shocked to learn that our peers disapproved of our performance. I'd assumed I'd get some congratulations for facing tough men and taking responsibility for the actions of the community. Instead, our constituents felt misrepresented. This was my first encounter with a pattern that came to define my band experience: friends and fans perceiving some noble facet of my personality and then bitterly expressing disappointment when I failed to live up to expectations.

•••

THREE YEARS LATER, THIS disappointment came to its logical conclusion. The ABC No Rio crowd largely disavowed Born Against. Former friends (including Charles Maggio) publicly denounced me in fanzines. I'd given my detractors more than enough ammo. I frequently backtracked on my own loudly stated principles. Within our immediate social circle, my incompetence was renowned (after one terrifying flight lesson, I abandoned the dream of becoming a pilot). We demoted ourselves out of the city, and started playing shows under the defeated banner of the New Jersey state flag.

My expulsion followed a template I myself helped perpetuate. In college, I'd badmouthed the members of Dag Nasty for the sin of performing music I found inauthentic. And Dag Nasty's members had been genuine and genial people. In contrast, I'd deliberately made myself despicable. I had no right to complain about being despised now.

More humiliating, I had been entirely unable to keep my wealth a secret.[133] Warped in the echo chamber of fanzines and hearsay, the "inheritance"—I didn't dare call it a trust fund— became its own entity. In 1992, a stranger wrote of two friends physically fighting over my having turned down a million dollars (one thought it was a "cool, anti-capitalist thing to do" while the other believed I should have bought a bunch of land and declared it "a free nation"). When I went broke in the spring of '93, this played out in the community as one final stain on my character. Born Against's last show booked out of state, I fled New Jersey with a $3,000 tax bill I couldn't afford.

Without the outlet of a popular band, my previously camouflaged mental health issues accelerated. By the mid-1990s, I suffered daily, debilitating panic attacks. After one episode of dissociation, I could no longer fully distinguish reality from fantasy.[134] In the years since, Adam and I debriefed each other on our interlocking years of "cuckoo craziness" (his term). I had to reassess my poor choices: antagonizing strangers, throwing cash at every problem, living with an ex-girlfriend. How many of my own bad decisions came from average stupidity, and how many mistakes had been sparked by mental illness?

The band's small-scale legacy became something to navigate. As a leftist hardcore act in the vein of Dead Kennedys, we'd produced some interesting art. As a lifestyle choice, the experience left a bitter aftertaste. Singing for a "confrontational" band, it turns out, sits in the shallow end of the pool of human activities. What is band touring but the use of resources—yours, others', everyone's—to move from town to town, striking poses in front of witnesses? If the poses are good, artistic fulfillment can cover lapses in motivation. But if the poses are politically confrontational, and thus dependent on audience reaction, motives can wither. Commenting on the world isn't the same as engaging the world. I could only ignore that truth for so long.

•••

EIGHT YEARS AFTER THE debate, I sold some rare records online. The sale included several test pressings from my own label, including a few Born Against releases. My early nineties incarnation would've thrown a fit over this auction: speculation in hardcore records was a major outrage for me and Adam. My late nineties self recognized that this wasn't a real-world issue. Test pressings cost thirty to forty dollars to manufacture. As far as I was concerned, the auction simply recouped an expenditure.

I was surprised to find Steve Martin posting about my sale on a Usenet forum. I hadn't thought about him in years. In the back of my mind, I'd assumed that all the SOIA guys had victoriously moved on. Instead, Steve bitterly denounced me as a trust-fund brat, "raping" buyers through my auction. His fury had clearly built up over time. Most disturbing were the fresh accusations of hypocrisy. Apparently my reputation was stuck in 1990.

This was my first inkling of the debate's online resurrection. Not having foreseen the invention of a global computer system, let alone the creation of an easily tradable digital audio compression format, I was slow to take this reappearance seriously. It had never occurred to me that the debate could be anything other than a bit of audio memorabilia, one traded on cassettes through the grubby back channels of hardcore completists. By the turn of the century, the recording had transformed from a curious asterisk in the band's history to an essential part of the band's discography.

In one sense, this was good news. Most of Born Against's bad behavior had, somehow, escaped the Internet's attention. We'd made some bloopers. Our lyrics trafficked in anti-racist, ironic racism whose sarcasm would be difficult to explain to a layman listener. One show flyer featured a photo of a New Yorker's corpse. The band mocked the deaths of US soldiers, on shirts and buttons, in a style eerily foreshadowing the Westboro Baptist Church. If the

WNYU fiasco was the worst thing to get dredged up, I often told myself, I'd gotten off easy.

And yet, there was something sinister about the debate's persistence. Being audio, it existed in real time and present tense. The immediacy of the recording, combined with the revelation of the recording's existence—*listen to what these guys did!*—created a living version of my former self, one continually representing me at my worst. A new phenomenon emerged: people informing me, with sly little smiles, that they'd discovered it online, as if the debate was a naughty secret I'd tried and failed to hide.

Common knowledge of my cash flow made this representation all the worse. I would eternally be the idle rich kid pompously lecturing others on how they could and could not eke out a living. In one sense, mine was a common problem of the digital age. After all, the idea that every mishap goes on one's permanent record is a load-bearing girder of the Internet. But most exposed blunders—drunk posts, mug shots, sex tapes—automatically imply regret. My prime mistake was more like a calling card, loosed upon the world without further explanation.

The debate sparked smaller debates on message boards, with many of Born Against's fans offering contorted defenses for our poor behavior. In some versions, my wealth made me incorruptible, a hardcore Bruce Wayne (or at least Ross Perot). Some versions of the recording could have been made by fans or foes. I bought a bootleg CDR of the recording on eBay. The disc came packaged as a Born Against release, and the elaborate insert reproduced all the minutiae of paperwork—photos, columns, exchanges from *Maximumrocknroll*— including a letter I'd written to a customer apologizing for a one-year delay in mailorder. The CDR sits in the back of my closet, as if it's a bottle of botulism. I've never listened to it. It's there right now.

···

OVER THE YEARS, I encountered more and more adults who'd wrecked their own finances just as badly. Life, I now know, offers ample opportunities to screw up. Even without addiction, there are windfalls to squander, debts to accrue, taxes to underpay, businesses to bankrupt. Such defeats only feel public when viewed through the lens of an in-progress autobiography. On the fiscal irresponsibility front, I was in good company.

But I never met anyone who'd sabotaged their own reputation like I had. In the early 1980s, Tim Yohannan staged a radio debate with rock impresario Bill Graham; without a matching recording, this event lived in lore as a victory for Yohannan (before WNYU, I'd envisioned our own debate as a companion piece). Even dramatic public failures— Bill Gaines' disastrous 1954 Senate testimony, Jane Fonda's 1972 Viet Cong photo op, Bill Clinton's painful 1988 DNC address—had been followed by dramatic public successes.

Then there was the wonderful 1979 showdown pitting John Cleese and Michael Palin against Mervyn Stockwood and Malcolm Muggeridge. The Monty Python members defended *Life Of Brian* with a grace and humor that stung. Besides Adam, there was no support group for the predicament of the debate. And he and I didn't have much to say about it anyway.

···

TWENTY YEARS AFTER SITTING in the WNYU studio, Vice magazine paid me to interview Glenn Danzig. I was happy for the work, and excited to see inside his infamous Los Feliz craftsman bungalow. On Danzig the artist, I was agnostic. I admired his first album to the same degree I scorned his videos, and always viewed the Misfits as less of a band than a very successful clothing company. He and his music weren't part of my adolescence. I might as well have been interviewing an accomplished bagpiper.

Danzig's publicist had one iron rule: don't mention the video. Five years earlier, he'd gotten punched out during a backstage argument. Video of the knockout went viral (the week of the interview, it was the first YouTube listing under his name). The twenty-second exchange plays out with the clarity of an *SNL* spoof. Danzig argues, Danzig strikes first, Danzig gets clobbered. It was all there. There was no other way to spin it, despite how hard his diehard fans tried.

The ban was fine. I had nothing interesting to ask on the subject, and no interest in antagonism. There was a time, long ago, when I wasn't above making people look bad in interviews. All that did was mark me as a lousy writer and a jerk. Danzig met me in a back office, and as he turned the TV (Fox News) low and we each took our seats, the strangeness of the debate was my obvious callback.

This stayed with me during the interview. We discussed things neither of us much cared about— two people miming the rituals of publicity—and I nodded duly and found my mind wandering. It suddenly felt cruel, to be denied my lone opportunity to discuss crushing public humiliation with another human who had lived it. That this other human just happened to be Glenn Danzig was irrelevant. Weren't we both distant brothers in Jersey hardcore? Well, now we had two things in common. He and I were in a teensy tiny club of people who'd made punishing unforced errors—a second of unprovoked belligerence for him, a one-two combo of obliviousness and wealth for me—and had to figure out how to soldier on. We could start a support group. At the very least, we should discuss it.

It felt urgent to say this. We rattled on, two strangers stuck in an automated Q&A, and the full weight of my real question bore down. The things that could've been built, the places that could've been seen, the stink of failure that followed me from city to city, from state to state: how do I forgive myself? We rose, shook hands, I lingered by his door. I kept tumbling the words over and over in my head, kept fumbling with a way to phrase just one question before being forever cast from his compound. *Mr. Danzig; How do I shake this piece of shit off my shoe? How do I erase the horror and shame of fucking up so badly?*

•••

A MONTH LATER, I read through the Danzig interview online comments. I knew they'd be harsh; as I used to do before anti-depressants, I sought some sharper pain to pierce the dull ache of depression. Ten comments down, I found what I'd come for. One anonymous person, just one more person out there, somewhere, asked in unrelenting all-caps if I remembered THAT TIME YOU GOT YOUR ASS BEAT BY SICK OF IT ALL.

ALBERTI RECORDS, RIP

1946–2001

ALBERTI RECORDS OF CALIFORNIA has closed its doors after fifty-five years as a vinyl manufacturer. Although I've covered four states since first dealing with Alberti, fate had me living a mere half hour down the freeway by the time they'd called it quits. The final announcement came by mail. Being the closest label owner made me the first to receive the letter, and the bearer of bad news to other label owners. We had been given exactly one week to clear out. *After next week there will be no here at all* [sic?], *the doors will be locked and the keys to the company will be turned over to our lawyer*, read the impenetrably bleak announcement. *After that point anything remaining here will be sent to the dump.* "No here"? The dump? That sounded hopeless indeed. A lot of record labels started emailing me. I suddenly found myself popular.

When I and Andy arrived at their Monterey Park plant, I came armed with a mandate to retrieve all parts for nearly every Vermiform, Kill Rock Stars, 5RC, Punk In My Vitamins and Paralogy record pressed in the 1990s, over 180 titles. I also packed: one clipboard, detailed notes on every release by name and catalog number, magic markers, liability waivers (removing our right to sue in case of injury on their now-uninsured premises), a bottle of Bushmills whiskey, a red Christmas bow, and two pairs of woolen winter gloves, unearthed from the pre-California section of my closet, as insurance against the jagged metal we planned to handle. Ebullition Records owner Kent McClard greeted me at the door with a hearty handshake. The last time I'd seen him was eight years earlier, and I'd placed my first call to Alberti from his living room.[135]

The Christmas bow was for the Bushmills, and the Bushmills was for Frank. My eight-year phone relationship with plant manager Frank Scalla had left me anxious to meet the man in person. But then again, it was a tad jarring to see the whole place in person. For all the rumors surrounding Alberti, I didn't know a single label owner who'd ever set foot in the place. Kent admitted this was his first time at the plant. Several years earlier, I'd made arrangements to "swing by" while on tour. I'd heard later that my last minute no-show had been considered as rude an offense as the $500 bill I'd temporarily stiffed them on.

Frank arrived, along with Bill Alberti, the middle-aged and mannerly grandson of the company's founder. We made our introductions and ceremoniously signed the waivers. "Any injuries around here?" I asked in half-mock nervousness. "Welllll...let's see," Frank said, stroking his incredible mustache. It was like seeing a famous radio DJ in the flesh. "One guy got three fingers crushed in a press a while back. That's about 2,000 pounds per square inch."

Kent directed us into the snarled interior of the assembly room. It was a little hard to get a visual grasp on the place. Stuff, stuff, and more stuff sprawled in all directions, crammed into loose boxes, shoved under tables, piled around trash cans. Andy and I arrived at six tidy, narrow aisles along the east wall. "Here's your stuff," said Kent, pointing to a neat stack of all my Mothers, the solid nickel master record that the more brittle and short-lived pressing plates are born of. Almost every release I'd ever pressed was here. One aisle over I found the endless stacks of paper labels and pressing plates.

"Isn't it disturbing seeing everything at once?" asked Kent, laughing. It was. All my triumphs and all my mistakes were neatly arranged and covered in a fine layer of dust. The entire space resembled a monastic library, maintained over eons by dedicated monks.

The relevance of particular artifacts made it hard to concentrate. Here and there were the very plates that had pressed some of the most significant albums of my formative years. Andy threatened to stab me with the (presumably) sharp edges of the *Fresh Fruit For Rotting Vegetables* mothers. I menaced him with Flipper's *Gone Fishin.'* Long Gone John of Sympathy For the Record Industry emerged from a further aisle, looking morose. "I've got over five hundred titles here," he said to no one in particular.

Behind the assembly room we found an equally spacious loading dock. Here were hundreds upon hundreds of boxes, frozen in bankruptcy, some loaded on pallets, some buried, some loose. A bound tower of Lookout Records cartons teetered off an eye-level ledge at a crazy forty-five-degree angle, like part of a lame Universal Studios theme park ride. The clutter extended across the breadth of the room and continued into a second story loft, receding into darkness. Andy pointed to a series of aisles underneath the loft, also dark. Bill told us this was "mostly old stuff."

We flipped the lights and gingerly started down the corridors of this auxiliary lost library. Faded boxes of labels hinted at the company's history: "Wild West Recordings of Rialto, CA," "Kick Khadafy's Butt," the "Erotic Sounds of Love" series, the "Black Political Power" series. Andy swooned at the sight of paper labels for old Nuclear Crayons records. The timer light for this section kept shutting off, forcing him to fumble back through the darkness to reset the switch, and leaving me a few private moments to contemplate my immediate finds.

One week earlier, a bunch of world-class assholes had knocked down the Twin Towers. Reality had revealed the barbarism that lurks below the skin of civilization, and nothing much seemed to matter anymore. I was concerned that I had temporarily stopped feeling emotions. So it was nice, in these brief moments, to stand in this dark, sauna-hot space and pretend that the planet outside hadn't fallen apart.

•••

ON WEDNESDAY WE BROUGHT a truck.[136] My mandate widened to include more record labels: Jade Tree, Troubleman, Slap A Ham, Mr. Lady. We spent the morning loading pallets. Alberti had always kept strict East Coast business hours, 6:00 a.m. to 2:00 p.m. I'd been told this was because Monterey Park is "a hellhole." Standing by their loading dock in the cool dawn air, surveying the hills and swaying cypresses behind the plant, I wondered why. By eleven, I understood. Outside the sun was merciless, the perhaps forty feet of loading area a scorched airport tarmac. Inside, the air hurt to breathe. Bill Alberti chuckled at my discomfort. "This is like heaven to us. When those presses start up, it gets to 110 degrees in here."

Ken from Prank Records and Mike from Broken Rekids [sic] arrived mid-morning. They'd left San Francisco at 2:00 a.m. and appeared grim. Andy and I clawed through boxes with the enthusiasm of those unaccustomed to hot manual labor. When Bill Alberti found me perched between shelves and pallet, six or seven feet over the concrete floor, he politely asked if I might consider using their ladder. "No, we want to do this! We signed waivers! Fifty-five years and only one behanding," Andy said, giddy. "I think your safety record speaks for itself!" Later in the day, Long Gone

John unearthed a dozen boxes of old Redd Foxx 7"s. A very quiet and intense period of looting occurred until someone pointed out that we couldn't all sell these on eBay at once.

On the third day we reverted to scavenger hunts from my list. The dark loft was revealed as a graveyard of Alternative Tentacles jackets. Andy and I discussed which important mother would look the prettiest mounted on his wall and installed with one of those crafts store clock innards. On the envelope for the KRS 250 stampers I read: PUT BACK IN NOTHING WRONG WITH THIS PLATE SOMEBODY WAS LOCO. I overheard the familiar disembodied Frank voice, explaining to the telephone, "This would've been our fifty-fifth year." On a Kill Rock Stars box I found a sad, hand-drawn heart, crudely crossed out with magic marker. It seemed emblematic of something.

I used a lull to question Bill Alberti. How long had they been in this building? (Since Eisenhower.) How long had Frank worked here? (Since Ford.) Had they ever refused anything on grounds of content? (Never.) Did he listen to any of the records he'd pressed, for enjoyment? (Back in the seventies). Any problems with bootlegs? (They'd been raided by the FBI thirty years ago, but CDs had made the issue irrelevant by the eighties. "After a while the FBI wouldn't even return our phone calls.") We discussed some of the financial events that had led to the company's demise. An estate battle resulting from the death of Mr. Alberti (Bill's father and the plant owner) earlier in the year had triggered the final cash drain. But the economics of vinyl, no surprise, had been on a steady decline for the last decade. By 2001, their main customers were Mordam labels and Ebullition. And certain Mordam labels had stopped paying (he didn't mention any names and I didn't ask).

"McClard always paid up front," said Bill. "He's a hell of a guy." Andy picked up a chipped label and said, "Hey…it's *Brown Reason*

To Live!" Bill examined the shard, then looked up, stumped. "Is this a good record?"

•••

ON FRIDAY WE MADE one last van trip. Loading finished before two. Our repeated offers to treat Frank and Bill to lunch grew awkward. Bill hemmed and hawed and finally said he wouldn't have the time. Frank laughed and roared off on his forklift, cigarette dangling. A representative from a rival plant arrived, thumbing through his own inventory for different record labels. We introduced ourselves.

"Our place is nothing like this," he said, nodding toward the disorder of the assembly room.

"Actually, their plates and mothers were exceedingly well organized," I said, blushing at the man's rudeness. Insulting Alberti at this stage seemed like writing nasty lyrics about a lymphoma patient.

"Yeah, okay," he continued. "But…I mean, look at this place. We're nothing like this."

Bill agreed to a quick tour of the pressing station before we left. This was behind the assembly room, a dark cavern I'd only peered in. He hit the lights, illuminating the mechanical guts of the operation. The drama of insolvency had seemed to overwhelm Bill, but here he was in his element, a guy as versed with steam-release valve mechanics as he was with a spreadsheet. We passed sacks of shiny pellets from Keysor Corp of Saugus, CA. This was Alberti's prime number: raw vinyl. I'd pictured it simmering in vats of blurpy liquid. In person, it more resembled cattle feed, bagged and unpretentious.

We were shown to the record presses, large Semi-Automatic SMT's (for Southern Machine & Tool). There didn't seem to be anything automatic about these monsters. Each stood chest level, a jumble of pipes intersecting pipes, secured at points with five-inch bolts that would be better suited to the bowels of a supertanker. "These cost us seventy thousand dollars apiece." Even with the overheads, the room remained a dreary and atmospheric place. Sunlight strobed through the roof fans onto random tangles of machinery. Years of calcium deposits clouded the windows. Nearby, a woman in a bikini gazed at us from a faded 1986 calendar for Thermo King Of Indiana. "They're worth about two hundred dollars now," Bill added softly.

He tugged on a jutting tube and a set of metal jaws rolled out and popped open with a faint hiss. He showed us where water cooled the system, where steam entered, where to fit the plates and hot blobs of wax. I asked how many records one machine could make in a shift. "1,500 records can be pressed on one machine in any eight-hour period. That's if there's no bullshitting around." My heart sank at the inhumanity of the work I'd commissioned without regard for labor, as if I had been ordering up an endless series of pay-per-view movies. Bill added, "This is where it really gets hot."

I asked to use the office phone. A pang of gloom registered when I found my own name at #27 on the speed dial. I'd lived in California for two years at this point. Why hadn't I visited earlier? Why, at the very fucking least, hadn't I sent a sympathy card when Mr. Alberti passed away? The opportunities to verify your humanity are rare and irretrievable. Clearly I hadn't been the worst financial offender. But I had acted in collusion with every other stupid, thoughtless record label by default. It was too late.

We shook hands out front. Bill and I exchanged email addresses. I told him I'd send lists of AWOL plates. Bleached cardboard spilled out of an overflowing dumpster.

"Well." I paused for a moment, unsure of what to say. "What now?"

Bill shrugged. "Start over, I guess."

PLEASE DON'T STOP THE MUZAK

Psychic Carpet Bombing as Mass Marketing

I ONCE HEARD A radio interview with songwriter Sara Allen, frequent collaborator with 1970s/1980s soft rockers Hall & Oates. Allen dated musician Daryl Hall for thirty years, and Hall & Oate's first hit single, 1975's "Sara Smile," was written in her honor. Not long after Sara and Daryl broke up, she was shopping in a supermarket when the song came on the storewide speakers. Overwhelmed by emotion, Allen simply abandoned her shopping cart and walked out the front door.

I, too, have left supermarkets over this song. Although my reasons were more practical. I've left because I had to, and I had to because this song MAKES ME WANT TO LASSO COPS WITH MY OWN INTESTINES WHILE SHRIEKING THE LAUGHTER OF THE ABYSS.

Then again, I hear a lot of music I don't like. At the store where I buy the food I need to survive, it's the groveling white flag of Dave Matthews Band. In the pharmacy where I buy the medicines I need to stay healthy, it's the sociopath pageantry of Nicki Minaj. At the gas station where I must refuel my vehicle, it's the music my mom calls "that shrieking stuff, where 'I love you' is stretched out to eighteen syllables, it's *horrible.*"

Some businesses force me to hear music that I might actually like under different, less mandatory, circumstances. But I'm not always in the mood to hear Bill Withers croon about what a lovely day it is. Sometimes it's raining outside. Or it's raining in my brain. Or a madman has been elected leader of the free world.

•••

WHAT HAPPENED TO THAT jaunty, brassy music America used to be into, music a fella could strut down the street to? Muzak once ruled America. It played in JFK's White House and aboard Apollo 11.[137] But the counterculture made the pippy tunes sound fusty, and sinister.[138] Because Muzak is so mismatched to almost every human experience, it became a proxy for hypocrisy, a sarcastic commentary track looped over reality. The word itself devolved into an insult and then, worse, a generic trademark, like Kleenex, or Xerox. Only this lower-case "muzak" also came to describe something more than music (one of Muzak's original slogans), a sort of general soggy moral rot that permeated all of postwar America. *Dawn of the Dead* of 1978 adds silly bells and slide whistles to its Muzak, which keeps on playing long after the dead have devoured the living.

If cultural changes hadn't doomed Muzak, its own history of manipulation would've done the genre in.[139] In the 1940s, the company pioneered Stimulus Progression, a workplace soundtrack designed to boost employee productivity through subtle tempo changes (proven effective through the company's own "internal research"). Postwar America migrated this concept to retail, using fast tempo to get customers in and out (supermarkets), slow tempo to boost browsing (high-end retail), its twangy guitar licks and ethereal synth lines and sleepy sax solos used strategically to lure certain demographics and subtly repel others.

Muzak acclimated civilization to the constant soundtrack. After Americans soured on its cheery manipulations, pop music rushed in to fill the silence. Where Muzak was instrumental, pop music is insistent, demanding, song after song, that we pay attention to words. Where Muzak was once confined to discrete speakers, pop music blares from ring tones, popup videos, gas pump TVs, and subwoofers in passing cars. And in this version of pop music, no popular song ever really dies, so that, *even forty fucking years later*, I still have to hear Heart's Ann Wilson pleading with her mom to understand that the shitty pot dealer she shacked up with is a magic man.

While I was writing this book, Target—the lone music-free holdout among major American retailers—began subjecting its customers to music that is "upbeat, positive and has a playful personality." In 2015, someone hacked the intercom system at a Target store in Campbell, CA, in the heart of Silicon Valley, and blasted the sounds of porn. What kind of priceless sales data did Target glean from the incident? Perhaps they learned what cults have known for millennia: sound that is loud, monotonous, constant, and inescapable is a textbook indoctrination tool.

•••

THE "WHY" IS WHERE things get fuzzy. Why has pop music become inescapable? It's a mystery of some complexity, like "when did 'racist' become a universal insult?" or "why did top hats go out of style?" These questions have answers, but these answers are as convoluted as changing weather patterns. What is clear, from our lowly, limited vantage point, is that two consensuses have emerged. First, there is the general agreement that music should play in every privately owned public space, at all times. Then there is the more insidious, unspoken assumption that everyone is cool with this.

Here's another big "why." Millennials: why do you tolerate this crap? You lead custom-tailored lives, from your social media feeds to the fancy drinks you expect your barista to get right day after day. You've grown up with the accumulated knowledge of humanity literally at your fingertips. You're the first generation since the dawn of the Industrial Revolution without actionable levels of lead in your bloodstream. You should be far smarter than all of us who came before.

When U2 forced their music onto a half-billion devices in 2014—what the *Washington Post*'s Chris Richards coined "rock-and-roll as dystopian junk mail"—you joined the chorus of bemused outrage. So why do you tolerate businesses pulling this crap every single day? And if you won't stand up for yourselves, won't you at least take a stand for the ironclad egalitarianism you've been raised to believe in? For the depressed, isolated people who get clobbered every year by Christmas music? Or for all those autistic people who suffer sensory overload every time they have to buy anything?

Isn't your generation in some sort of perpetual tizzy over triggers? Well, consider: According to a 2017 American/Australian study, 90 percent of western music listeners cry because of certain songs. No one's yet constructed a study of all the emotions forever tagged to seemingly random melodies, the unexpected flashes of embarrassment or disgust. Not all evoked emotions are bad (most Americans my age can, I suspect, sing at least one *Schoolhouse Rock* song in a fond trance). But everyone has songs that can crush them through grief, or heartache, or depression. I counted, and I've got at least five. Two of these songs would be problematic if ever heard in public.

At the very least, the sheer arrogance of it all should give your generation rage headaches. The liquid nausea of Throbbing Gristle's "Hamburger Lady" is something I feel viscerally. "Dust In

The Wind" by Kansas sickens me existentially. Guess which song can be played in public? Who decides these rules? How come stores that have no problem with Merry Clayton and Mick Jagger literally screaming "rape" and "murder" in "Gimmie Shelter" would have me escorted off the premises if I started loudly singing along?

I can, and have, taken news breaks when I go for a day or two without going online. But I can't take a break from the relentless, endless barrage of pop music. I shouldn't have to hear Drake or Pink or Kanye songs. Ever. I don't want their voices inside my mind. We're strangers. I shouldn't even have to know who they are. I should not, for example, even know that Carly Rae Jepsen's music makes me want to hop on the freeway and pop out my eyeballs. I shouldn't even know who she is. We should just be two random people living our separate lives in different cities.

Why do I have to write any of this? The math here seems obvious. Don't cram gum into other people's mouths. Don't make strangers sniff your fingers. Don't force music onto people you don't know.[140]

•••

IN THIS ERA OF audio branding and mandated channels, employee preferences are irrelevant, even the preference to keep one's senses intact. Twenty-first century restaurant audio, for example, increasingly veers into the seventy to eighty decibel range, an eardrum destroyer to those who must endure it shift after shift. In 2017, American workers comp hearing loss claims totaled almost a quarter billion dollars. But American consumers spend that amount every ninety minutes. In this equation, customers have all the power.

Only in numbers, though. One individual customer—say, me—can't plausibly complain about music to a cashier. It'd be like a prison visitor complaining to an inmate. And sometimes even the inmates aren't sympathetic. Once, in Virginia, I asked my waiter to turn down a TV blasting anguished 911 recordings. He and the waitress laughed at me. Why would I ever waste my time complaining about the Taylor Swift song being shoved down my brain?

•••

PERSONALLY, I LIKED MUZAK. It was made to stay the fuck out of my way. And if you can separate the art from the manipulation of its creators, Muzak is the most emotionally honest music there is. There are no singer-songwriters desperate to share their hopes and dreams, no divas trying to cement their brands, no rappers trying to sell you on their realness. There's nothing real at all about Muzak. Below the surface, there's just more surface. Obviously: I'd prefer silence. But smooth instrumentals—background music that allows one to *think*—is an acceptable runner-up.

Most important, Muzak made things simple. To be involved with 1980s hardcore was to be ever mindful of the Us vs Them thing of 1980s hardcore. Until grunge, there was a consensus that Us, the good guys, operated underneath Them, the overhead culture of false values as advertised through MTV and commercial radio (or the values of liquid oblivion as advertised through Muzak). There was once a time when anyone wearing a hardcore shirt was your secret friend, an ally by default. Now there's not even that. There are no more secret allies, no one to even commiserate with. The overculture is omnipresent, and the Us vs. Them of yesteryear feels a lot like Me vs. All. It's a system that seemingly evolved to make each of us despair in isolation.

How about some fair play? Maybe, for a change, we start listening to the songs I like:

—Geza X's "Mean Mister Mommy Man," a seedy spurt of horror in which the singer is forced to sniff "stinky pie."

—Techno Animal's "City of Glass," a relentless nightmare I listened to on repeat for six hours on 9/11 while watching muted footage of crashing skyscrapers.

—Clint Mansell's "Coney Island Dreaming," from 2000's *Requiem for a Dream* soundtrack, a foreboding little elegy that became my soundtrack for the unending 9/11 of life after the 2016 election.

—Saccharine Trust's "Human Certainty," a song descending into the depths of grief and never coming back.

—Joy Division's "Exercise One," the soundtrack to something terrible illuminated by car headlights at night.

—Cosey Fanni Tutti's "Time To Tell," a slow-rolling fog of unease, twenty-three minutes long, in which the barely audible Tutti narrates her time as a sex worker.

I know, droll suggestions, Sam. Very funny. Ha ha. So allow me to propose a real-world compromise. *Let's all listen to stuff no one likes.* That certainly seems like an equitable solution. If the arc of the moral universe bends toward justice, I think you'll find my solution has the ring of inevitability. Supermarkets can play ambient penitentiary noises. Pharmacies can play the Halloween sound effects and animal screams once blasted at the Branch Davidian compound by the FBI. Bring back the porn and 911 calls. And "Sara Smile"? With its mincing, wincing, caught-in-my-own-fly falsettos? Play it 24/7. Never ending. No escape. Let's get everyone everywhere just screaming and screaming and screaming. Fair's fair.

BACKGROUNDING FOR
THE SMELL

Poseurs On Premises

AS AN EAST COAST immigrant to Los Angeles County, one susceptible to the glamor of Hollywood, I still have a hard time thinking of movie shoots as bad news. And yet there they are, clogging up streets and office lobbies and public sidewalks, one more intrusion of private, moneyed interests into the public sphere. I've crossed Union Station when two separate film crews congested two different parts of the building. A friend once showed me a notice taped to his door, informing him that his neighborhood would be subjected to "full-load automatic gunfire." Driving home one spring night, a cop stopped me at the intersection of Hope and Sixth while a film crew detonated a fireball that climbed eight stories then just as quickly vanished, as if nothing had happened.

So when I was approached for a one-day job as an extra, my enthusiasm shocked me. Australian actress and aspiring pop star Holly Valance had rented out The Smell for a full-scale, eighties-punk-themed music video shoot for her new song, "State of Mind." LA's exceptional all-ages music club was currently closed, shuttered for six long months as a casualty of the post-Station Fire safety crackdown. Volunteers had labored to get the place up to code. Being an extra on the shoot seemed almost an extension of this labor, one final task to replenish empty coffers before The Smell could reopen.

A few days later, I arrived to find the club's side lot transformed into a bazaar of tents and trucks and well-stocked catering tables. I joined a group of about fifty extras, half Smell regulars, half clients of an LA casting company called, sadly, Scottie's Bodies.[141] We formed lines, signed contracts, posed for photos, and then subjected ourselves to costume tent triage based on our 1980s style. It seemed odd that I was deemed sufficiently eighties. I was wearing my lucky cowboy shirt, and the black frame glasses that have come to define my face. Over the course of the day I would be called many names—"Cowboy Bob," "Buddy Holly," "Drew Carey"— with no root in the 1980s. The day's theme would be "Eighties Punk," and the costume department referenced Jim Jocoy's *We're Desperate* photobook for a particular cheap and exploitative style.

Scottie's Bodies were indeed desperate. To work in entry-level Hollywood requires a pathological lack of self-respect found in few other professions. For example, when we discovered that we were not to be referred to as "extras" but as some even lower caste called "background," only regulars from The Smell groaned. And when one such regular attempted to heist a pineapple from the catering table, Scotty's Bodies all looked the other way, unwilling to acknowledge any infraction to the rules that bound their acting careers.

The sun crept up and up, eating into our cramped shade. Women disappeared into the costume tent at a much higher ratio than men. At high noon, two caterers shoveled tables of leftover food into several oversized trash cans. In the distance, the leg-shaped wind sock on the roof of the Ronald Reagan State Building waggled down at us in mockery. We were to spend nine hours in this parking lot.

Here's what I did with my time: huddled in the shade of the producer's Toyota 4Runner, read the first eleven pages of *Red Badge Of Courage* in an attempt to convince myself that I am a smart person and make healthy life decisions, eavesdropped on two Scottie's Bodies debate file sharing with the gravity of a high school bioethics debate, ate several hundred Red Vines, read the entire *Los Angeles Times* from cover to cover, attempted to make a paper hat from the Sports section, and tipped my chair back onto the concrete to see how much it would hurt.

Pigeons flapped in and out of the old Linda Lea sign next door. Vacant for twenty years, this Japanese chambara theater (samurai movies!) stood abandoned in place, all its gorgeous pastel signage left to fade in the sun. Before The Smell's shutdown, there had been some not-quite-daydreaming about buying the Linda Lea, knocking down some walls and tripling the size of The Smell, making it a central venue for independent music, film, theater, and performance. Now the sign stood as another cracked and spattered relic of ancient Los Angeles, just one more mile marker on the highway of lost possibilities.

•••

THE SMELL MOVED TO its current home, just two blocks from city hall, in late 1999. The neighborhood was then derelict, and the new spot offered three times the square footage for what they'd paid in North Hollywood. Unattended lots meant free parking. I'd moved to California right around the same time, and I'd been struck by the *Omega Man* desolation of downtown LA at night.

The club's unwritten charter (all ages, volunteer-run) was an attempt to import the audience of the recently closed Jabberjaw.

The Smell also looked twenty years back to the freewheeling days of The Masque, and a dozen blocks away, to the staunch purity of Bob Baker's Marionette Theater. Patrons of two nearby Mexican bars might fight in the street using belts as whips, but there was no violence inside the club.

Not that everything always went smoothly. In late 2002, The Smell booked Oakland sludge/crust/dirt punk band Dystopia. One volunteer urged them not to, and further urged that they hire "a lot of security" if they did (The Smell has no bouncers). This would have been like hiring security for an earthquake. Dystopia the band were nice enough folks, but their followers took the band's name on its word.

Punk has always bred strains of super-scammy assholes. Eventually these strains evolved into their logical conclusion: hoards of able-bodied apocalypse hobos, with such cartoony contempt for "authority" that all things became authority. It was that caricature entitlement bullshit from *Quincy*—or, in a more general way, Fox News—brought to freakish life. In the urban folklore of this show, the Dystopia members could barely get their gear to the stage, mired in an ocean of their own fans cursing out the band members as "rock stars" even while awaiting their set. The club quickly reached capacity, but the throng outside found it incomprehensible that anyone could get between them and their entertainment.[142]

The hoard ripped open the front doors and bum-rushed the black hole of Calcutta. "It was like a home invasion," organizer Jim Smith later told me.[143] In the crush of people, there was a real possibility of catastrophe. Cops arrived and asked the flummoxed volunteers how they wanted to proceed. "Do whatever the fuck you need to do to get rid of these people," a volunteer told them. "Because we cannot." But for some reason lost to time, the cops let the show continue, and Dystopia did wind up playing. That the night ended without injury seems like pure luck.[144]

A few months later, 100 people burned to death in the Station nightclub fire in Rhode Island. This wasn't just a glimpse at what could have been. It also set in motion a wave of fire-safety crackdowns rippling outward from New England. By the time the crackdown reached California, Jim's crew had plenty of warning. But even with a sturdy new stage (exactly forty-four-inches from the wall, in strict compliance with fire codes), it was only a matter of time before the law found The Smell.

The last band to play the club was The Whip, featuring my old pal Joe Preston, and Scott Maniac and Jared Warren from the band Karp. The fire marshals politely waited until the end of the set to urgently usher everyone out of the building. The Station disaster was still fresh, so I don't remember any complaints. But as the weeks wore on, it became clear that the venue would have to overcome huge financial and bureaucratic obstacles to reopen.

Scott Maniac was dead just four months later, killed at age twenty-eight in a boating accident near Seattle. I only met him once, the night before the show, when the band stayed at my house. He seemed like someone I would have been friends with.

•••

SCOTTIES BODIES AND SMELL regulars trudged inside at dusk. I'd been warned that set decorators had made the place unrecognizable. Indeed, a phony aluminum light rig bordered the stage, and the walls advertised fake graffiti;

187
NYHC
HATE
NO WAVE

PAY TO CUM
REAGAN YOUTH
LEFT TO SUFFER
SCREW THE LAW
BLOOD BROTHERS
PROTEST & SURVIVE[145]

Seemingly overnight, the parody fairy had transformed a real punk club into a fake one.[146] It was a reverse Pinocchio scenario. Huge, red-gelled banks of light lit the bricks like a dungeon, and within minutes all of us dripped sweat. Shocker: Background got no respect. Instead of even a "quiet on the set"—and when will I ever get the opportunity to hear these words again?—we were told to "shut the fuck up if you want to get paid."

Holly Valance emerged to weak applause. We'd already seen her, briefly, after lunch, bantering with an interviewer next to a fast food bag as a prop. She was beautiful and physically flawless in that Who Gives A Shit way all twenty-year-olds are beautiful and physically flawless. Before us now, she appeared nearly naked, an unripe android wearing only a skimpy miniskirt with a sleeveless Ramones shirt slit down both sides. This was her "punk" look. Staffers were on hand to keep her PG-13 bits concealed with double-sided tape.

Director Jake Nava arrived. Nava is known for Beyonce's "Crazy In Love" video, and he spoke with an accent that kept switching between British and Australian. On his command, smoke machines spewed and bad music surged. "Okay people, let's see lots of that crazy, rock-punk en-ah-gee!" Nava ordered. "Wild, wild, wild...just keep moooving!" With the crew high on stress and the background high on heatstroke, unreality set in and we leapt and careened to the cheap music.

Things got ugly during the "mosh pit" scene. Crew arranged Background in a circle around a writhing Holly. Stagehands sprayed Holly's arms and face with glycerin for a postcoital sheen, the song again pumped and we all jumped like dummies in a music video. At some point I slipped into the Frankenstein dance. I don't know what this involved, and I haven't been able to replicate it for friends. I think I was on the verge of a stroke at that point, I'm not sure. I do know that I wasn't very happy with the way my life was going at that moment.

After the first take, an angry cockney cameraman roughly yanked my shirt to indicate that I was being removed. "We 'ad our lit'le chat about those lights, din't we?" he said without explanation. Not yet knowing that my favorite shirt had been ripped, I felt some relief. I no longer wanted to be in this video. Then Jake Nava parted the crowd, pointing directly at me. "You...Cowboy Bub!" My smile wilted. "Ay...like...yah...ENAGY! Back in!" I trudged back into the middle of the paused mob, the song started back up, and Holly wrapped herself around my leg, unwittingly referencing the cover of Black Flag's *Slip It In*.

You have some time to think when an Australian pop starlet is wrapped around your leg. If the Dystopia show was a home invasion, what was this? Subletting to sociopaths? At the very least, it was that slow-mo bait and switch of capitalism; by the time you realize what it is that you really are expected to do, you've already invested so much time you might as well continue. The "punx"— that Mr. Hyde id of a complex subculture—had already had their way with the space. Now it was the poseurs' turn.

Afterward, I collected my $125 check and wrangled an additional $30, reimbursement for my destroyed cowboy shirt, from a man carrying an impossibly large bankroll. I did some math. $125 (pay) plus $30 (shirt) minus $8 (parking) minus $5 (wagering)

= \$142. At thirteen hours, that gave me \$10.92/hr., probably union wages in a flyover state. So why did I feel dishonored?

As if sensing my confusion, a crew member, an American, shrieked at me from across the thinning lot. "Holy SHIT dude, I can't wait to see that fuckin' Frankenstein dance! Man, your eyes were rolling back in your *head,* bro!"

•••

IN THE HISTORY OF The Smell, the video shoot was a net plus. The club did reopen, and in surmounting the shutdown, the community emerged revitalized. The new Smell managed to bridge a gap that had stymied weirdo music people since the late 1970s; the audience grew younger but remained unafraid to channel the artiness of the early LA punk scene. The space hosted punk bands along with weirdo folk acts, and improv, and ultra-indie movies, and experimental nights.

And in a city whose power structures and physical distances sustain stubborn levels of segregation, The Smell became a crucial melting pot, the one place where kids from downtown, East LA, Hollywood, Compton, and both valleys could all comfortably congregate and pollinate ideas. As downtown got safer in the twenty-teens, soccer moms felt comfortable dropping off kids for a safe night. The venue somehow combined the best attributes of a dozen different scenes and clubs without significant pushback.[147]

•••

BUT THEN THERE'S THE "State of Mind" video. In the nightmare world created by Jake Nava, Holly plays a tough rock chick strutting and grinding before (and through) a suspiciously enthusiastic audience. After her punk club set, she zips into a respectable dress, zips out to a modernist manor in the hills and plops onto an expensive duvet at dawn, exhausted from a night of slumming. It is, somehow, both the most poseur-positive video ever made and a stab of nihilism far darker than any Dystopia song.

Personally, I'm not so bothered by the *Quincy* punks posturing of "State of Mind." 2003 wasn't 1983, and this video didn't contribute to an ongoing narrative about amoral punk rockers. But the anti-women bits are dumb, and sad. At one point, Holly stops at a red light and gives the finger to two women in the car next to her. Because…they're weak? That's what tough chicks do? It's a depiction of "punk" (or driving a car, or being a person) designed by people with seemingly no experience or interest in the subject matter.

The song didn't get past position eight in the UK charts, and Holly retired from music in her mid-twenties. In 2016, her billionaire husband bought her a $38 million yacht as a birthday present, but she had some troubles with seasickness, and it remained in the dock. So, you know, fart.

UNCLE!

Drunk, Long-haired Suspect Running Now

THE CITY OF NORWALK is located in the seat of north Ohio's Huron County, a region seeped in small town Midwest fiber but still only an hour from the bright lights of Cleveland. Although the town took some lumps in the 1970s for spawning the Norwalk virus—a nasty infection transmitted by fecal-oral contact—it is also home to the International Hot Rod Association, and is renowned for the stately maples planted along its Main Street in 1830. Neighboring Milan is the birthplace of Thomas Edison. As of the 2000 census, Norwalk's population stood at 16,238, enough people to fit comfortably inside LA's Staples Center.

In July 2000, I found myself in Norwalk after the summer tour of Men's Recovery Project had gone terribly wrong. In San Francisco, our bassist quit three shows into a three week journey. The surviving members managed to recruit a replacement (John Michaels, of the SF band Towel), teach him the set, enlist his van, build a loft and retaining wall, and arrange for insurance and new tires, but there was still the matter of driving from California to Indiana to salvage as many dates as possible. John had been planning to move to the East Coast anyway, so in addition to holding our merchandise, luggage, sleeping bags, and equipment, his van—a 1979 Ford E-150 Econoline affectionately dubbed "Angie"—would need to haul all of John's worldly possessions, including several hundred pounds of science fiction paperbacks and physics texts. We established a reference section under the cramped back bench and raced east.

This meant a fantastic amount of weight on an engine and suspension running for three days at full speed for over two thousand miles. Approaching Cleveland, Angie whimpered and died at a rest stop just north of Norwalk. Some helpful locals gave the band a ride to the club, where I promptly split the cartilage in one knee, ending the portion of the tour where I was able to walk unassisted. The locals donated a pair of mismatched crutches and allowed drummer Grant and I to sleep on the floor of the club. A drunk guitarist Neil and new bassist John were driven back to Norwalk by a nineteen-year-old. When we reunited in the morning, our prognosis was grim. A mechanic pronounced the carburetor cracked, and all we could do was wait for another. The band was bleeding cash.

We retreated by cab to Milan, a town whose name is pronounced less like the European fashion capital than the layer of insulating fat that surrounds the brain's neural sheath. Milan did not have the cosmopolitan glamour of Norwalk. I withdrew my last forty dollars from an ATM, and further withdrew into the depression of an Econo Lodge room. My notes on this day are sparse. At some point I watched a VH1 documentary on U2. The following morning, we moved to a cheaper room at the nearby Royal Motel. At some point I watched all of VH1's "Bad Boys Of Rock" special.

Since I was effectively confined to bed, my understanding of that Tuesday's events have a *Rashomon* feel. Grant told me he swam in a neighboring motel's pool and "had a really nice evening" at the local Glass House Bar. John and Neil bought a six pack and took a long walk through what John called "the netherworld of pavement" linking the little stretch of motels, fast food joints, and convenience stores that seemed a poor homage to a world class inventor. All agreed that Neil's attitude was quickly deteriorating.

•••

SOMETIME AFTER 9:00 P.M., Neil and John realized they had come full circle, arriving back at the Wendy's opposite our motel's parking lot. Although the restaurant had closed for the night, a live human still manned the drive-through. The men politely requested provisions, and were just as politely rebuffed. Here was our predicament laid bare. One needs a vehicle to eat. At this point, John recounts, Neil got "all aggro." Words were exchanged. A beer was smashed to the ground in anger.

At that moment, Grant was being interrogated by a Milan police officer at a nearby phone booth. "We don't have many people use this pay phone," the suspicious cop explained, reading Grant's ID into his radio. A curious reply came from Milan Dispatch. "Drunk long haired suspect," a voice crackled. "He's opening another beer and running now." From his vantage point, Grant realized he could just make out two figures running from the Wendy's window to our motel room. The revived policeman hurriedly thrust back the driver's license. "Today's your lucky day."

Milan takes civil unrest seriously. Five police cars materialized to subdue Neil, who had descended through the Three Stages Of Crapulence from pissy to pissed to pissing. As Grant later recounted in a private email, there was "no resistance of arrest, just a broken man in a bad way who didn't have an actual automobile to get a potato at the strictly enforced drive-thru-only and couldn't take another 'no' on a tour riddled with negation." An MPD cruiser tailed MRP's unemployed rhythm section on the four-mile walk to the city jail. Sixty-five dollars of the band's remaining $180 paid for bail, and the desk officer kindly returned the remaining half of the six-pack. Neil remained defiant. "The least they could have done was refrigerate it."

The next morning we caught a taxi back into Norwalk. The van still wasn't ready. At the library, Grant asked if the town needed any more drummers. "We have our fill," the librarian responded coldly, perhaps making a pun at our expense. I searched the web for signs of hope. The day before, a Concorde had crashed in flames just outside Paris, killing 113 people and providing our downtime with appropriate visuals. Only after an hour of aimless browsing did I realize that Neil had loaded the adjacent public computer with explicit porn and walked away. Norwalk would feel his wrath.

I hobbled to The Invention, Norwalk's Thomas Edison themed diner. To kill time, I asked about Lorain, suburb of Cleveland and my and Angie's birthplace. "They've got a lot of Ukrainians," one waitress offered. "A good place to go if you want to get shot," said another, having none of our big town ways. All we could do was wait, and ignore an obvious mathematical truth: the band might not have enough cash for another motel.

Mild misfortune requires a punch line. The afternoon's triumph of a working van was neatly mirrored by the evening's failure, when Angie conked out in Philadelphia, four blocks from the club. The next morning, a Greyhound delivered me to Albany, New York. The city I'd left as a confident, competent young man greeted a bitter thirty-year-old stumblebum, broke, sleepless, and unwashed, on mismatched crutches, unable to even grow a decent mustache.

John eventually revived the van and broke down again in front of the Smiles II Go Go Bar in Ledgewood, New Jersey. Over beers,

Michaels met a helpful stranger who suggested he check the spark plugs. Sure enough, one was loose. John screwed it back in and "nothing ever happened again."

This story has more than one possible villain: the disloyal first bassist, the deceitful mechanic, the wanton spark plug. But all along Neil has assumed primary role as Not The Hero Of Norwalk. Would he, I recently asked, acknowledge this role?

"I wasn't looking for trouble," Neil said with a tone of evasion, seeing himself as the Rambo of Norwalk, a long-haired but innocent stranger harassed in a small town. I pressed the matter, reassuring him that I dredged old memories in the service of truth.

"That's the truth?" he exploded. It was as if the last six years of healing had been a hazy dream.

"That's the truth? Dragging a man down into the sewer and calling it truth?"

TOUCHABLE SOUND INTERVIEW
Someone Must Make the Socks

THIS INTERVIEW ORIGINALLY APPEARED in *Touchable Sound: A Collection of 7-inch Records from the USA* (Diego Hadis, Brian Roettinger, Mike Treff, 2010), a book dissecting the design of 1990s independent weirdo music, hardcore and otherwise. I appeared in my capacity as owner of Vermiform Records. Interview by Mike Treff.

1. Why was the record—the tactile, physical manifestation of the music—so important, in terms of visual aesthetics and personal self-worth, to those who defined themselves by collecting these records?

2. Why would a label/band/designer want to contribute/ create/make something that had near-zero potential to return on investment (against any parameter—time/money/effort)? What was the reward, then (and how was it measured)?

Both these questions [1 and 2] have the same answer, and it's one that took me a long time to figure out. When I was younger, in my early twenties, I was interested in the hidden conflicts of interest in powerful institutions (record labels, big music magazines, mass media). I only slowly came to understand that persona can present just as strong a conflict of interest. I've known anarchists who dressed and acted like leftist stereotypes because they convinced themselves that's how anarchists were supposed to dress and act. Likewise, I've known record label owners who defied all common sense and economic realities simply because they'd invested so much of their personality in the persona of Record Label Owner. This was my fate in 2002—I fought as hard as I could to keep Vermiform from bankruptcy, simply because I'd come to think of myself as someone who ran a label.

Underground records are deemed important artifacts because they have been deemed important artifacts. It's self-definitional. Culturally, the indie / punk / weirdo scene has been the most exciting game in town for the last thirty years. That dynamic is changing quickly, but adherence to tradition will probably ensure a slow demise for vinyl. People love tradition, even traditions that only span a few decades.

3. What were the inspirations, graphically, for your aesthetic(s)?

My mom is an artist (multi-medium), and many of the artists and concepts that interest me today I picked up from her—"Tintin," Japanese kids' comics, late seventies color xerox art. I also used to pore over her old copies of *Graphis* magazine. She gave me the collection a decade ago—thirty-six issues from the 1960s and 1970s—and I still use these for reference at least once a month.

When I was a teenager, my dad took me to a Patrick Caulfield retrospective in Buffalo that made a big impression on me. Caulfield was an English pop-art painter whose best work looks like details from Hergé's comic panels. Caulfield died just a few weeks before Jean-Michel Folon, a Belgian illustrator whose spooky alien landscapes also made a big impact on me from the pages of *Graphis*.

I mail ordered lots of Raymond Pettibon's fanzines all through high school. Mat Brinkman, a founding member of Rhode Island's ForceField and Fort Thunder crowd, was a big influence in my late twenties. In my mid-thirties, I learned how to use Flash as a poor man's vector graphics editor, so I've been returning more and more to the airbrushed illustrations of Robert Grossman (another *Graphis* childhood discovery) and cartoons of Terry Gilliam.

In general, I don't much go for modern fine art. When I visit The Getty Center, or the Norton Simon Gallery in Pasadena, I find myself growling at almost everything produced after 1800. If I knew more about fine art and art history, maybe I wouldn't have such a reflexive antagonism; Jackson Pollock drippings just seem like a crummy joke to me. The art that I respect and admire is almost entirely commercial design—product logos, cartoons, packaging.

4. What made you, as a designer and label owner, take it upon yourself to make these objects (in other words, choosing the hard road of designing or making them yourself instead of farming them out to someone)?

I did farm all the Vermiform record covers out to other people for the first four years of the label's existence. And even after then, I had to have help when prepping crude art for production. The cover of Born Against's *9 Hymns* LP only looks good because a friend with a BFA (Melissa York) knew exactly what she was doing. And the only Men's Recovery Project records that look good are the ones that Neil Burke designed. Contrast this with the BA side of the Born Against/Screeching Weasel split 7". I labored over that cover for weeks, and I remember there being cut marks clearly visible on the final product. Disgraceful.

5. As the mass consumer industry made it less and less difficult to make, manufacture, distribute, and sell singles (especially

once digital came into the picture), how did that affect your design, construction, and approach to physical records?

My own design probably suffered because of the ease of credit and production in the late nineties. I released a lot of records I shouldn't have, simply because I could and didn't know what else to do with my life. Some of these releases didn't look so hot. They didn't sell so hot, either.

I see now that the economy of the punk and weirdo scenes has the same dynamics of a pyramid scheme. I mean that literally, not figuratively. I started going to hardcore shows in the mid-eighties. Even though I looked fairly normal, and even though I lived in a fairly safe city, I still got threatened twice for being a "punk rocker," once by a stranger with a baseball bat. This tells me two things: 1) the people who came before me had it a lot harder, and 2) the people who came after me had it even easier. These days, I go to Target and see babies with mini-Mohawks and cashiers with purple hair. No one thinks twice.

That's fine for the cashier and the baby, because I'm guessing neither has any interest in punky weirdo music. But for all the high school punkers in my neighborhood (and I see these kids every day), identification with this lifestyle means pressure to "get involved." Modern kids probably aren't so interested in starting a record label or making a fanzine, so most of them will join bands. This is a classic pyramid scheme setup. The folks at the top (in this case, the punk/weirdo/DIY crowd of the late seventies) had the high visibility of pioneers. And because dressing like a punky oddball had actual safety consequences thirty years ago, this crowd generally drew the most committed people (meaning the best and brightest) from the available pool of artists and musicians. Meanwhile, the people at the bottom (the punk/weirdo/DIY crowd of 2009) are left with exponentially greater competition for audiences and buyers at the same time that the avenues of expression have been flooded with mediocrity.

Throughout the 1990s, the disincentives to identify with underground music (violence, ridicule) plummeted at the same rate that the cost of production (CD pressing, online distribution) plummeted. But the subculture's core message—*anyone can do this!*—stayed constant. So bands and fanzines and record labels became the default pursuits of a generation. A lot of people think this is a good thing. I don't. I know too many folks who plod along with their bands or record labels simply out of momentum, because underground creativity is a tradition that extends just far enough past their own lifespan that it seems like an enduring lifestyle. That was certainly my sorry state for a few years there.

I understand this is an elitist sentiment, but consider the big picture. This specific era—the massive wealth of post-Cold War America—is an anomaly in history. Not everyone should make art. Not everyone should be in a band. Some people have to farm, and repair bridges, and make socks. Sometimes it's okay to be a spectator.

6. What role did geography, or location, play in influencing your graphic design choices (since you've lived in a lot of places around the country)?

None, as far as I can tell. I do wish I'd kept my label in New York instead of dragging it through New Jersey, Virginia, Rhode Island, and California, but that has more to do with consistency (of releases and concept) than design aesthetics.

7. What role(s) did technology (equipment, as well as modes of production) play in affecting how you designed the records?

There's no exciting answer to this one. Photoshop expanded design possibilities in ways that were unimaginable when I was in college (and I have more than one friend who got their BFA in the early nineties only to have their entire education trashed by personal computing just a few years later). This impacted my design style both overtly (my liberal use of the "stamp" filter in the 1990s) and covertly (scanning and doctoring my own drawings to make myself seem like a more skillful freehand artist than I really am).

8. Is it possible to force-rank the compelling aspects of a record (such as design vs. music...band vs. label)?

I might have been able to do this ten or even five years ago, but I definitely can't now.

Except for one box of records I myself released or appeared on, I no longer own any vinyl. I've lost all perspective on what it was like to be a record collector or record creator.

But I can tell you that I was very interested, toward the end of Vermiform, in navigating the hidden conflicts of interest particular to small record labels. Some are easy to spot; if a band hands you an unreleasable recording, for example, then the conflict is obvious. This happened to me only once, and I dealt with it by choosing label over band and refusing to release the record. Not so obvious are the smaller conflicts: distributor deadlines versus art (this tripped me up dozens of times), touring deadlines versus art (same deal), or having a band hand in an amazing recording with terrible artwork (happened to me twice). And if you run a small label on a small budget, any sort of deadline imposed from outside has the potential to take a toll on the quality of your output. I've released more than one record with flawed art, simply because I didn't have the time or cash to correct a sloppy proof. Even when I had the organization to plan ahead, I didn't always have the means.

9. Expand on the idea that, in many cases, a 7" was not just a single, but served as the band's record. It was an end unto itself, not an invitation to obtain more...or a sampling. Why did

such a dichotomy exist between how the 7" was perceived in the "underground" versus how it was or had been perceived by mainstream labels and the general public.

I think you're assuming a consensus of opinion that didn't exist. Some bands placed lofty expectations on their records, some used their records as interchangeable business cards. The bands I worked with certainly ran this gamut.

10. As a designer, what are some of the advantages and disadvantages, and challenges or opportunities, of working on the scale of a 7"(versus an LP, a CD with booklet, etc.)?

As a canvas, the 7" only has one disadvantage: economy of scale. It's harder to package a product you can only sell for three to five dollars (like 7"s) than one you can sell for ten to twenty dollars (LPs and CDs). I could never budget more than a hundred bucks toward art for any 7" with a run of 1,000 or less. Meaning, if I put in more than fifteen hours on artwork I'd be making less than minimum wage. Sometimes I could convince myself to make such a sacrifice for my own label, but I certainly couldn't convince anyone else to. And when I do art for other people's records now, I keep very close track of my time, so I don't wind up earning sweatshop wages for someone else's record.

A BOOTING

Bargain Bin Postmortem

2002

TIMING'S THE THING WITH this piece. I'm writing from six weeks before my record label gets the boot from Mordam Records. It is probably inaccurate to assume that you, the reader, are familiar with Mordam. The company is, after all, only a distributor, a backstage player. I've long been awed by the availability of bottled Starbucks Frappucinos in every single gas station in America, but I couldn't for the life of me name the corporation that works this magic (perhaps I should find out in the next six weeks). I should add that, for reasons of propriety, I'm not supposed to be mentioning my discharge publicly until after the fact. So this column has the chintzy gloom of Yul Brenner's posthumously aired anti-smoking commercials, a bit of kvetching from the past.

This would be the appropriate place to complain bitterly over the split. Such complaints would follow in a grand tradition. I can count a half dozen labels, magazines, and ex-employees that have felt the need to vent their bottled spleen along these lines. *MRR's* Tim Yohannan and Jeff Bale both took regular potshots at their own distributor. Mordam's own accountant sent several anonymous emails to all the labels after he was fired, urging them to jump ship. Just this last year I received a more somber and signed mass mailing from one of their ex-employees, angered at Mordam's decision to carry a label with links to GG Allin. As should be no surprise to anyone dealing with this wide a range of underground personalities, the complaints come in all flavors, and from every direction.

Here's the thing, though: I have nothing bad to say. Mordam gave me a fair deal. I'm proud to have been associated with them. The heave-ho six weeks hence is at least justifiable, if not deserved. When one pays no bills and cleans no catboxes, one eventually gets kicked out of their parent's garage. This is a bedrock principle of America. Only assholes challenge this principle. When my label started with Mordam in 1994, I'd already known half of the staff. I had far fewer friends on hand when the ax fell earlier this fall. No business is immortal.

That Mordam is still here is itself an accomplishment. In the last three years, this company has lost Lookout Records, Kill Rock Stars, and Man's Ruin (twice). Mordam managed to lose the catalogs of both the Dead Kennedys and Green Day, those absurd, towering bookends of the Bay Area punk scene. It's been a several million-dollar chain of doom, one that would have creamed a lesser company. Add to that the San Francisco real estate explosion, the growing gravity of digital music distribution, and the stresses of interacting with the punk community on a financial level…well, it's mind grinding. The Green Day boom of the year of my arrival left impossible expectations in its wake. The tightening cash flow could be traced through the catering of Mordam's annual conventions: in 1995, a massive gourmet buffet spread in Japantown; in '96, a nice meal in a bar's backyard; in '97 a less nice bar in the Mission with stray dog poop under the tables. The 2001 convention picnic was held in a public park.

I talked recently with fellow bootnick Bob, owner of Vinyl Communications, and we agreed that there was an element of relief in expulsion.[148] Mordam's monthly catalogs, filled with a merciless tide of mediocre independent music, have started to trigger mild clinical depression. At conventions, I'd hear about the commercial viability of something called "street punk" that made me feel supremely out of touch with my own business model. Of all the things I've gotten kicked out of—jobs, apartments, relationships, scenes—this was the softest blow.

And the element of community is a hard thing to nourish. My first convention was also the first in years without hostility (Tim Yohannan and Jello Biafra had already decided to avoid each other) and, consequently, the least exciting in years. Karin Gembus left in the late nineties, and with her the most vocal conscience of the Mordam machine. Gembus was once responsible for Bob VC having to fly from San Diego to San Francisco to defend a rather innocuous techno record recorded by a porn star. I didn't always agree with her, but the pesky straightforwardness was refreshing.

And I am going to miss Ruth.[149] Ruth Schwartz, owner of Mordam, the closest indie music will ever get to a Winston Churchill, was the only person on Earth with whom I could plausibly use the sentence "I don't want to get buttfucked on the shipping."[150] That this heartfelt sentiment—I don't want to get buttfucked on the shipping, not now, not ever—no longer has a proper conversational outlet in my life is…heartrending. I once shared a surreal car ride with Ruth and her husband Rene (former lead singer of ferocious Dutch hardcore band BGK), their precocious grade-school daughter, and Suzanne, my daily contact, who was leafing through color proofs from a recent lingerie photo shoot. *Just another wild day at Mordam. We're unpredictable folks, we lead exciting, rich lives and we're glad to have you on board, McPheeters.*

In *Loud 3D*, the incredible book of 3-D photographs of early eighties hardcore bands, there's a picture of the *MaximumRocknroll* crew taken in 1984. In the photo, a dozen people crowd a radio station studio. I only recognize a few. Jeff Bale is the most prominent, arms stretched toward the viewer like a stoned grad student. Ruth is in the corner of the frame, wearing a DRI shirt, beaming toward her buddies. Tim Yo is directly behind her, frozen in time with a pair of headphones suspended over Ruth's head. Everyone smiles. That a future Ruth never once took the public bait for a feud from either Jeff or Tim was admirable. That I actually became friends with two people from this book meant a great deal to me. Ruth and I remain friends now. And she probably wouldn't mind if I called from time to time to tell her how very much I still do not want to get buttfucked on the shipping. But, frankly: it won't be the same.

The year I started with Mordam I tracked down the equipment used to shoot *Loud 3D*. This was in the final days before the Internet (for me), and I spent months on the hunt. The camera is a Stereo Realist, manufactured by the David White company of Milwaukee. They stopped making these things thirty years ago, so one is reliant on a small and cranky crowd of 3-D enthusiasts for tech support. Far from being a nifty gizmo, I found the camera painful, unwieldy, something that could draw fatal attention to me in foreign countries. I had an impossible time finding anyone who would develop the oddly spaced negatives. Digital three-dimensional cameras have already arrived. There's no reason for me to keep it.

And yet, facing an impending online auction, I find myself seeped in sadness for that lost potential. As with all things, the time has come to let it go. But how?

ENDNOTES

1   This whole thing started with the creation of a new market. Punk, and all its offshoots—"alternative," "indie," "underground," and most important, "hardcore"—began as a correction for the lost promises of the sixties. This market was an emotional one before it was a financial one. It popped into being as a nameless yearning, a collective reaction to the gap decade when the sixties counterculture stalled on its promises.

2   These different meanings could directly contradict each other. One suspiciously perfect story nails it. Sometime in the mid-1990s, musician Richard Hell and author Legs McNeil found themselves walking near Tompkins Square Park in lower Manhattan. The park's fringe had become a hub for grubby street punks, and when neither man offered up any spare change, one punk loudly dismissed them as yuppies. Hell had directly inspired the Sex Pistols and McNeil had literally coined the word "punk." A pal of both men stopped and yelled back, "Are you kidding?" He pointed to McNeil. "That guy invented you." But the chasm was too wide for anything but shouts. Both sides saw the other as ludicrous fakes.

3   ISIS pulled this same trick. Before gelling in 2014, its members toiled in unaffiliated terror groups—Baathist, Sunni insurgent, Al Qaeda—with mixed results. ISIS took the barbaric energy of past organizations, both stateless and official, and made the "hardcore" version of terrorist groups. The repackaging worked; only three years after launching, ISIS edged out climate change as "top threat to the world" in a Pew global survey.

4   This usage of "scene" is a holdover from beatnik times. It's a slippery word, since the thing it refers to, a "milieu," can be any size; a small enclave, an entire city, or the entirety of a genre (national or international). *The rock scene. The Montreal jazzmetal scene. The bloodmosh scene. The freaky forest people scene.*

5   There's another way to look at this, that these were the final years of a system that had served humanity for millennia, a system of written communication with no viable competition. The pre-Internet communications between cities and the scenes of cities were not that far off from Lewis and Clark days. You waited for correspondence. Travelers pollinated. But instead of tobaccy twists and beaver pelts, it was dances, fashions, fanzines, tapes.

6   In the mid-eighties Albany hardcore scene, "punk" was considered passé and foolish. We, the hardcore kids, relentlessly mocked The Sex Punks, a much smaller and utterly benign rival scene who dressed in spikes and leather. When a girl from my high school arrived at a show with eyeliner lightning bolts on her face—a look I now understand is awesome—I joined pals in laughing her off the dance floor. Those distinctions were real, and had lasting psychic power. I used to call Born Against a "punk band" as a joke.

7   Although if America can take credit for this industriousness, it also shares the blame for hardcore's chronic amnesia, and ravenous consumerism, and casual cruelty. Not to mention its epidemic of self-congratulation. Bands that performed in the very recent past are "classic," "old school," "legendary," "seminal." Books and documentaries breathlessly recall glory days within recent living memory. Bands reform and re-reform like drunken high school football stars cornering strangers to share tales of touchdowns past. In a few short decades, this thing has devolved into a tradition, one with elaborate codes and expensive relics.

Even discussing punk and hardcore has become a semantic slog, a carsick-icky, molasses-sticky swamp of placebo words, demeaning in their lack of meaning. Anyone who once fronted a visible hardcore and/or punk band is, forever and for all time, a "punker," always running from or returning to their "roots." It's the schmaltz and self-congratulations of *The Road Not Taken*, except the road less travelled has been utterly trampled by now, clogged with generations of would-be iconoclasts, everyone high-fiving each other for their dinky deeds of daring-do. It's infantilizing.

8   Is it common knowledge that "show" means "concert"? I once had a Who's On First type conversation with my dad about a show I was driving to in Manhattan. He'd thought I had tickets to a Broadway play. Well, why wouldn't he?

9   In our second zine collaboration, *Plain Truth*, my pal Jason O'Toole drew a comic called "Paper Blowing Around." It was just four panels of paper blowing around. In a fanzine devoted almost exclusively to interviews with tough-guy NY hardcore bands, the comic's wordless weirdness was its own punchline. It was this cartoon that got the attention of Adam Nathanson and Neil Burke, who later became his bandmates in Lifesblood and then my bandmates in Born Against. Those four panels determined the direction of my adult life.

10   I bought a cheap board at Woolworths, covered it in quality band stickers, and went for one harrowing thirty-foot ride that ended in blood. I think I left the board at the Salvation Army. Skateboarding heads a list of things (drumming, learning Arabic, becoming a voiceover actor, getting a pilot's license) I threw myself into and immediately bailed on.

11   In 2017, issue 1 of *The Archies*—yet another reboot for the septuagenarian comic series—showed Archie in a hardcore band. In one panel, he's wearing a Born Against shirt. The shirt was real but a bootleg; actual BA shirts were NSFW in the worst possible ways.

12   In the mid-1980s, consumer laser printers and scalable fonts were still the stuff of science fiction. This meant a clear and dramatic difference between the official look of typeset text (things cut out of newspapers or magazines) and the amateur look of every other type of text (handwriting, typewriter, Letraset). Snippets of text from the real world looked more official than blocks of text in the fanzine world. Which meant that

amateur text could look more authentic when placed on the same page of a snippet of newspaper text.

Example: In 1985, if you cut the plastic label off a two-liter bottle of soda and copied the part that read WARNING: CONTENTS UNDER PRESSURE, you could collage this into the cover of your zine and it would read as ironic appropriation. If you did this in 1995, it wouldn't be clear to the reader if you'd appropriated this or made this yourself on a laser printer, and if it was the latter, what exactly were you trying to convey? It's the emotional difference between what's printed in a Hallmark card and what you write by hand.

13   In hindsight, this seems like an odd problem, as I was already a published author. When I was twelve, in 1981, I and my best friend Mark cowrote *Travelers Tales: Rumors and Legends of the Albany-Saratoga Region*, a collection of folklore, ghost stories, and tall tales from the five counties surrounding Albany. My parents put up the cash for two print runs. Although it was not a kids' book, we'd leveraged my youth into press in all the local papers, and a spot on *PM Magazine* (which was sort of a TV news show for people who hated news). We spoke to an elementary school class about writing, marking my very first experience addressing an audience of bewildered young people.

There's far more to the story (Mark was nineteen and I was twelve, we met in a hippie school run like a cult, Mark later married my mom), and this book is not the place for any of it. This thing's complicated enough already.

14   Not much to work with here. I see "blazing" is in quotes, since the album is not literally on fire. So kudos to me there. Initializing "NYHC" assumes that all my readers were familiar with New York Hardcore, which seems off for an artzine. I make "apocalyptic lyrics" sound like a real genre, although I guess it kind of was in my limited musical sphere ('80s hardcore had a lot of songs about the end of the world). My underlining the word "ever" hints of frustration with not having the right verbal tools to make the sale. It reads like the distress of a fourth grader who "really, really, really tried" to write a book report (in this case, on *Ulysses*). Weirdly, this is still my favorite album.

15   And I have written some stone-cold dogshit in my day. Forget those feeble music previews for various weeklies ('09-'15), or my unintentionally comedic Angry Young Man shtick in *Maximumrocknroll* ('91-'93). I'm talking about the stuff that didn't even make it to full public consumption, like my freshman year college newspaper column—"In Your Face"—in which I equated the pot leaf with a swastika and dabbled in pro-life rants.

Then there's "The Straight Edge Movement," an article which ran in the Albany weekly, *Buzz*, when I was a high school senior. I and my buddies had asked guitarist Brian Baker some questions when he was in town with Dag Nasty, and—based on his authority as a founding member of Minor Threat—decided it would be okay to list his name on the byline. Wikipedia references this piece even today. Of all the unethical boners I've ever bonered, this has to top the list. Oops.

16   *Dear Jesus*, my fanzine from 1989–1992, was a mean-spirited mess, filled with cruel reviews and lewd doodles. For some reason, this zine has had a curious afterlife. Some fans of my bands bring up this zine more than the bands themselves.

17   David Byrne has pointed out the absurdity of expecting bands to be both great recording artists and great performers. Even when I went to shows religiously, I still favored recordings over live performance. I love all those little details that can't happen onstage. Think of Cindy Wilson's faint, sensual groan, fifty-four seconds into The B-52s' "Dance This Mess Around."

18   An odd detail hides in the background of one Black Flag photo. Henry Rollins grimaces at a tangle of heads. Behind him, a pair of hands holds up a two-lens camera. With a bit of squinting, the device is discernable as one of two cameras used to shoot *Loud 3D*. One photographer has captured the other.

This bit of self-reference points to the book's central mystery. In our own era of mass nostalgia, how has this book fallen by the wayside? Photographer Glen E. Friedman has made a name for himself with photos from this same age. *Loud 3D* came and went in one printing. Used copies are hard to come by, and not cheap.

I spoke with Rob Kulakofsky, one of *Loud 3D*'s three authors, in 2011. I was a little scared to ask about this obscurity. My specific fear was that he'd confirm what seemed obvious, that the book's negatives had since been lost or destroyed. Digital scanning, with its hostility to dot screens and unpredictable moiré gremlins, might not be able to resurrect a work this technically fragile. RGB scans for computer screens would work— I've seen serviceable JPEGs from this book on various websites (although resolution had been lost, and staring into a computer screen didn't feel great). But in no way would a *Loud 3D* memorial website substitute for the sheer thrill of holding the physical book. Human history is lousy with nonextant masterpieces. What if this book was also lost forever?

When I finally worked up the nerve to ask, Kulakofsky sighed. Although the plates had long since deteriorated, the photos, he assured me, were quite safe. The problem was labor. With two negatives for every picture, complete alignment is essential. Working long before personal computers or digital photography, they'd had to painstakingly line up every set by hand, then test each with glasses. Based on a bad tip from an alleged 3-D expert, they'd spent many long, fruitless nights experimenting with fluorescent inks. And after the printer miscut some of the lustrous black bleeds, the three photographers had to riffle through thousands of books to spot the defects. The beauty of the end product seemed to coexist, for him, with the memory of grueling artisanal toil. None of the original photographers has the time to recreate this project.

19   Three-dimensional is perfectly suited to concert photography. We hear live music in three dimensions, through layers of filters. We focus on specific instruments, or melodies, or performers. Music reverberates off objects, every unique venue layout and sound system competing with the moving mix of clothing and flesh within every unique audience.

More than that, we perceive the world like we watch live music, through constantly shifting focus. The human eye makes saccades—rapid visual movements from one fixed point to another, like a mountain goat leaping from ledge to ledge—more often than it blinks. This might explain why jump cuts in film aren't more jarring; our brains perform thousands upon thousands of jump cuts every day. Being able to make saccades within a photograph mimics the experience of watching bands live.

20   Three-dimensional photography comes from a rich tradition of exotic revelation. This was true through every era of its innovation: stereoscopes, anaglyphs, vectographs, stereo cameras. Throughout nineteenth and twentieth century 3-D photography, there was a strong emphasis on exposing the viewer to things almost nobody could see in person: the Grand Canyon, the arctic, the depths of a coal mine or an Ottoman palace. Because of the cost and size of the original equipment, 3-D photography was a medium of display, not motion. Stereoscopy never developed a tradition of action photography. It had to show action by its aftermath. Which makes *Loud 3D* unique. Of 111 photos, 105 are action shots.

21   Or natural science: pits (both mosh and circle) are flocking behaviors found in birds, bugs, and bacteria.

22   I experienced cognitive dissonance the first time I saw photos of Black Flag, in this book. I'd already decided what the singer of "My War" looked like (small, ratty, leather jacket).

23   Do all these poses also count as virile abandon? Meaning, is a sweaty dude posing on a tiny stage playing good music somehow different from a sweaty dude in an arena playing boring music? I don't know anymore. The question gives me a headache.

24   According to Steven Blush, author of *American Hardcore*, "few gorgeous women participated in hardcore—many of them were nasty, ugly trolls." In a book peppered with racism, misogyny, and dogshit prose, this was the line that really enraged me.

25   She is seen from below, looking down toward her bass at sharp enough an angle to create a temporary double chin. The viewer can examine her body in a way that would be impossibly intrusive in person. The photo is fascinatingly intimate, borderline voyeuristic.

26   Someone (not me) should do a blog or documentary or coffee table book about that magical period in the late 1970s when big city punk shows

were basically costume balls. The epitome of this era has to be Cheech and Chong's "Earache My Eye" in 1978's *Up In Smoke*, although little glimpses pop up elsewhere. The shockingly excellent 2007 documentary *You Weren't There: A History of Chicago Punk, 1977–1984*, showcases some of these weirdo bands: Tutu and The Pirates, The Mentally Ill, Strike Under. It's a very particular slice of an era, not quite the rawness of early seventies Leee [sic] Childers' photos, but one step further on in the evolving weirdness, at the point when audiences realized they could rival performers in outrageousness. It's a personal ideal so utopian it becomes political: anyone can dress any way they want, whenever they want, using all the joyful creativity at their disposal. How long did this era last? Less than a year? Six months? I would imagine it was different (but still fleeting) in every city. Maybe in some towns it only lasted the length of one show.

27   I interviewed DK bassist Klaus Flouride in early '05. He was charming and chatty, and totally up for discussing his old band with Billy Squier. But there was no way to write the piece without mentioning the obvious, that it is grotesque and downright farty to reform the Dead Kennedys without their original singer. Imagine if The Rolling Stones replaced Mick Jagger with Jared Leto, or Jim Belushi, or a fire hydrant. Similar deal here.

While I was writing the piece, the reformed DK's manager had been pestering me with inappropriately chummy emails. Within fifteen minutes of my badly written article going online, he sent a bitter follow-up to let me know how disappointed he was in me. It was preposterous.

28   On October 13, 2016, a woman walked into the US Bank Arena in Cincinnati in a shirt reading TRUMP CAN GRAB MY over an arrow pointing down to her crotch. The message was hand-drawn, and something about its amateurish red and blue marker gave the woman a distinct air of demented menace. She'd arrived for a rally in a presidential campaign that had itself grown so demented (pundits had predicted the candidate's withdrawal for days) that the shirt wasn't even close to making the news. But a writer for *The Guardian* got her to pose for a quick cell phone photo, and when he posted the photo on social media, it predictably went viral.

A week earlier, the candidate had been caught bragging about grabbing women "by the pussy." A dozen women corroborated. In fifty-five previous presidential elections, such a moment would've vaporized a political career. This T-shirt signaled a change. Republican voters now openly supported their candidate's freedom to sexually assault women, and, by implication, to do whatever else he pleased with his hands, wealth, or (soon) nukes. This wasn't a photo of a mentally ill person stumbling into public. It was a photo of a dangerously irrational demographic.

The moment happened and then was gone, swallowed in the endless, blurry montage of horror that now passes for modern life. But for those of us who noticed, the shirt was an epiphany. We'd thought we were tits deep in the rising nightmare, only to discover it was barely up to our ankles.

For a much smaller group of us, this photo had an extra, hidden meaning. It wasn't just the queasy realization of what that shirt meant. It was the recognition of something we'd seen before. In a presidential race run by two aging Baby Boomers, rock and roll served as both history and soundtrack (riot cops had to escort reporters out of the arena—site of 1979's The Who concert stampede—while the Rolling Stones' "You Can't Always Get What You Want" blared overhead). Now one side had gone punk.

This wasn't the twenty-first century pop punk of bratty boy bands. This was the punk of bands like Millions of Dead Cops and Dayglo Abortions, of Carter-era HANG THE HOSTAGES buttons, and the Black Flag *Police Story* T-shirt every wearer dreads getting arrested in. Those of us bound by this recognition had long shared a secret: society needs norms just as much as it needs laws. And norms can be brushed aside like cobwebs.

For anyone who's ever designed a shocking shirt, or worn a shocking shirt, or drawn an arrow pointing to their crotch on a piece of clothing— and I, somehow, have done all three—the mysterious woman with her terrible message gave notice that conservative America had finally discovered this secret. Even the inevitable co-opting of this shirt felt eerily familiar (in the following weeks, online stores sold professionally screened TRUMP CAN GRAB MY shirts, hoodies, tank tops, and, oddly, tote bags). The candidate himself gleefully scorned norms. Why wouldn't his followers?

It's the premise of all zombie movies: what happens when everyone stops behaving rationally? In other words, what happens when everyone goes punk? *Night of the Living Dead* director George Romero has himself called those zombie films his punk phase. But Ivanka Trump says she had a punk phase, too.

29   The Face was a staple of eighties hardcore performances. It's easy; make your mouth a shocked oval, open your eyes as wide as possible, flare your nostrils, and yell into a microphone. The late Steve Irwin, Australia's "The Crocodile Hunter," made The Face when mugging for cameras with dangerous reptiles.

30   In eighth grade, I acted in Albany Civic Theater's production of *Fanny*, an unfortunately titled musical in which I "sang" the second-act showstopper, "Be Kind To Your Parents." Halfway through the run, I decided to add a cocky little twirl to my choreography. That night, the director told me in no uncertain terms to knock it off.

    I had no such guidance in hardcore bands. The only rule was "authenticity," and even that was a stupidly easy thing to fake.

31   My closest brush with a spiritual experience happened in the doorway of this unit. Three months earlier, my pals in the Orange County hardcore band No For An Answer arrived at the apartment. These California boys seemed excited to experience the Big Apple for the first time (days later, I found them marveling wide-eyed at exposed rivets on a subway platform), but their jet-lagged drummer asked to stay behind at my place to sleep. I was also tired, and hoarse from band practice, so I stayed behind to nap as well. I drew a map to the nearest pizza place, the remaining band members departed, and I retired to my room. For some reason lost to the ages, the front of my apartment had filled with junk, and there was only enough room for the drummer to slumber on the floor directly next to the door.

    I'd just fallen asleep when someone knocked on the door. I groggily tiptoed so as not to wake the sleeping drummer, and had to step around him to peer through the peephole. Through its fisheye lens, I found myself staring at a military man in full dress outfit and medals. It looked like a still from a cheesy music video.

    "Yes?" I called out in a hoarse croak.

"Mister Smalls?" the military man asked, hat in hand. "Mister Dick Smalls?"

Mister Dick Smalls. My roommates and I had spent hours calling toll-free numbers from TV commercials and ordering free mailings to the most ridiculous names we could think of. Somehow, impossibly, one of these youthful larks had resulted in an Army recruiter at my doorstep. I was too bleary to think up a plausible excuse.

"One moment," I rasped. The door had to be opened with a screwdriver, and only after I'd jimmied it free did I remember that I was wearing my plaid pants with the word LOVE written in magic marker on one of the legs and an arrow pointing to my crotch. We stood in my doorway, in full view of the prostrate body of No For An Answer's drummer, me holding my screwdriver, the military man presenting a thoroughly convincing pitch for enlisting in the armed forces. The man was a pro.

Several times during this pitch, I nodded my head in agreement and looked down at the floor, so as not to seem rude. Each time, I'd catch a glimpse of my ridiculous pants. I looked like a circus clown. What was I doing with my life? My roomies were up to no good, college was awful, I'd lived in Manhattan for two years and had yet to meet any ladies. In the entire cluttered apartment behind me, there wasn't one possession I actually needed. My life, my interests, my goals; it was all a bunch of crap. In the most explicit terms possible, I was being offered a reset. All I had to do was take that step out the door and leave with this man. Just one step.

When the band returned, they clearly didn't believe my story. Their drummer had slept through the whole encounter. It was as if nothing had happened.

32 "From what I've heard about this music book you're writing," Neil recently told me, "I'm hearing best seller."

33 Maybe this was a New York game. James Sclavunos (Teenage Jesus And The Jerks) and James Chance (The Contortions) used to play "catch" with a hammer in their twelfth street apartment.

34   I and my bandmates had an irrational vendetta against Venus Records, on St. Marks Place. For some reason, I extended this vendetta to include the store's owner, Bill "Crackers" Shor (of the great Art, The Only Band In The World). Crackers and I once argued over the valuation of a rare punk 7", and I recognize now that he was arguing in good faith while I was arguing with a brain that did not fully work. When I became co-owner of Reconstruction Records just one block away, I lobbied hard to name the place Uranus Records. I was outvoted.

35   We're now far enough from this past that nostalgia has buried the brutality at its roots. In 2016, Green Day revived the ferocious chorus of MDC's "Born To Die"—*No war! No KKK! No fascist USA!*—and the moment threatened to transform the American Music Awards into something relevant to reality. But the song itself wasn't written as a slogan, or even as generalization. Back when MDC hailed from Austin (as The Stains), the Klan actively recruited at Texas hardcore shows. Green Day's use was defiance without risk. No one in the audience had to worry about getting clobbered by white supremacists outside the Microsoft Theater in downtown Los Angeles.

36   Maximumrocknroll ceased publication after this interview. See Green Day chapter.

37   I also hated bar codes. For a few years in the late eighties and early nineties, I and my bandmates convinced ourselves that bar codes (at least on music recordings) were evil. Although our beef was symbolic, we acted with the same conviction as fundamentalists who believed the Antichrist was going to tattoo unbelievers with Universal Product Codes. At least the fanatics had scripture to back them up. Our distaste of UPCs was arbitrary. It was like waking up one day and deciding to hate the color blue.

38   MRR has what must be the world's largest collection of punk and hardcore records. At some point, Tim decided to make their office the Library of Congress for this one small genre, and the collection has just kept growing. To thwart thieves, each record is bordered with thick green

electrical tape, so that the collection doesn't immediately present itself as what it is; all those beautiful album spines have been erased.

39   The future journalist AC Thompson was the first person I met in Richmond, Virginia, years before I knew I'd move there. He warned Born Against to tread lightly with the between-song banter, as a punk frontman had recently gotten knocked out, on stage, by some rednecks. It was the first of twenty shows below the Mason-Dixon. We still had a week to go before even hitting the Deep South proper. I was scared stupid.

40   This rabid anti-cop rhetoric lives on, although not where you'd expect. Every time you read a right-wing pundit rail against "jack-booted government thugs," or some keyboard warrior quote that Thomas Jefferson horseshit about "watering the tree of liberty with blood," remember: they're fantasizing about killing cops. Millions of Americans have bought into the myth of guns as insurance against law enforcement. It's absurd. These people should be blasting the first Crucifucks LP from their pickup trucks.

41   Michael Smerconish, attorney for the Philadelphia Fraternal Order of Police, later became a nationally known CNN commentator.

42   I have very little grounds on which to critique a film about a historical period I was not part of, and self-consciously idolize.

43   I worshipped Nation of Ulysses. I once had a talk with their Godard-character frontman Ian Svenonius about *Raw Power*. It took longer than it should've to realize he was discussing the Stooges album and not the blazing hardcore band from northern Italy. Even though my reference was more obscure, I felt so supremely uncool that I started blushing.

44   Pinky was the girlfriend of Fonzie, who was a character on *Happy Days*, which was a TV show, which is what people used to schedule their lives around before streaming video. She was a tough customer.

45   The middle section of this book was inspired by *Jigsaw*, and Tobi's luxuriously long, free-range band essays. So if you complain to me that the band chapters of *Mutations* aren't, strictly, about the bands themselves, I shall refer you to this footnote and you will be shamed.

46   By 1992, everyone I knew thought Millions of Dead Cops had passed their expiration date. Toward the end of Born Against, a peer called us "the MDC of New York." It was a piercing insult.

47   The last time I saw Bikini Kill, I saw this process in action. At a sold-out show in DC, a guy walked in wearing a hand-drawn shirt that read RIOT GRRRLS GIVE GRRREAT HEAD. I kept an eye on him throughout the night, not just because of the potential for confrontation, but because I was curious how this would play out. Would anyone throw him out? Instead, everyone ignored the guy. By the end of the night, I found him sitting alone at the bar. He looked like he was going to cry.

Where is that guy now? Does he regret what he did? Or is the shirt part of a fanciful tale he tells his core group of transparently lame pals?

48   Don't trust a band that doesn't have a Zeppo. All the great rock and roll groups had one: George Harrison, Charlie Watts, Larry Mullen Jr., Doug Holland. You know who didn't have a Zeppo? Mötley Crüe.

49   In the mid-1970s, *Time* magazine started using a "faux page fold" on its covers. This was a design element in the upper right corner made to look like a perfect flap of the cover had been pulled back, thus revealing a little looksie inside. It was a wink toward the reader. *Hey, you're cool, right? Here's a sneak peak!* In its own hokey way, that faux flap perfectly captured all the slippery hipness of the 1970s.

It was such a slimy decade. Everyone thought they were so goddamn cool. Adults talked openly about "making love." "Bull" and "mother" were used as wink-wink stand-ins for curse words. Calling someone "uptight" was like calling someone "racist" now. The slippery slang of a million two-bit dope dealers seeped into the general language. Henry Kissinger became a Studio 54 swinger. Even as a child, I remember being grossed out that everyone (even magazine covers) was always *winking*.

50   Except *Dawn of the Dead* was still two years in the future, so this person had no obvious inspiration. *DOTD* and the Sex Pistols loomed as twin terrors of my pre-adolescence. One was a film rated X for sheer violence. The other was a band whose members (so I'd heard) fired guns into the audience. I vowed to have nothing to do with either.

51   In the noble roll call of upper Midwest American hardcore (Hüsker Dü, Mecht Mensch, The Replacements), the closest anyone came to the terror of Die Kreuzen was Negative Approach, another battalion of ghouls with a disembodied-flying-head of a frontman. But Negative Approach drew on British oi, and although they crafted their own sound, the influences are easy to hear. Early Die Kreuzen's influences sound Lovecraftian. Non-Euclidean. *Wrong*.

52   In the US, Republican outrage over the "pacifist" themes of *The Day After* actually compelled ABC-TV to make *Amerika*, a miniseries depicting life after a Soviet takeover of the United States. It was fourteen hours long.

53   Then you've got the Feederz. Their singer, Frank Discussion, once played a show using a dead dog as a shawl and a dead cat, swinging on a noose, as an oversized necklace. The dog still had its collar and tags; it was someone's euthanized pet. If anyone pulled this crap today, they'd be run out of civilization, or worse. So social media isn't all bad.

54   Including some, unfortunately, on my own record label.

55   ** NON-LAYPERSON FOOTNOTE ** The debate between Cro-Mags demo and Cro-Mags debut album often overlooks one important point: the album is better. It's not that the *Age of Quarrel* tape is bad. It does what demos are made to do, in that it provides a rough blueprint for a greater work of art. But it's raw in ways that betray the band's influences. Harley Flanagan's bass tone matches Darryl Jenifer's subway rumble from the Bad Brains' ROIR cassette, and vocalist John "Bloodclot" Joseph sounds merely like a New York hardcore singer (perhaps a hectic impression of Antidote's Louie Rivera).

There is nothing raw or derivative about *Age of Quarrel* the album. Joseph's vocals may be more polished, but he croons and yelps with a neat little swing that is all him, despite belting out all fifteen tracks in one day. And Flanagan clearly came into his own on this record. His bass sounds weaponized. Like he has a great big bass guitar weapon and he's just using it to explode people and buildings and stuff.

And then there's the back cover photo of the band, huddled in a graffitied grotto somewhere inside a failed metropolis. It looks like a production still from *Escape From New York*. Harley and Bloodclot are all muscle and menace. This photo hangs heavy over the entire recording. In the history of recorded music, how many bands' physical appearances have so perfectly matched their music? A pal's exasperated girlfriend once asked, "Would you guys even *like* the Cro-Mags if they didn't look like that?" It was a philosophical direct hit, one I ponder to this day.

56 Throughout this book, I use the phrase "selling out" under protest. It's an imprecise descriptor. Many underground bands change styles for reasons other than careerism. It gets boring playing the same kind of music. Good musicians challenge themselves. Sometimes bands have valid reasons to antagonize their old audience. "Level up," a phrase from video gaming, would be more accurate.

Also, the phrase is going obsolete. In the space of one generation, social media has completely altered the boundaries of what is considered authentic. Writing for CNN in 2014, Douglas Rushkoff asked young sponsored "influencers," kids, if they worried about selling out. "None of them could even tell me what 'selling out' meant. They thought it had something to do with there not being any tickets left for a concert."

57 A few minutes online gave me twenty-seven: Disaffect, Disbeer, Discard, Dischaos, Disclose, Discontinue, Discover, Disease, Disface, Disfear, Disfortune, Disfuture, Disgust, Dishammer, Dishumanity, Diskonto, Dislike, Dispair, Dissystema, Disrage, Distrabe, Diskobra, Disthory, Distruct, Distrust, Disturd, and Diswar.

58 According to my three-time ex-drummer Brooks Headley, "The D-beat is so stupid that it's easy to fuck up. And when you fuck it up, it

goes from brutal military pictures of dead bodies straight to Benny Hill theme song."

59   Bessie Oakley, of The Wrecks (America's first all-female hardcore band), was a schoolmate during my undistinguished college career. I remember a conversation we had in the computer lab, when Bessie said, "I don't understand anyone who only listens to aggressive music." At the time, I rolled my eyes and was all, *okayyyyyyy, Bessie.* But this simple rule has guided me, with startling accuracy, for the last thirty years (although I personally would insert "trust" for "understand.")

60   Then there were those artists (Art [the band], Diamanda Galas, The Units, Pere Ubu) I never connected with but still valued, at least in their roles as vanguards. And then those other, later artists (Add N to (X), Melt-Banana, Stretchheads, OOIOO) I deeply loved and saw continuing in this direction.

61   Although some of us had more complicated reactions to Fugazi. For years, I and my friends were deeply threatened by this band. My own relationship with them, as a listener, had at least five distinct periods:

1) Irrational hostility. In an interview for my fanzine in 1988, a good pal called Fugazi "a piece of shit trendy band" (I remember nodding somberly in agreement).

2) Stunned Disbelief. There was a stretch in the early 1990s when a series of beloved underground performers became bona fide celebrities, and their fans underwent a steep adjustment period. These adjustment periods were induced by Beck, Chumbawamba, Green Day, Nirvana, or Rancid. For me and my pals, it was Fugazi. We loved Minor Threat in a way that felt almost mystical. Having normies hone in on "our" guy, Ian MacKaye, was cognitively jarring.

3) Grudging acceptance. For the entirety of my band career, "Fugazi" served as a metonym for standards and practices that all punk bands were subject to. This spotlight of integrity was good news when aimed up (larger bands reconsidered ticket prices) and bad news when aimed down (bands with exponentially smaller draws than Fugazi,

but with all the normal expenses of touring musicians, having to make do with five dollar admission charges).

4) Belated respect. At a certain point, it became obvious that Fugazi were a net positive for humanity, even if their collective persona balanced precariously between two traits—rectitude and grandiosity—that, on their own, would seriously turn me off.

5) "I was into these dudes before anybody."

62   Online discography resources are notoriously iffy. But even if it was a third, that would still make for forty-seven separate appearances. Which remains nuts.

63   I once saw Rollins debate Jack Thompson, the crusading Florida attorney who'd tried to prosecute 2 Live Crew for obscenity. The "debate," held at NYU, was more of a public censure session, with all the Hero Versus Heel transparency of a pro wrestling match. And Thompson was the heel. When he hemmed and hawed through his pro-life convictions, the audience roared. Rollins was only asked a few questions toward the end. At one point, someone yelled, "what about *Slip It In?*" but his quick defense of yucky, fucked-up lyrics was accepted without question.

This was only a few years after his song "Hey Henrietta," in which he rapped, poetry slam style, about raping and killing a policewoman. If the debate were to happen today, the audience would have been armed with this knowledge, and the good-guy/bad-guy polarity would have been reversed (although such a "controversial" exchange probably couldn't happen on a college campus now anyway). Afterward, Rollins confidently declared himself the winner, a debate tactic I could've used in my own life.

64   I was in a bad way by the end of my 2012 book tour. I'd gone broke again, a good friendship collapsed, my cat died, and I had to cancel the last few weeks of tour due to malfunctioning retinas. Depression had me. I could barely pull myself together for my last readings in Texas.

Some friends put me up for those final few nights. These friends had built a full-scale, Chuck E. Cheese-style ball pit in their backhouse. At night, I would sink to the bottom of this ball pit and listen to *The Secret Dub*

Life of the Flying Lizards (Cunningham's elaborate remix of an unreleased Jah Lloyd LP). Once you get to the bottom of a ball pit, it's pitch black. You can position your body any way you want and remain in that pose. It's like diving into Jell-O: I've never felt so relaxed. In the years since, this album has retained the hypnotic power of those serene intervals on the ocean floor. It's not entirely safe for me to play this record while driving.

65   It wasn't just Cunningham. In a 1979 interview, Deborah Evans explains of their LP, "It's the best we can do under the circumstances. Very few of us can play. I mean, David can play the bass guitar very badly…and I can't sing."

66   Although not a live band. When I mentioned I'd read that The Flying Lizards only played seventeen shows, Cunningham laughed and said, "that seems a lot." If he had to play live, he preferred appearing on television. But benefits were not as bad as regular concerts, removing some of the pressure on performers to fully perform.

67   Chamberlain designed the cover art for *Flying Lizards*, which incorporates work made on a Xerox 6500 color copier. This had period-specific significance. The 6500, a late entry in the race for color copies, was a huge, groaning beast, capable of less than two prints a minute. It was made for business, not art, and had a reputation for setting itself on fire. But Xerox made color technology affordable. In the process, the company created a spooky new medium. By the laws of the universe, electrostatic charges are weaker in the center of an object than at its edges. On an electrostatically charged copy, toner clings to the charged edges and drops back into a pale ghostliness in regions of heavy coverage. At the same time, the 6500's heavy dry powder development process rendered the colors in a jarring gloss. Solid objects obtained a corona of lymph that is impossible to precisely replicate in Photoshop, at least in color. Nothing else looks quite like it.

In the same way that the Civil War speaks to us through its daguerreotypes, the late 1970s and early 1980s reveal themselves through this visual style. Color xerography's biggest drawback is what gave this medium its look; the world, washed of depth but insisting on vibrancy.

The 6500's limited output lives on in record covers from this period: Foreigner's *Head Games*, Television's *Marquee Moon*, Billy Squire's *Don't Say No*, Def Leppard's *High N Dry*.

Canon's four-color laser copier killed the 6500 in 1986. Xerox retaliated by creating the Graphical User Interface used on every computing device in the world.

68   Cunningham: "Punk opened the door to all sorts of possibilities. One of which was a different idea of what 'British' was. It's not something I've thought about much, but the 'British' aspect of 'Money' is more like the older world of Noël Coward juxtaposed with something more contemporary and international."

69   More connections: the model for the "man's head" logo used by Discharge—a blocky face brooding like Rodin's *Thinker*—is Pop Group vocalist Mark Stewart.

70   There's a connection here. I'd just turned eight when I saw the first ad for *Star Wars*. The memory is sharp: the commercial plays, and everything beyond—the 12" Trintitron frame, the living room, the city of Troy, NY, outside—fades to a gray murmur. It was a coded message, received with dog-whistle intensity, intended for me and me alone. I remember thinking, *how did they know?* I saw the movie eighteen times that year. Often, my parents would just drop me off at the theater. Obviously, I was aware that there were other people in the world who enjoyed the film. But I processed this information as an abstraction. *Star Wars* was mine, my own private thing, in a way that felt fiercely childish in its insistence.

The same thing happened with hardcore. I'd convinced myself, against all evidence, that something I liked was private. Again, the thought wasn't rational (or conscious), but experienced with a similar childlike urgency. As with *Star Wars*, I'd squatted property that wasn't mine. I'd placed myself in the ridiculous position of allowing both artistic entities to break my heart when they continued to evolve and dilute with age.

I'm still in this stage with the Flying Lizards. I don't care who else likes them. *Mine.*

71   I've only found one equal to Fort Thunder: the transcendent Bread & Puppet museum in Glover, VT. If you happen to find yourself driving between New England and Montreal by way of I-91, do yourself a favor and take the detour through Glover via VT-122. No spoilers. Just go.

72   Letraset was a company that made dry-transfer fonts for graphic design layouts. Every letter of every word had to be transferred by hand, one at a time, by rubbing a pencil on a plastic sheet. Every. Single. Letter. If you didn't use guidelines, the words came out skewed and a little crazy looking (which was also your mental state, after several hours of this). LA band X used Letraset on part of the lyric sheet for their first LP, and I liked the strange emotional distance of the presentation. After my mom bequeathed to me her old cache of Letraset letters, I spent several months of '94 in my bedroom, using Letraset to produce a twenty-page CD layout.

73   No one was hurt.

74   In December 2016, an Oakland artist warehouse named Ghost Ship burned down, killing thirty-six. It was the deadliest building fire since The Station disaster. The parallels between Ghost Ship and Fort Thunder were unsettling. Brian Chippendale wrote a genuinely moving online response to the disaster, one whose sorrow reflected the more general mourning of post-election America.

75   Despite their own pyrotechnics having killed 100 and maimed 200, Great White continued touring and plays shows to this day. Three weeks after The Station Fire, the Dixie Chicks told a British audience they were ashamed of president G. W. Bush. Enraged fans boycotted the band, publicly bulldozed their CDs, and bombarded their members with death threats. Dixie Chicks didn't tour for another seven years. I tried to sell a freelance article exploring both bands' treatment, and the outrageous double standards facing female musicians. No magazine wanted it. And after viewing a few minutes of actual Station Fire footage—don't ever watch this—I abandoned the project for good.

76   *Is* Green Day a punk band? Does it matter? If enough people agree to believe in something, that kind of makes it real. It's like money.

77   It's hard to tell how much physical picketing their major label debut, *Dookie*, inspired. The whole thing lends itself to rumors that distort with age. One documented show at the Phoenix Theater in Petaluma attracted a picket line, complete with literature, urging fans to boycott the band. Even if, as I suspect, the picket line was only four or five people, it's still kind of disturbing.

78   "High on outrage": The wonderful writer Sara Marcus coined this term, although intoxication on all sorts of emotions is a hallmark of both youth culture and extremist fringes. My pals in the band Lifesblood once nixed making HIGH ON HATE shirts. I tremble to ponder the tens of thousands of nincompoops who would've shelled out cash money for those things over the years.

79   The line "fuck YDL" made me nervous to hear even in a recording. Youth Defense League had the reputation of being the most overt "white pride" skinhead band from New York. They terrified me. A few blocks north of CBGB, on the side of a building, someone once scrawled *YDL ARE SHIT AND FOOLS FOLLOW THEM.* Below this, in angry Magnum Marker, someone else had written *IF I EVER FIND YOU.* This anonymous public threat gave me the willies, like I might somehow get blamed for the anti-YDL message just by walking by it.

80   It wasn't really a cooperative, as many employees discovered when the time came for the company to be sold.

81   As was the classic lefty infighting. This was a scene in which people accused each other of working for the CIA and debated, with straight faces, phrases like "Sternhellian definition of fascism." *MRR* itself eventually turned on Lookout, Jello, Mordam, and Gilman. Tim was dead for half these feuds.

82   Lookout Records was originally set to release the Born Against catalog on CD. I reneged, which derailed my relationship with Larry for a few years. Which was a shame. I like Larry. Also, I probably would've gotten some of the $12,000(ish) in royalties my own record label was never quite solvent enough to pay me. (Although after Larry left, Lookout Records went famously bust owing far more than the $13,621 in royalties—against $32,440 paid—my label still owed when it went belly up.)

83   This verbal economy allowed the mag to document every single punk release, a decision that would bite them in the ass a dozen years later. By the mid-1990s, the explosion of indie labels led to a crisis that would've once been unthinkable; MRR had hit its physical limit. After the printer informed Tim that the magazine couldn't add any further pages, Yohannan decided to accept and reject records based on an entirely subjective criteria that struck many as arbitrary. The endless, infinitely tedious argument about what is and isn't "punk" suddenly had a cash value: for many small labels, MRR ads were vital marketing real estate.

84   The infamous MRR rolodex held the home phone numbers of every possible hardcore luminary. How many visitors (besides me) copied these numbers for later pranking? In the early aughties, one of their "shitworkers" returned my own index card with several numbers I'd left behind three states earlier. No prank calls for me.

85   I suspect a lot of people could have said this about Tim.

86   As this book went to press, *Maximumrocknroll* announced it would cease its print publication after thirty-seven years. It's criminal that this announcement wasn't made in the April Fools issue.

87   Tim Yohannan had a hearty, disarming laugh. You can hear this laugh now on reruns of NPR's "Car Talk." One of the Magliozzi brothers unwittingly did a spot-on Tim Yo cackle.

88   CBGB's role for punk and hardcore functioned like Jerusalem's Temple Mount. The club was a sacred site for two different, entwined

movements, one built using tenets of the other, each with habits and rituals that looked very similar to outsiders. So Missing Foundation probably made serious enemies with this particular act of vandalism, both among the old guard who remembered (or at least idolized) the initial, world-famous punk scene, and the far more dangerous hardcore matinee crowd.

Weirdly, there was very little crossover. In my experience, the matinee crowd couldn't have cared less about Blondie, or Suicide, or The Ramones. That scene could've happened a thousand years earlier.

89   Cheetah Chrome Motherfuckers claimed to be Italy's oldest punk band. The band also claimed (believably) that their singer Sid once punched a cop onstage, and (unbelievably) that they did not get their name from Dead Boys guitarist Cheetah Chrome.

90   Thorn/EMI was the perfect villain for the 1980s hardcore scene, being a company that sold (among many other things) both punk records and missile components.

91   There is no direct comparison for what Dischord did, but there are echoes of the supernatural curation of other American artistic institutions: Currier & Ives, *The New Yorker*, City Lights.

92   Although the status afforded the Dischord crowd made for a weird stratification in a scene that fronted like it didn't have famous people. The shows I saw in Washington always felt awkward. There were invariably moments of disconcerting eye contact in a crowd, meeting the momentary gaze of someone quasi-famous, who knew that you knew they were quasi-famous. I've lived in California for two decades now, so I've had a lot of random Hollywood celebrity encounters. None has ever made me feel as uneasy as I did at those DC shows.

93   In the vast sweep of humanity's entire recorded output, Void is the only band it is both tacky and profane to write about. How can I explain this band to you? Here is my best attempt. Imagine you are a tenth-century Viking on a long journey. You're homesick, and exhausted, and your brain is Swiss cheese from all the syphilis. Unfortunately, you have

to battle a bunch of schizophrenic horse skeletons who are each high as shit on super-PCP. Later, when the victorious horse skeletons fall asleep in nests made of dead bodies (including yours), they will dream about the music of Void. Does that make sense?

94   That rap-beef thing of 1980s hardcore was quite real. There was the anti-Black Flag band (White Flag), the anti-Jello Biafra LP (*Jail Jello* by White Flag & Necros), and the anti-Ian MacKaye LP (Poison Idea's *Ian MacKaye*, with its can't-be-unseen cover art). No Trend's jabs at the Dischord scene might have seemed pretty oblique in comparison. But No Trend were smart, and it's always harder getting made fun of by smart people. I suspect their jabs and barbs stung their targets.

95   Like the line "there's no girls that want to touch me," which held a stinging falsity when sung by Ron Reyes or, later, Henry Rollins, both of whom girls *very much* wanted to touch.

96   For those interested, there is a wealth of printed and online information parsing the nuances of the skinhead lifestyle, which skins are "good" and which are "bad," the political distinctions, and black hat/white hat dress codes, and political strata. It's a needlessly complex subculture, one in which anti-racist skins can be just as terrifying as their Nazi counterparts.

I never considered it my duty to figure out any of this. The defense mode I once employed for skinheads—courteous vigilance—I now use for desert tweakers and Orange County Republicans.

97   I was part of an effort to establish a Positive Force NYC. I remember the group accomplishing two meetings (both about convincing Fugazi to play a benefit for us) before disbanding.

98   The raw sincerity of this line—"give a fuck"—stands out in the twenty-first century, now that "I don't give a fuck" has become such a popular mantra. Of course, anyone who now says they don't "give a fuck" means the opposite: the phrase has become as potent a dismissal as "fuck you." I've always assumed that LA band Fear directly influenced this

phrase with their glorious 1982 song "I Don't Care About You," whose chorus ("I don't care about you / fuck you") cemented the contradiction. Guns N' Roses covered the song in 1993.

99   Straightedge: part of me still wants to define this word whenever I use it, even now that it's in most dictionaries and has kinda sorta achieved mainstream usage. I was a belligerent child teetotaler before straightedge existed, and relied on its label as a calling card from age fifteen on. It's weird to remember how psychically *heavy* that word/world got. In the wonderfully bonkers, unwittingly campy 1982 Faith song "You're X'd" there's a throwaway line, at the end, when singer Alec MacKaye mutters— of those who drink or "fuck" behind his back—"if you defend them, you're no better." I remember there was a time when I agreed with this line, that I felt its underlying premise was not only sane, but reflected a healthy thought process.

I also bitterly remember all the abuse I endured, well into adulthood, for not drinking or doing drugs. People who imbibe can get crazily aggressive with people who abstain. There is something about the perception of separateness, expressed through lifestyle/dietary choices, that generates an irrational offense. People who don't grow up straightedge have no way of understanding this.

I stopped being straightedge at age forty-six. I'm high, right now, typing this. I feel like a rainbow.

100   One of the strangest disconnects from high school years was this perception that "the hippies had failed." I give myself a pass for treading this line (violently binary worldviews being the right of all teenagers). And as these records remind me, I wasn't alone. Recently, someone asked me if I thought hardcore had failed. It was such a bizarre question I didn't quite know how to respond. How can an artistic genre fail? It's like asking if a painting needs new batteries.

101   Goofus and Gallant were two cartoon youngsters who went around providing examples of moral clarity. Up With People is a churchlike youth group that goes around providing examples of how dull life would be if all the Goofi died.

102   These logos had the same significance as old hobo markings. When spray-painted on a wall, they communicated a specific message: cool people were here (and communicate, in this century, that cool people once walked the Earth). Unlike hobo markings, it's only a matter of time before all these logos are unwittingly repurposed by corporate America. Think of the Target video symbol, or the friendly sphincter of the Butthole Surfers symbol resurrected as the cold, gaping anus of the Walmart logo.

But here's the thing: hardcore logos won this race. Four decades in, the Crass circle and the Misfits skull are more recognizable than nearly any corporate insignia from 1980. The Microsoft flag only lasted seventeen years; the pictographic flag of the Black Flag bars is still instantly identifiable. That's a feat. Go forty years backward from 1980, and you'd find an entire stable of cheery prewar logos—animals and fonts and food dudes—none of which survived even to my childhood.

Oddly, debates over best American hardcore/punk symbol always overlook the obvious winner: the beautiful masthead of Flipside fanzine, with its neatly curled F and S, like Al Jaffee's signature or the Lawry's spices emblem. Gorgeous!

103   Ah, the Consumer Rights wing of the underground lifestyle. It was a potent combo of bad behavior: the fake fellowship of hippies ("that's not a very cool price, man"), the busybody bean-counting of punks ("I know what it costs to make a T-shirt"), and the oblivious entitlement of Big Box consumerism. Take the five dollar door price for shows. Over the fifteen years I toured, inflation rose by 55 percent and gas prices by 75 percent. But the five dollar admission rarely budged. Essentially, audiences pressured promoters to pressure bands to accept diminishing resources in the name of bargain entertainment. It was Walmart logic on a local level.

104   Reagan Youth faced a deadline on both words of their band name. I'd always heard they'd planned to break up, or at least change their name, once Reagan was out of office.

105   "Spoken word" is not a great format. But it's appealing to punk and hardcore band people precisely because everyone understands it's not a great format. Expectations are low. I've thoroughly humiliated myself

doing spoken word, many times over, and I got the distinct impression that it didn't really count.

106   Sometimes I forget the harrowing *powerlessness* of witnessing or fleeing violence at shows. When I read now about the twenty-teens festival culture and all its humiliations—the steep prices and ridiculous lineups and cattle-herding lameness of it all—I have to remind myself: no one at a concert festival has to worry about getting clotheslined by skinheads.

107   DYS frontman Dave Smalley later helped launch "conservative punk," a G. W. Bush-era website for right-wingers in underground music. He posted a few timid, poorly written essays, but never assumed the role of figurehead for a widely despised organization. My hunch is that he didn't have the stomach for the fight. Who can blame him? Being hated is never fun. It's much easier, as everyone discovered during Obama Times, to simply cloister yourself behind social media walls and trade complaints with like-minded allies.

108   There was something equally admirable in their refusal to reform, or visibly care about their legacy. The self-seriousness of Lou Reed and Nick Cave always rubbed me the wrong way. I like Frank Zappa's attitude: "Ronald Reagan is the kind of guy who worries about being remembered. I don't give a shit."

109   In 2008, Barile thwarted Springa's attempted SSD European reunion tour with an amazing 750-word open letter. The acidity of his outrage is a treat. One section of this blistering post, labeled MOTIVES, is an actual laundry list of supposed treacherous intents (example: "4) Escape their miserable lives and US wifes and girlfriends to pursue their sexual fantisies" [sic]).

Barile writes, "I am a fucking fighter and I don't take well to people ripping me off and tarnishing the name of my band." It's not a bluff. When *The Kids...*LP was expertly bootlegged in 1987, a friend of mine was able to track down copies at wholesale. Barile and other ex-members then tracked down my friend with a private detective. My pal had some 'splaining to do.

It's rare to hear any pushback against the Hobblety Hardcore Reunion, all those chunky frontmen huffing and puffing through impersonations of their former selves. You could read this phenomenon as another indignity imposed by capitalism, but you'd only be half-correct at best. Most reunions are for comfort junkies. Bravo, Barile.

110   A few words about racist anti-racism versus anti-racist racism. The first was the realm of the hippies (think of Robert Crumb's big-lipped caricatures), and its icky paternalism has aged worse than almost any other relic of sixties hysteria. The second approach came from punk, although it required a bit of evolution. Sid Vicious and Siouxsie Sioux wore swastikas to shock, and they succeeded to the extent that they spawned (along with racist rants by David Bowie and Eric Clapton), the Rock Against Racism concerts. In their wake, punk and hardcore maintained a complex relationship with the N-Word.

The defense of Patti Smith's 1978 song "Rock N' Roll N*gger" is, I guess, that it came out in a different era—pre-"woke" NYC—when artists and audiences simply didn't know any better (although Lester Bangs' deft essay, "The White Noise Supremacists," bulldozed this argument just a year later). In her lyrics, Smith references Lenny Bruce's infamous, ugly standup bit, when he singles out "n*ggers" in the audience and then tries to magically disarm the word through sheer repetition.

The New York N*ggers (not to be confused with the Detroit band The N*ggers) explicitly took cover from Patti Smith's song. Despite being ¾ white, they played shows with near-zero pushback from late-seventies audiences. The early punk scenes had lots of white musicians in similar positions (like The Bad Seeds, and The Avengers, and Gun Club, and Elvis Costello), artists who sought exemption, not collision. Each one was hip enough, apparently, to get a one-time waiver to use the deadliest word in the English language.

The Dead Kennedys did seek collision. "Holiday In Cambodia" of 1980 used the word as a weapon, a boomerang, its anti-racist mock-racism similar to Mark Twain's withering (and flawed) caricatures of nineteenth century bigots. More such American hardcore songs followed, by the Big Boys, and Millions of Dead Cops, and the Dicks, and SSD. This was the inverse of Lenny Bruce's bit, something closer to Bob Dylan's use on

1976's *Hurricane*, or the 1972 Lennon & Ono song, *Woman Is The N*gger of the World*. It was caustic artistic protest, no different from any other fictional medium depicting humans at their worst. Except, of course, that it was absolutely different; no white lyricist could use the word now without grave consequences (when Foo Fighters feat. Serj Tankian covered "Cambodia," they changed the word to "brothers").

More confusing were the bands that fell in between. The 1986 film *X: The Unheard Music*, opens with perhaps the most graceful intro in documentary history. Under the gentle strum of Billy Zoom, we see a series of micro-vignettes, each with conspicuous glimpses of Mexican culture: a Guadalupe virgin candle, serape car drapes, a cross made of papel picado flowers. Then the film abruptly cuts to the song "Los Angeles";

She had to leave Los Angeles
All her toys wore out in black and her boys had too
She started to hate every n*gger and Jew
Every Mexican that gave her a lotta shit
Every homosexual and the idle rich

As a teenager, I felt like I "got" the song, that the lyrics were second-person satire disguised as third-person narration. But the film made me question this when, at the offending line, the filmmakers cut to a shot of black hands handling cash in an alley. And in light of singer Exene Cervenka's twenty-first century descent into Alex Jones-style conspiracy villainy, the whole thing takes on an ominous odor.

I am, to the best of my knowledge, the only hardcore singer to use the N-word twice, in two different songs. I'm not defending this. Both songs were attempts to continue in the vein of dark, Dead Kennedys-style satire, and in the context of that razor-thin slice of the musical Dewey Decimal system—anti-racist mock-racism—we soared. But you can never bind intent to interpretation. Cultural context evaporates in a way that printed words cannot. Satire always runs the risk of being taken seriously (1729's *A Modest Proposal*— in which Jonathan Swift proposed eating poor Irish children—now requires textual notes). In a band career marked by many errors in judgment, this particular error stands out.

I didn't realize this was a problem until years after those songs were recorded. In my small record label office in Richmond, I met one of my neighbors, Ron the Muzak Man. I offered him a record, and, because Ron was black, suddenly had to backtrack through my catalog so I didn't give him one with the "wrong" lyrics. The realization stuck, that I'd have to attempt to explain the nuances of anti-racist mock-racism to a layman, and that, minus this explanation, music I'd recorded and released could appear as dehumanizing as that of David Allen Coe, or Skrewdriver.

111   Choke fronted three Boston bands: Last Rights for just one show, Negative FX for six shows, and Slapshot, which feels like it's been a band for the last nine centuries. He's a granite-jawed burly man, if not quite Sgt. Rock, then at least a Corporal. In 2012, he posted an odd video in which he apologized for the Slapshot song "Fuck New York," which was both wimpier than the Blatz version (the lyrics slag Central Park and Woody Allen) and ballsier (the lyrics include a 9/11 zinger). Toward the end of the video, he glances furtively offscreen, as if someone is standing nearby, compelling his *mea culpa*. The whole thing reads like a hostage video.

112   Like everyone else, I went through a brief and intense period of trying out new personas. Unfortunately, my own teenage ID crisis came in college, not high school. Right around the time of this exchange in the deli, I spent a week strutting around Manhattan wearing suspenders down, so they slapped uselessly on my thighs with every step. I looked like a grade-A a-hole. This experiment ended abruptly when, between bands, I caught one of the useless suspenders on the edge of the stage at CBGB—quite literally the worst square foot of Earth for this to happen—and I locked eyes with a bouncer and he faintly but firmly shook his head. *No.*

113   At the end of that trip, at an Anchorage Subway, we'd just sat down for lunch when a man walked in wearing a homemade shirt reading WHITE PROUD over a badly drawn SS logo. It was time to go.

114   It was the guys from Nirvana!!

115   1996 film about a man who built a suit of bear-proof body armor. I never saw it, yet reference it often.

116   Roadies may look like the interns of this world, but their role is more complex. Roadies pull their weight by driving, loading equipment, and selling merchandise, yet they live under the simple math that they are expendable while the band members are not. Anyone traveling with a band for more than one night becomes the roadie. By my count, the roadie has eight types:

1. The Fifth Beatle
2. The "Pro" Roadie
3. The Real roadie
4. The Mascot
5. The Infantilizer
6. The Freeloader
7. The Antagonizer
8. The Sociopath

In my own week and a half as a roadie, I covered type 1 and 4 (with Soddamn Inssein) and type 3 and 6 (with Screeching Weasel). I've met every kind, and the type 8 roadies are people I will not forget.

I may have once presented myself as a type 8, although hopefully it was just a six. I put the hard sell on Swiz—the retro DC hardcore band beloved by me and my pals—to let me ride with them across the country. I did NOT know them well enough to do this. They found some polite way to rebuff me. Years later, I was told they came close to naming an album "Sam McPheeters." This would have been either the best compliment I'd ever receive, or the most mortifying insult, depending on an intent I would've never known. Lois Maffeo named her pre-grunge band Courtney Love after the worst person she'd ever met. Although I doubt I was the worst person the Swiz guys had ever met, I could definitely be a pushy, unpleasant weirdo with the power to confuse and alienate people.

117   His pals in the band Isis presumably had it worse a few years later.

118   The Adoration Problem is most conspicuous on TV. We've all seen it on national awards shows. A beloved star—usually male—tells lukewarm jokes to roars of laughter and applause. Scale this down and you'll get the same outcome. For example, I saw The Evens play in 2000. Flea from The Red Hot Chili Peppers sat in on trumpet, but no one seemed to notice. All eyes were on Ian MacKaye, and everything he uttered earned a round of hearty applause and implausibly sincere chuckles. My guess is that he long ago came to terms with this reaction, and treats it as one more hazard of life as an approachable celebrity. It's certainly nothing he can control. But it was still uncomfortable to watch.

In the excellent 2007 autobiography, *Born Standing Up*, comedian Steve Martin describes the logical endpoint of this phenomenon. He was at the peak of his standup career, playing sold-out stadiums, and audiences howled with delight the moment he set foot on stage. "I was performing a litany of immediate old favorites," Martin writes, "and the laughs, rather than being the result of spontaneous combustion, now seemed to roll in like waves created far out at sea."

119   Not to be confused with the mid-nineties Massachusetts band Fit For Abuse, who, because they released records, became the official Fit For Abuse. It's weird if you're from mid-eighties Albany. Although Born Against did the same thing by stealing the name of a west coast Born Against who never released anything. And there was an Ohio version of Born Against after us. In time, I suspect, all band names get repurposed. *MRR* columnist Mykel Board once fronted a New York band calling itself The Rolling Stones. No club would book them.

120   I once read the account of an ex-deaf person who attended his first symphony with a new cochlear implant. The word used to describe this experience—*overwhelming*—felt familiar from that afternoon at the Pythias. For those of us who've never experienced a prison riot, there is no frame of reference for a mob of humans intentionally colliding with each other. As a kid, I'd glimpsed slamdancing on *Saturday Night Live* and in *Repo Man*. In person, it made no visual sense. It was that familiar sensation of watching a car accident in slow-motion. My brain couldn't keep up with my eyes.

I thought of this moment two decades later, the final time I played live. I knew it would be the last show I'd ever play, which means I was conscious of making my final stage dive. During our encore, I found myself upside down, being hoisted through a sea of exuberant Japanese men. At one point my arms got pinned, and I remember looking down (up?) at the floor I hoped I wouldn't get dropped on, thinking *this still makes no sense.*

121   I only saw Capitle once, at a 1986 Albany street fest. It was their farewell show. The city had built a stage on the intersection of Lark and Central, blocking off the cultural main drag from a major east/west artery. There was a bottleneck a few blocks in the opposite direction, near a beer garden, leaving several hundred drunks no escape from the music. And Capitle knew how to capitalize on a captive audience. The singer Jim had done up his hair in colored rubber bands and seemed to delight in tormenting the normals. I watched the set from inside a nearby drug store (too loud) and learned something about myself; I liked antagonistic bands. Although I couldn't really picture life as a frontman—I can't hold a tune—Capitle meant I couldn't completely rule out the idea either.

122   A half-dozen years later, my band embarked on a sixty-city tour. From Birmingham to Bellingham, New York hardcore had saturated every town we visited. In some scenes, it was all anyone wanted to talk about.

123   I'm quoting from video. I don't have a photographic memory.

124   I know it's a tad unseemly to get upset over a musical group's choice of lettering. But seriously, fuck this font in the face. Collegiate-ass heavy line bullshit fratboy roofie typeface.

125   I had an eleventh grade dishwashing job at a suburban mall. Every night I'd cross an empty parking lot to catch the last bus home. And every night a punk rocker would get on this bus about a mile into my ride. I didn't know him. I'd never seen him at shows. He was like a character in a recurring dream. Every night I'd watch this person take abuse from other riders on the bus. Sometimes it was just chuckles and insults—"hey, pubic

hair" got laughs—but sometimes people physically threatened him. It was a cautionary tale, played out night after night. I didn't dress conspicuously for years (and then only in New York, where I could get away with it).

126   Another small but significant style shift: Youth Crew frontmen didn't make The Face, that classic expression of first-wave hardcore vocalists (see the *Loud 3D* chapter). They preferred the stiff-pointed finger, often delivered during a chorus, with eyes squinched shut. It was a telling change of theatrics, from confrontational to evangelical.

127   Once, in '92 or '93, a pal lightly scolded me on the importance of conducting myself correctly, as my band had fans who paid attention to what I said. We were standing on a sidewalk, in San Francisco, and I had a flash of Déjà vu as sharp as an ice-cream headache. Later it hit: I'd delivered the exact same speech myself, four years earlier, on a NY sidewalk, to Walter Schreifels of Gorilla Biscuits and Youth of Today.

128   In light of what Born Against became, it's weird that it once seemed plausible we might not make any dangerous enemies at all. The band debuted at the Pyramid, across the street from the site of A7—the infamous club where Henry Garfield first sang for Black Flag—during a brief period of scenewide accord. Just that morning, a skinhead named Bags had gotten out of prison (he'd bitten off a man's thumb and had allegedly been charged with cannibalism), and his joyful reunion took over one corner of the room. The Sick Of It All guys were there, as was, oddly, Keith Morris, the first singer of Black Flag. Nobody fought. I paid close attention to details like this. The night felt like an omen of safety.

129   As the country has swung left culturally, the right wing-stink of 1980s NY hardcore has not aged well. It's shocking to remember how pervasive all that stuff was. The revered all-hardcore store Some Records sold *Blood & Honour*, a UK neo-Nazi fanzine. *In Your Face*, an otherwise mild offshoot of Token Entry, had a song called "Faggot stomp" (with the strangely telling lyric, "because of you, I might get AIDS!"). On its 1988 NYHC compilation LP, Revelation Records balanced the leftist group Nausea with the hard-right Youth Defense League.

Some have made amends. I was startled and moved when Nick Solares, former YDL frontman and now an accomplished restaurant critic, publicly apologized in 2016, without reservation, for being part of "the right-wing skinhead scene." I'd only known of the guy as a bogeyman. It'd never occurred to me that he could be an actual person, with thoughts and emotions, capable of change just like everyone else.

130   The scene (meaning the network of scenes) has long prized likability over art. Aaron Cometbus once neatly summed this bias: "bands are measured not by their quality but by their amiability."

Adam and I strongly disagreed with this bias. We shared a feeling that your art was your more authentic self, and bad art was to be battled loudly, and with great ridicule. We acted on this belief at every opportunity. It was call-out culture, pre-social media, harnessed with absurdist fury. This put us at odds with potentially everyone, and gave us very few friends at the end.

131   In 2017, I accidentally went off my antidepressants for three days. I'd prepared for a lapse back into depression. Instead, I found myself *enraged* by everything: traffic, strangers' tattoos, airplanes in the sky. I wanted to punch birds. Then I remembered. This was how I felt all through my early twenties. So was Born Against—meaning whatever portion I contributed—just the product of a serotonin imbalance?

132   It's not a coincidence that the same city gave us New York hardcore and Donald Trump. Each side sprang from opposite poles of the class divide, yet share so much. As Trump rallies grew increasingly dangerous in 2016, I kept thinking of CBGB matinees, the gravity of violent spectacle that draws more and more meatheads into the howling scrum. And, like Trump, NYHC is unequaled in self-congratulations. There is literally a plaque at the site of the A7 club congratulating all the old bands for a job well done.

133   What if I'd just gone for it? What if I'd played squats dressed as Richie Rich, dancing the can-can while fanning myself with Monopoly money? At a certain point, you have to ask yourself: how bad can I make this?

134   Once you've experienced random, non-trauma dissociation, it's hard to fully trust your senses. Three months after the dissociative panic attack, my band played a show in DC and my dad showed up. Except it couldn't have been him. I'd just arrived on a bus from Albany, 350 miles away, and he'd dropped me off at the station. There was no logical explanation. I spent the entire night circling this impossible imposter. Finally I approached him. I was as close to his face as your face is to this page. The man was identical to my father.

"Do I know you?" I finally asked, shaky with adrenaline.

"No, I don't think so," he answered in the shrill voice of a stranger. I spent the rest of the evening wobbly. I'm still not sure what happened that night. Except: if you live long enough, you're going to experience some statistically improbable shit, and sometimes this shit will be timed to sink your confidence even lower than you'd thought possible.

135   Kent McClard ran Ebullition Records from Goleta, just up the coast from Santa Barbara. We were peers, and, for a few years, pals. I was never crazy for Ebullition's aesthetic, which poached the Health Food Co-op Bulletin Board graphics of DC's Revolution Summer and cranked the wheat germ to eleven (I remember every Ebullition release containing poetry, or a drawing of a flower). But Kent himself was a decent, likable guy. After Born Against disbanded, he and I seemed to have had a soft falling out, which I regret.

136   Andy, my future bandmate, spray-painted a giant penis on the side of this truck. Driving through traffic, it looked like I worked for a company that sold cartoon penises. Even though I'd fully insured the truck, I was worried about what the manager of the rental company would say when I returned it. In the early part of this century, it was considered poor form to decorate someone else's vehicle with huge genitalia. I felt rude.

But the manager was a professional. He didn't say a word. Perhaps he was happy, in this new, post 9/11 world we'd all found ourselves stranded in, that I hadn't filled his truck with explosives and killed people.

137   It's a compelling visual: three astronauts sitting ramrod straight, listening to smooth jazz as they stare out into the endless black void.

138   Cartoon music also has this sinister undertone. Think of those eerie snippets of *Looney Tunes* in the background of *The Shining*, or *Close Encounters*, or *Twilight Zone: The Movie*. Born Against used to play a tape of Carl Stalling songs before our sets. We toured in an era when young people would just sort of stand around aimlessly between bands, as if every audience member were an inactive video game avatar. It was a ridiculous phenomenon, for which we'd found the appropriately ridiculous soundtrack.

139   All of us live on one side of a bright line in history. For eons, music was an activity. It's been a commodity for less than 150 years. And this commodity leverages a flaw in human consciousness; audio can hijack emotion. Among other things, this means audio is a cheap yet powerful tool for curating specific shopping environments. Music's ability to trigger old emotions is second only to smells. The theme song to National Public Radio's *All Things Considered* still makes me carsick, forty years after all those long family drives across New England.

140   I once worked closing shift in a fancy health food restaurant. At the stroke of nine, we'd blast the speedmetal cable radio station to communicate to customers that they were no longer welcome and, in a certain sense, no longer even human to us.

141   According to the Internet Music Video Database, Scottie's Bodies also provided cannon fodder for Rob Zombie, Staind [sic], and Nickleback. Maybe it was a social club for people who despised themselves too much for suicide.

142   Ugh: the Get One Over contingent. For years, every other catalog order to my record label included a curt note insisting I return the stamps, so they could be soaked and reused. Some customers demanded I soak the stamps myself. On one of my last band tours, I found myself standing in someone's living room while two grown men, both dressed in zombie tatters, earnestly explained how to shoplift from Whole Foods. I remember thinking, *but I'm 35.*

143   Jim Smith is the lone holdout from those early days. He's emerged as the Hilly Kristal of the early twenty-first-century downtown Los Angeles punk scene, the one constant throughout years of whackadoo shows and wacky celebrity cameos. Despite Jim's relentless pleasantness, "Smell kids" instinctually hide their drinks when they spot him at parties.

144   I was at this show. My wife's band, Amps For Christ, had been scheduled to play. We arrived to find a mob, far more people than would ever fit inside, but only after we'd parked and lugged her Chinese Dulcimer over the throng—literally carrying it overhead, like a small canoe—did we realize that this was a mistake, that her band would not be playing, and that we needed to immediately evacuate before we and the delicate instrument were pulverized. We reverse-portaged the thing back over the unfriendly audience, somehow got back to the car, and got the fuck out of there.

145   Much later, I learned that most of these slogans had been solicited by the authenticity-famished production company. It would have been easy to sabotage the entire video with the name of just one Nazi skinhead band.

146   Of course, punk is itself a parody. The first Damned and Sex Pistols LPs came out the year after the fall of Saigon, and the new genre wasted no time in digesting the deadly struggles of the twentieth century and regurgitating it all back as ironic art. Band touring is a caricature of military tours; mosh pits mimic civil unrest. Think about all those 1980s hardcore photos channeling the urgency of the 1960s, all those old flyers using imagery from WW2 or Vietnam. In the afterword to *We're Desperate*, X's Exene Cervenka writes, "We did not like poseurs but we liked to pose for pictures." But viewed against eons of human cruelty, the whole thing is a pose. All of it.

So this video was a parody of a parody. And if Holly Valance's song had been a hit, some up-and-coming Weird Al type may have made their own parody. Humanity, etc.

147   I was a frequent audience member and sometimes performer, but no more. My time at ABC No Rio, in New York, a decade earlier, made me wary of getting too close to The Smell. It wasn't just the aftertaste of 1993, when a series of friendships all soured at once and I departed NY in disgrace. It was the knowledge that volunteer-run spaces can swiftly shift clienteles. At ABC, we in the nerdcore scene (or whatever it was called) had the place to ourselves for less than a year. After Scottish punk band Oi Polloi played in autumn 1990, a whole new crowd of retro-punks barged in. Vibes changed.

Ironically, that original nerd scene was itself retro. That's not a dig. For three years, I was part of a small but vibrant artistic explosion that produced some great records, superb live performances, and hilarious fanzines. But ABC No Rio hardcore matinees were just that: events where people could watch hardcore bands in (relative) safety. It wasn't a scene that prized experimentation. Fans didn't want noise bands, or bleep-bloop keyboard duos. They wanted that old-time hardcore music from one decade further back.

148   I met Vinyl Communications' Bob Beyerle on tour, in 1991. My bandmates and I came close to kidnapping his dog, Pedro (we'd mistaken canine arthritis for abuse, and mistaken ourselves for plainclothes animal avengers). For some unfathomable reason, Bob decided to forgive my mistake and we've remained pals ever since. Through both his VC Records and his band, Tit Wrench, I came to know Bob as a kindred spirit. We each ran labels that curated increasingly unsellable music, and both fronted bands that thrived on confusing an ever-shrinking fan base. I think the world of this guy.

149   Sometime in the early 1990s, Ruth approached me and several friends about forming a Mordam East. I wasn't able to bluff my way through even baseline competence or confidence. She'd caught me at a bad moment in my life.

150   Am I the kind of person who uses words like "buttfucked"? I'm no longer sure. I've spent so long trying to craft whatever writerly persona I'm attempting to put forward here, and I don't know if that version of

me uses this kind of language. But it's not like my earlier public self, Smart Hardcore Guy, was any more genuine. *That* fellow used words like "buttfucked" all the time, despite the little voice always whispering that maybe I wasn't really the kind of person who swore as much as I liked to think I did.

I've never resolved this question: must a good writer also be a genuine writer? What, exactly, does that even mean? The masterful Jia Tolentino manages to pen a funny and (mildly) graphic account of getting fitted for an IUD, and somehow maintains the same polite distance one finds in her essays on Texas congressional races, or heavily capitalized biotech companies. How do I write like her?

THANKS

26, Freddy Alva, Lisa Auerbach, Jill Barron, Felicia Berryman, Jello Biafra, Christina Brown, Noelle Burke, Julia Callahan, Brian Chippendale, Bryan Connolly, Andy Coronado, Zach Cregger, David Cunningham, Evan Dart, Steve Dore, Sean Dowdall, Vernon Dowdall, Kerry Dowling, Diego Hadis, Oliver Hall, Kathleen Hanna, Brooks Headley, Coco Howard, Leandra Gil, Guy Intoci, Hailie Johnson, Aaron Kenyon, Jeff Krulik, Rob Kulakofsky, Joel Kyack, Ron Labbe, Laffy, Lowly, Susan Lutz, Josh Marshall, Mickie McCormic, Tom McPheeters, Spencer Moody, Slim Moon, Adam Nathanson, Arwen Nicks, Lars Panquin, Joe Preston, Brian Roettinger, Gretchen Rognlien, Portia Sabin, Ken Sanderson, John Skaritza, Jim Smith, Dean Spunt, Mark Steese, Chris Terry, Mike Treff, Rich Unhoch, Sarah Utter, Brian Walsby, Joe Wangler, Kathi Wilcox, Allison Wolfe, John Woods.

SPECIAL THANKS

Anthony Berryman, Neil Burke, Zack Carlson, Aaron Cometbus, Tyson Cornell, Jesse Pearson, Tara Tavi, Tobi Vail.